GERMAN FIGHTING VEHICLES

TIGER & KING TIGER TANKS

AND THEIR VARIANTS

GERMAN FIGHTING VEHICLES

TIGER & KING TIGER TANKS

AND THEIR VARIANTS

WALTER J. SPIELBERGER

A FOULIS Military Book

First published 1987

English language edition published 1991

© Copyright Motorbuch Verlag 1987
English language edition © Haynes Publishing Group 1991

Published by:
Haynes Publishing Group
Sparkford, Nr. Yeovil,
Somerset BA22 7JJ, England

Haynes Publications Inc.
861 Lawrence Drive, Newbury Park,
California 91320 USA

A catalogue record for this book is
available from the British Library

Library of Congress Catalog Card No. 91-71120

Typeset in 10/12 point Times Medium Roman
Translator: Gilbert F. Burns
Editor: Michael G. Burns
Page Layout: Pete Kay
Printed in England by J.H. Haynes & Co. Ltd

CONTENTS

FOREWORD

Seldom have the minds of amateur and expert alike been so stirred by an armoured vehicle as by the tank which today is almost a legend — the Tiger tank of the German Army of the Second World War. In the post-war period books giving accounts of the development and deployment of this vehicle were written not only by those competent to comment but unfortunately also by those who were not. Dr Erwin Aders, who held the responsible post of Head of Development, was aware how difficult it really is to record the unprecedented achievements of German industry objectively when late in January 1945, he gave the following account based upon his own close knowledge of the facts:

'As late as September or October 1942 the Tiger Ausf E was called a lame duck in influential circles and the cylindrically moulded turret produced by Krupp after mature consideration was compared to a tin can. That gave rise to a rather absurd situation. Several months later, all those involved were taken by surprise by the exaggerated glorifications of the press which produced in us as great a feeling of distaste as the earlier disparagements.'

Today, analyses go even further. The few remaining of those who served in Tigers — those who know what it's all about — to whom the vehicle gave a real chance of survival, are still convinced today that the Tiger was on the whole the only reliable tank. Taking the matter above and beyond subjective experience, however, it became our duty to preserve the technical development of the vehicle for posterity by giving as fully detailed an account of it as possible.

When the aggregate value of the Tiger development and production costs, conservatively estimated at about 500 million Reichsmarks is considered and the result is then brought into perspective, it is a fair question whether this vehicle really was what the troops needed. Hitler's detailed influence will also become obvious as we go on, again and again. As with any venture towards the boundaries of technical development the identity of each participant soon becomes clear. The achievements of industry are remarkable — it produced the first experimental vehicle starting from scratch inside twelve months. And the troops were at last provided with a vehicle which could take part in a tank battle with good prospects of success.

Scarcity of raw materials and the effects of Allied air superiority also prevented the troops from being adequately supplied. The Tiger tanks were not only feared by the enemy but by the troops who were apprehensive that this very scarce and extremely valuable vehicle was at no time made available in sufficient numbers. The history of the war as recorded today overlooks only too often that fewer than two thousand of these vehicles were in fact completed. Compared with the production figures of enemy tanks in the East and in the West that is a truly modest number. That the Tiger's reputation still persists today is recognition of the achievements of the industry which produced it and the crews who won recognition with it . This book should revive the memories of a bit of the past.

I am grateful to Thyssen Industry AG, to Henschel Defence Engineering of Kassel for their kind permission to use the memoirs of Dr Erwin Aders, and above all to Herr H.H. Schmidt for his assistance. A large number of the illustrations of the Tiger E production were also made available by Henschel. Data and illustrations from my archives date to some extent from my time with the Nibelungenwerken or were compiled from original documents and thanks is due to the German Republic's Military archives for their crucial assistance through which a wealth of relevant information, designs and photographs came to be made public for the first time. Most helpful were Colonel Robert J. Icks and Privy Councillor Dr Friedrich Wiener. Major H. Sculetus Dip. Eng. (retired) and Colonel Theodore Icken Dip. Eng. (retired) also participated in criticising it. Messrs P. Chamberlain and U. Feist have after years of work gathered together vital material which was of great assistance in the writing of this book. And last it is fitting once again to record the contribution of Hilary L. Doyle whose illustrations make the volume complete.

Such a documentation as this can only be made possible through the collaboration of many people and we hope that our readers will follow the example and take an active part in these researches so as to make further editions still more perfect. Every contribution helps, no matter how slight.

Walter J. Spielberger,
Trieblach 9,
A-9210 Pörtschach a.W.

7

Career of Erwin Aders Dr Ing. Habil Dipl. Ing

Paul Erwin Aders was born on 7th May 1881 in Dusseldorf. He studied at the Technical High School in Aachen where, in 1906, he passed the state examination.

Subsequently, he was employed as design engineer in businesses in engine and motor vehicle manufacture. During the First World War he served in the Motor Vehicle Unit and in the Motor Vehicle Experimental Department in Berlin. In 1919, he became Chief Engineer to the engine factory at Augsburg — Nürnberg, then in 1925, to the Vogtländ Engine Factory at Plauen and then, in 1929, to Daimler-Benz AG. In 1933, he became a University lecturer at the Technical High School at Aachen.

In 1936, Aders became head of the Development Unit of the firm of Henschel & Son in Kassel and took over tank development. The high point of his activity was the development of the Tiger tank.

Dr Erwin Aders died at the age of ninety-three at Dillenburg on 6th January 1974.

Note: The Glossary provides translations of items keyed in German in original technical drawings.

1. Development

The Tiger and Panther tanks came into being when the production of vehicles for the German Tank Service of the Second World War was coming to an end. Fundamental improvements in tank building were and are not least dependent upon suitable components being available, for instance, high performance engines which produce the greatest possible output consistent with occupying the smallest possible space. For that reason, in this instance intensive efforts to develop tank engines were pushed forward in the 1930s.

Since 1935, the Ordnance Department had been working on the provision of a high performance engine for heavy tanks. At a technical conference in October 1935 in the Army Ordnance Department, which dealt inter alia with '600 horse power engines for the large tractor', Daimler-Benz AG proposed the M 71 aircraft engine for use in tanks. This engine designed for a continuous output of 550hp and a peak performance of 600hp at 2,200rpm, was to be modified into a vertical cylinder model. Further development was to include petrol injection and diesel operation. The engines under consideration for the tank were the petrol model MB 503 and the diesel model MB 507. On 3rd June 1937, the Weapons Inspection Department 6 ordered two experimental engines whose delivery, ready for test bench running, was promised for the New Year of 1938.

As time went on, the application of these engines had however been changed repeatedly in the face of other priority tasks (Rheinmetal-Borsig 'Gerät 040'). Finally, two of the MB 507 diesel engines were modified and provided for installation in the VK 3001 (DB) tank.

Early in 1937, industry was under new instructions regarding the planned tank development. In accordance with these, Henschel & Son AG was given the task of developing the heavier tanks. Subsequently, Henschel produced the

first research vehicle of their own design. On the instruction of the Ordnance Department, the firms of Daimler-Benz, Henschel and MAN delivered plans in 1937 for a tank of the 30-tonne class. Late in 1939, Dr Ing. h.c.f. F. Porsche KG was instructed to partake in this development. While the designs of MAN and Daimler-Benz later led to the Panther tank, the experience of Henschel and Porsche with their prototype vehicles provided the initial basis for the later Tiger tank.

The Commander-in-Chief, Army, issued the next best thing to an order that the Henschel cruiser tanks be armed with the 7.5cm KwK L/24, but later changed this to the 10.5cm KwK L/28. This made a turret ring diameter of 1,650mm necessary. The order for the DW 1 (Durchbruchwagen: Breakthrough Tank I) followed late in January 1937 from Surveyor of the Works Kniepkamp of the Army Ordnance Department.

The stipulated 30-tonne tank had a two-part hull. Its rear part was secured by a bolted connection since the rolling mill was unable to produce a side wall of such a length in one piece. Escape hatches were provided in the hull floor to the right front beside the wireless operator and at the rear left in the engine room. An armoured skirt which could be wound up by means of a handle and a gear wheel arrangement was designed to protect the track driving gear. Testing under gunfire yielded no useful results. The armour plate was strong enough up to about 50mm.

A chassis was built and exhaustively tested. The powerplant was to be the Maybach HL 120 Motor of 280hp output. The turret was to be driven through a bevel gear directly from a permanent coupling of the headshaft line. For gear changing, a Maybach Variorex gearbox was installed. The hydraulic transmission system was to be

9

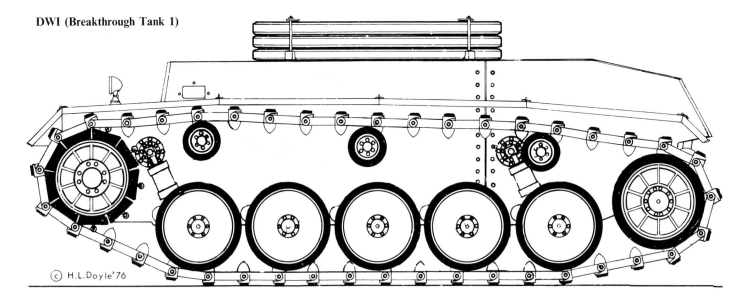

© H.L.Doyle '76

delivered by the firm of Treves. The reduction of the internally geared track drive was fixed at a ratio of 1:21.5.

The steering consisted of three ranks of CLETRAC connected in tandem. The steering gear was equipped with six brakes and four Ortlinghaus clutches but turned out to be of faulty design and had to be fundamentally re-developed. Henschel used external brake shoes of their own make with Jurid linings but, because of the generation of intolerable fumes during the braking process, they had to be changed to Götze chilled cast iron linings. The brakes were hydraulically operated.

A torsion bar sprung suspension through which solid section and hollow torsion bars (Röchling) were connected in tandem, served as the spring suspension for the disc-shaped cast steel bogie wheels shod with solid rubber dual tyres (constant spring rate of about 12-13kp/mm); whether springs were broken could not be ascertained. The bogie wheel cranks were individual forgings with shrunk-on axles. They were housed in Novotext sockets in the hull. Externally at the front and back of the running gear, special purpose articulated shock absorbers made by Fa.Boge & Sohn were fitted. The idler wheel axles were situated on the inside of the hull — their adjustment was effected from inside. The idler wheels were made from cast steel and had solid rubber tyres. The returning caterpillar track was carried on three rubber-tyred rollers. The track links had a pitch of 300mm. The link bolts were carried in greased needle bearings. Pro-

vision was made for an additional rubber cushioned mounting. The vehicle attained a maximum speed of 35 kilometres per hour.

On the occasion of a meeting with the Inspectorate of Transport (In 6) on 2nd April 1937 a successor to the DW 1, designated DW 2, was requested. The vehicle was supposed to be a further development of the Mark VI tank. The actual order for it was placed on 9th September 1938.

Compared with the DW 1 vehicle, there were differences in the steering gear, in the reduction gear, in the brakes, in the caterpillar tracking, in the driving gear and in the suspension. The triple radius steering gear operated on electromagnetic clutches. The direction of rotation was reversed and so alterations were needed to the caterpillar tracking and its brakes as well as to the mounting of the transmission unit and the torsion bar suspension. Since the original steering gear used was that of the ZW 38 (Panzer Mk III) and had proved successful on road running but not in the open country, the two large radii were completely foregone and only the original Cletrac arrangement, controlled mechanically by a steering lever, was retained.

The track was driven through a planetary gear by using a simple spur gear reduction. A Lorenz-Sykes herringbone gearing was used and the reduction gearing was set at 1:12, lower than in the DW 1. The greased track now had a pitch of 260mm and as a result, the running of the vehicle was considerably quieter. The driving sprockets were reset to the

The track of the DW2 had lubricated track links with track pin guide bearings for track pins.

The prototype of the DW2 tank with approved driving gear.

interval of 260mm, in the course of which various experimental applications of the driving sprockets using needle bearings and Novotext sockets were tested. At this stage, a simple torsion bar suspension was installed which sacrificed the smoothness of springing (a spring rate of 32 Kp/mm). It had proved itself to be adequate.

A chassis of this 30-tonne vehicle, which had a top speed of 35 kilometres per hour, was built and tested. The following model — VK 3001 (H) — had a one-piece hull with entry hatches to the right and left sides. Inlets for fresh air were built on the sides. Air intake through slanted open transverse louvres in the engine room cover was tried out.

DW2 (Breakthrough Tank 2)

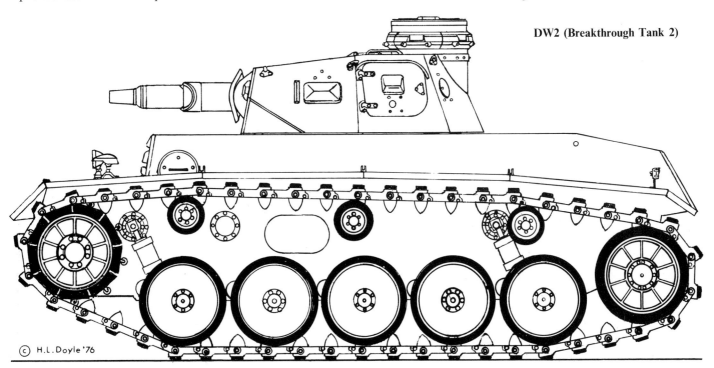

© H.L. Doyle '76

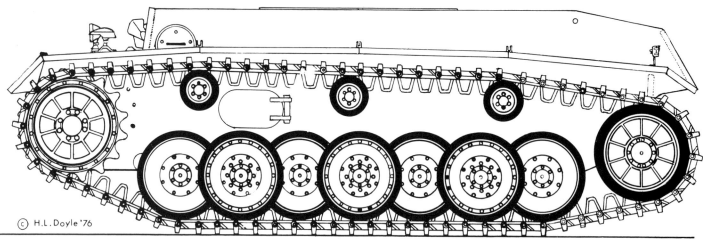

Tank VK 3001 (H)

The thickness of the armour was 60mm at the front and 50mm at the sides.

For motive power, a Maybach HL 116 six-cylinder carburettor engine whose output was 300hp at 3,000rpm was installed. Two radiators with four electric fans were mounted behind the engine as a cooling system. They were driven by means of V belts which were provided with spring-loaded idlers. As before, a Maybach Variorex gear change trans-

mission was installed. The type L 320C steering gear had a triple radius hydraulic steering and five oil-bathed clutches. Flanges to the track drive were dropped. This change followed from using the crankcase as support. The spur gear had flush sides and the tandem mounted planetary gears gave a gear reduction of 1:10.75. The mechanical Perrot internal expanding brake was largely adopted from vehicle ZW 38. As running gear, seven disc-shaped bogie wheels in stacked

Above *The VK 3001 (H) Vehicle with Tank Entrenching Fitment attached to the front.*

Above right *The bulldozer blade had deformed slightly under test.*

Right *The large heap of earth piled up in front of the tank after it had moved three times its own length.*

12

The VK 3001 (H) tank with the heap of earth it pushed in front of it at a speed of about 2.5 kilometres per hour.

The large compressed heap of earth piled up against the box-shaped bulldozer blade.

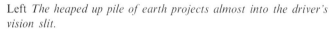

Left *The heaped up pile of earth projects almost into the driver's vision slit.*

Below left *This photograph shows the vehicle from the rear after its fourth forward travel. The effect of the entrenching device is insignificant.*

Below *In spite of considerable earth moving, the vehicle has still hardly dug itself in.*

Left: *The same VK 3001 (H) vehicle during a trial, left, with the Communication Trench Plough LP 500 made by the firm of Seheid and, below, a rear view of the vehicle with the plough mounted.*

The plough being got ready to work.

Ploughing begins. With a ploughing depth of up to 60 cm, depths of up to 80 cm can be attained, taking into account the earth thrown up sideways.

The plough hangs in its loading rack and digs itself in by short forward and rearward movements limited by the connecting rods.

The connecting rods are fitted.

Continuous trenches can be dug at 9 kilometres per hour.

The photograph shows the tank with plough fitted at a speed of 14 kilometres per hour. The plough became dirty at a greater speed.

Now the plough is ready for action.

Because of the rigid suspension of the plough, the radius of the trenches, all of even depth, could not be less than 90 metres.

order were installed. At this stage, ungreased tracks with a breadth of 520mm and a pitch of 130mm were used. The guide cog of the track lay in the middle.

As before, three track supporting rollers were fitted with rubber tyres and tapered roller bearings. The bogie wheel cranks were forged in one piece since there was no space for an assembled construction. They were housed in Novotext bushes in the hull and they were so arranged that

on the left half of the vehicle side they led forward and on the right half they trailed aft. Simple torsion bars with heads of different diameters linked the suspension components (Porsche patent). Torsion bars and suspension arms could be precisely positioned (Vernier operation) and the spring rate varied between 33 and 28kp/mm. Fore and aft on each side, Hemscheidt shock absorbers were fixed directly to the trunnions. The idlers reverted to cast steel, and the solid rubber tyres were dropped. The all up weight of the VK 3001 (H) vehicle was 30 tonnes, and its top speed 35 kilometres per hour.

In all, three experimental chassis were built and eight further vehicles prepared. A turret with the 7.5mm short cannon arrived from Krupps and a Maybach OLVAR gearbox of the 40 12 16 type came ready for trial. This was developed originally to team with an engine of 400hp output (40 = 400hp/12 = Md120mkp/16 = i = 16). It had eight forward gears and one simple reverse gear. For the seventh and eight vehicles a new steering gear of the SMG 90 type was planned. In September 1942, the speedy completion of these chassis was demanded for training vehicles.

One of the VK 3001 (H) chassis ran at Henschel's experimental establishment in Haustenbeck until the end of

The layout of the hull of the VK 3001 shows the typical step-shaped recessed frontal area with details of the armour thickness.

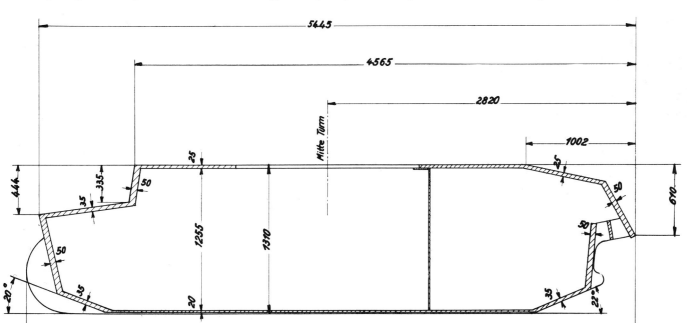

15

the war. It carried out experiments of a different kind. Inter alia, the vehicle was fitted with one of the tank entrenching devices planned for the Mark III tank. This consisted of an upper baffle plate and a lower shovel blade, with teeth for ripping up the ground welded on its front. Through repeated forward and backwards movement of the tank, a deep ditch was supposed to be dug which offered the vehicle protection up to its track cover plate. The device was fabricated by the firm of W & J Scheid Limburg (Lahn) but it was unable to do the job intended. Likewise, the firm of Scheid produced a communication trench plough which in contrast to the tank entrenching device was pulled behind the vehicle.

The salvage and rescue vehicle VK 3001 No 2 (without turret) stationed in Haustenbeck was also used as an experimental vehicle. A trailer coupling, which was directly attached to the rear of the tank by two long bolts provided the mounting for the plough itself, the heights of whose coupling could be adjusted. Trenches up to 80cm deep could be dug. The trials carried out in January 1944 showed that the vehicle, using a trench plough, could only produce large flat banks. Also the depth of the trench was insufficient. A portable suspended plough was ordered from Scheid for delivery in the middle of February 1944. This device was also earmarked for attachment to a Mark III tank. The implement was not, however, introduced.

On 25th May 1941, Hitler had ordered the development of self-propelled gun carriages for guns of 105 and 128cm specifically for the purpose of attacking bunkers and taking on the heavily armoured tanks such as were expected to be produced in Britain and America. While the 105cm gun was installed on a Panzer IV chassis, a variant of the Henschel VK 3001 chassis had to be used for the 128cm gun. The size of the guns necessitated the construction of a special tank hull with 30mm side armour and an open top.

The first experimental type of the 128cm armoured self-propelled gun Mark V was to meet a delivery date of August 1941. Communication was to be established with the General Army Department with regard to requirements. The 128cm gun with a calibre length of L/61 was the most powerful anti-tank gun in service during the Second World War.

Originally developed as an anti-aircraft gun, this Gerät 40 had been produced by Rheinmetal since 1936. The first production model was delivered to the Ordnance Department in 1938. The muzzle velocity (Vo) was 910 metres per second, the weight of the shell 26kg, the traverse was in all

14 degrees, and the depression/elevation was from -15 to +10 degrees. The gun weighed 7 tonnes. There was a five-man crew. Eighteen rounds of separate ready-use ammunition were carried in the vehicle. Because of the greater all up weight of about 36 tonnes as compared with the VK 3001, running gear of eight bogie wheels each side was installed. The arrangement of the inner and outer wheels (size 700/98-550) was so adjusted that 1,300mm at the front and rear respectively was allowed for the forward and return movement of the caterpillar tracking. As against the VK 3001 (H) the caterpillar track had to be correspondingly lengthened. Each track had eighty-five links. With a track width of 520mm, this gave a total track surface contact of 4,750mm. The two last bogie wheels of each vehicle were given additionally stronger suspension so as to avoid a situation where on gunnery trials there was such a strong pitching action that it would be impossible for the gunner to observe the fall of shot.

A Maybach HL 116 six-cylinder carburettor engine of special design provided the motive power. It was positioned higher than the cooling system and so the V belt drive for the fan as well as the inlet for cold air had to be re-designed. The track drive was set lower because the lengthening of the track required greater steering power. A dry triple disc clutch transmitted the power to a six-gear ZF SSG 77 synchromesh transmission. The fuel tank held 450 litres. The outside measurements were 9,800 by 3,180 by 1,670mm. A top speed of 19.6 kilometres per hour was reached.

Two 12.8cm self-propelled guns L/61 (Pz Sfl V) were built by Rheinmetal Borsig in Dusseldorf. Both vehicles were sent into action against Russia despite the original instruction. One of these fell, for certain, into Russian hands in the spring of 1943.

On Porsche's part, the Special Vehicle 1 with the Porsche work designated Leopard became the first experimental vehicle of the newly-built Nibelungenwerk. The official Army designation was VK 3001 (P), and the Porsche type designation was 100. Two experimental vehicles were prepared, but the revolving turret provided by the firm of Krupp was at no time mounted. Two Porsche engines of Type 100, built and tested by the firm of Simmering-Graz-Pauker AG in Vienna, were installed side by side and each was coupled to a dynamo. Each had an output of 210hp at 2,500rpm. The power generated was transmitted to two electric motors to drive the front-mounted driving sprockets.

Two of the VK 3001 chassis were extended at the rear and fitted by Rheinmetal with an open, armoured superstructure for the 12.8 cm gun. The lower photograph shows the gun at higher elevation.

17

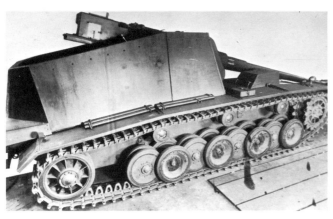

Both photographs show further details of the Armoured Self-Propelled Gun Mark V.

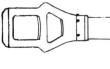
12.8 cm Self-Propelled Gun L/61 (Pz Sf1V)

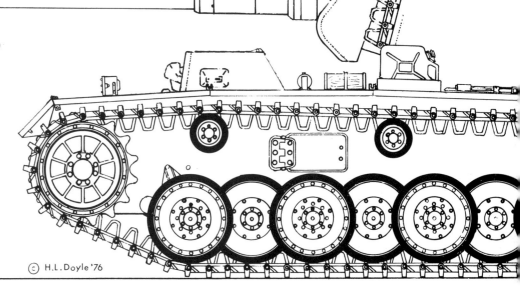

© H.L.Doyle '76

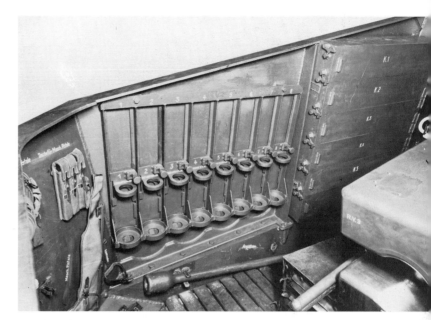

The three photographs above show details of the open fighting compartment of this self-propelled gun. The accommodation for the ammunition is easy to recognise. Cartridges and shells were separately stored.

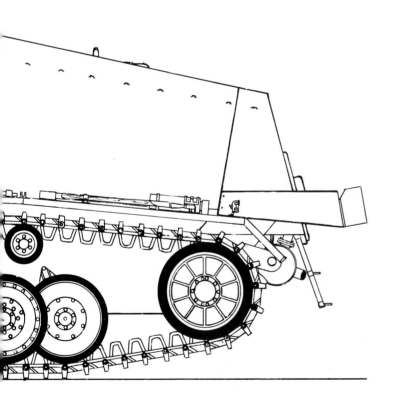

The gunner's position is at the left in the fighting compartment and that of the Commander at the right. Aiming and observation gear are above these respectively.

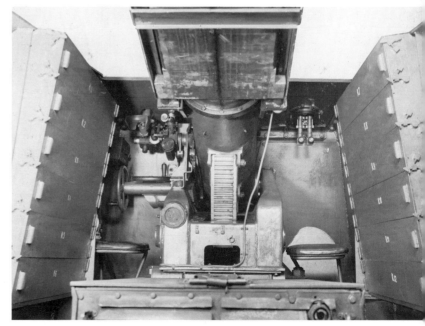

The experimental vehicle VK 3001, developed by the firm of Porsche, during driving trials in the country. The vehicle had a petro-electrical power plant. The driving sprockets were at the front.

The air-cooled powerplants each had a blower. The carburettor Type 100 engines had ten cylinders in V formation at 72 degrees, with a bore of 105mm, a stroke of 115mm and a swept volume of 10 litres. Steering and speed control was electrical through a NITA special transmission unit with a current transformer built by the firm of Voith/Heidenheim. For running gear, tread and track supporting rollers were to be provided. The tread rollers' suspension was of the knee action type with lengthwise lying torsion bars. Both chassis were subjected to exhaustive testing in 1941/42, in the course of which it was principally the running of the engines which caused snags.

For this vehicle, a diesel powerplant was also to be developed, and it was also designed as an air-cooled V-10 engine. A pre-combustion chamber fuel system was provided. The Porsche work designation for the engine was 200, but it was not built.

In the meantime, Henschel had started on a further development of the PzKw VI, with a strong emphasis on

The vehicle, also designated Leopard, turning off the highway in the neighbourhood of the Nibelungenwerk.

being 'the most powerful tank', which was ordered on 1st September 1939 by the Army Ordnance Department as PzKw VII (VK 6501). Under the order for a one-off series vehicle, Henschel were to provide the chassis and body while Krupp were responsible for the turret. Henschel's work designation for the vehicle was S.W. At the time the order was placed, there appeared to be no possibility of building such a large vehicle which would exceed the railway loading gauge. It was therefore planned to separate the vehicle into three parts and disassemble and reassemble it by means of a travelling crane. It was reckoned that it would take three weeks from start to finish at a different location.

The travelling crane made by Faun, Nuremburg, with superstructure by Demaq, Benrath, was the Faun type L 900 D 567 which the Army Ordnance Department ordered as a Mobile Road Crane (LK5S) in 1938. The first experimental model of the crane was tested in 1939, and seven of the first version were built. Individual vehicles came to the experimental station at Sennelager and later also to Kummersdorf. Two together would be able to lift up to 20 tonnes.

The hull of VK 6501 was designed in three parts; the side armour was 80mm thick. It was assembled using tension rods, crossbars and bolts by means of tapered seatings

VK 3001 (P) tank

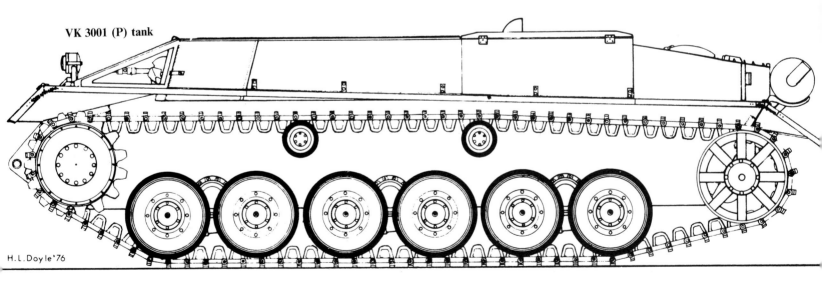

H.L.Doyle '76

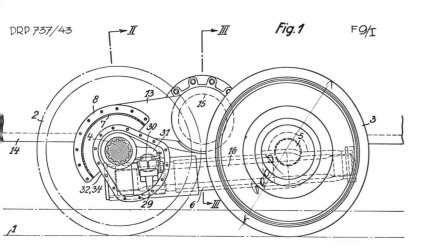

Fig.1   F9/I

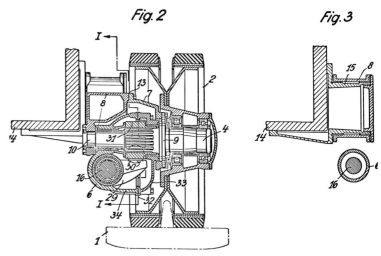

Fig. 2   Fig. 3

in the side walls (looked at from inside something like a Hussar's braiding). To keep out water when fording, the joints were treated with waterproof mastic. It was laterally strong, for example a shot would have to pierce through a series of small cylindrical castings arranged one upon the other and accommodated in milled-in grooves on both sides. The armour in front of the driver was 100mm. Alkett had designed the 80mm observation port to operate on a double-sliding principle.

The powerplant of the VK 6501 was to be a 12-cylinder Maybach engine of the Type HL 224 with an output of 600hp and 3,000rpm. Cool air flowed in from the side and the warm exhaust air was carried away through a broad louvre at the rear. The exhaust pipe was not to be led through the rear wall but be led away over it. The gear shift mechanism was newly developed by Maybach. The power

Porsche used a patented longitudinal torsion bar suspension for the VK 3001. The drawing shows the technical assembly of the bogie wheel suspension frame.

Opposite The layout of the hull of the Porsche VK 3001. The revolving turret was not mounted.

The track arrangement on the Porsche type 100 (VK 3001).

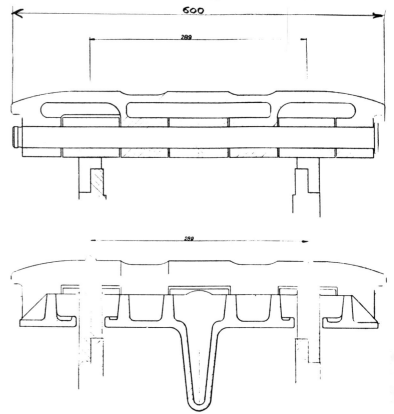

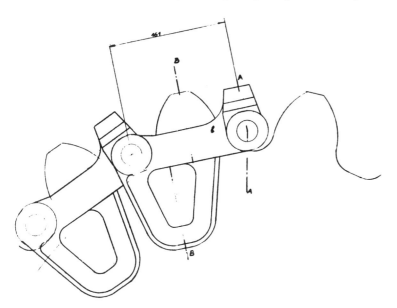

22

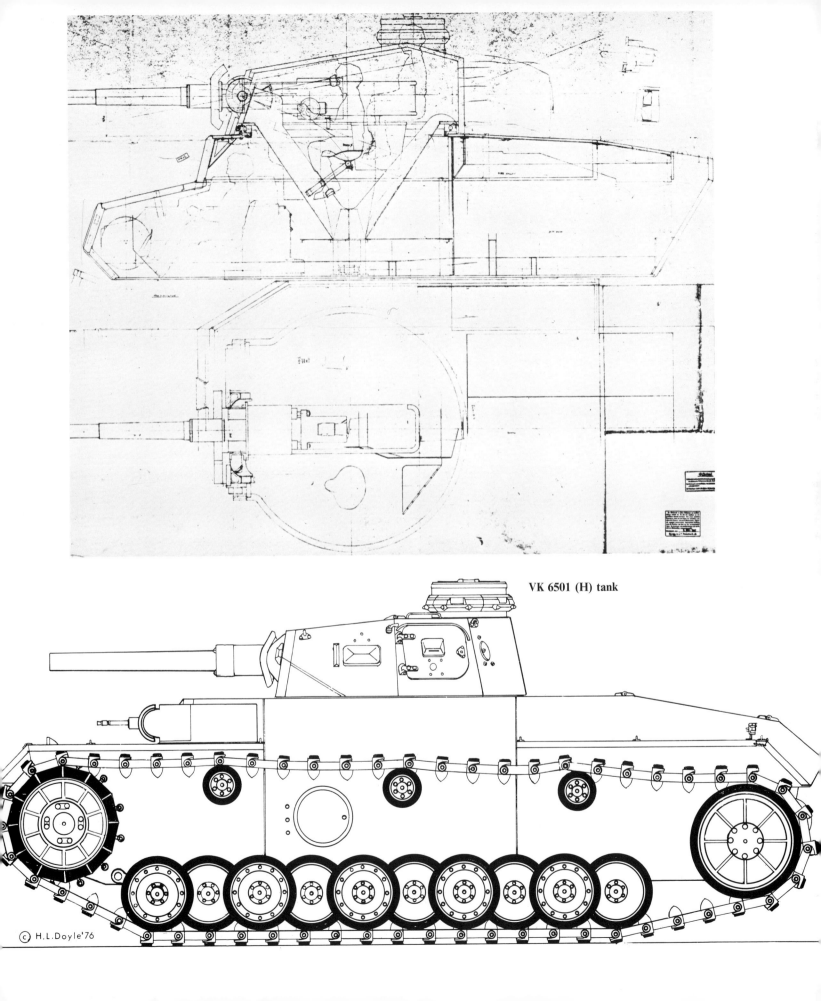

VK 6501 (H) tank

© H.L.Doyle'76

The heavy tank VK 6501 conceived by Henschel was to be conveyed in three disassembled loads. To meet the need, the Ordnance Department ordered a road crane. The photograph shows the Faun type L900 D 567 which was provided for the project.

bogie wheel cranks were drop forged (Krupps manufactured drop forged items). For the first time, there was an attempt to moderate a sudden shock to the road wheels by providing for stress and strain. The torsion bars were solidly designed and the splining at their ends was exceptionally strongly formed. At each side of the vehicle, four shock absorbers made by the firm of Boge were attached fore and aft directly onto the axles of the bogie wheel cranks. Sheet metal stops with rubber buffers for the cranks were fitted on all bogie wheels. The idler wheel consisted of cast steel with a forged armour steel hub. A torsion bar with a diameter of 70mm was used to cushion the idler wheel shaft. The adjustment was no longer achieved by rotation but through a movement of the whole idler wheel shaft. The idler wheel had a rubber tyre.

The 65-tonne heavy tank was designed for a top speed of 25/26 kilometres per hour. The crew of five were to man a 7.5cm KwK L/24 as well as an MG34 in the rotating turret. A further MG34 was provided beside the driver in a ball mounting. Two experimental vehicles were planned. The hulls were constructed of mild steel. Numerous parts such as swing arms were machined or supplied as rough castings. In view of the burdens imposed on factories and on the experimental department by the building of VK 4501 (Tiger tank), the Weapons Inspection Department 6/111 gave permission late in 1942 for the existing project to be completely scrapped and for trials of the VK 6501 to be abandoned.

On 26th May 1941, a meeting with Hitler took place at the Berghof at which fundamental questions about weapons were debated. Amongst other things, a tank was demanded which would spearhead tank formations with a ratio of about twenty per tank division and which would have the following characteristics:

A gun with greater armour piercing capability than that of enemy tanks;
More heavily armoured than before;
Top speed not to exceed 40 kilometres per hour.

From evaluation of the conduct of the war to date, and because of Hitler's command that the penetrative power of the tank guns be increased, production of the Porsche type tank 4501 with an 8.8cm gun as well as of the Henschel type tank 3601, with the 0725 gun with tapering bore, was ordered, with output to begin in May/June 1942. It was desired that both Professor Porsche's and Henschel's

transmission came through two shafts operating in parallel so that on gear change one of the auxiliary shafts would continue to operate and there would be no interruption in motive power. One was disconnected and the other put into the desired gear. Thereafter, the first was disconnected and put into gear and while this was happening the second shaft continued to transmit motive power. The motive power of the steering gear, which had three radius turns, was transmitted via two bevel spur gears. This assembly was designed by four of Henschel's engineers who stayed with Maybach in Friedrichshafen over a year to do so. The braking for the VK 6501 was by mechanical Perrott brakes. First, the arrangement of the track drive was reversed as in the DW 2 so that not a supporting lug but the cast steel casing of the track driving mechanism itself had to be carried on the side wall. These arrangements were the model for all future construction not only at Henschels's but at other firms. For the first time, the driving sprocket was cast in armour plate for protection.

Nine rubber-tyred steel bogie wheels in stacked order were visible in the running gear casing on each side. The

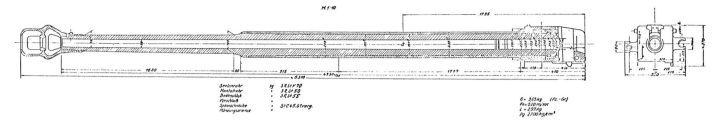

Late in May 1941, it was laid down that the 8.8 cm Flak be also used as a tank weapon. The drawing shows the longitudinal cross section through the 8.8 cm KwK L/56 for the Porsche VK 4501.

vehicles, both of which were in the developmental stage, should be expedited so that the six versions planned for each could be evaluated in the summer of 1942. In the event, the Porsche solution was adopted, namely that by using the 88mm gun, whose performance still had to be upgraded, armour of 100mm thick would be penetrated at a range of 1,500 metres. Inasmuch as the 88mm gun had originally been developed purely as an anti-aircraft gun, it seemed possible and desirable for it to be systematically developed for tank warfare. There was nothing exceptionable about using the 0725 calibre of the Henschel solution, except that the gun could only be put into large scale production if a satisfactory supply of tungsten were to be assured. Mounting the 88mm gun on the Henschel tank was to be tried out. The order to Krupps for the complete construction of the turret with an 0725 gun was given on 26th May 1941. The first 0725 gun — deferment of other work being a by-product — was made available for firing on 1st November 1941. The munitions development which took place in consequence probably had to be terminated at the beginning of 1942. As a result of the preference for the 8.8cm weapon, the first twelve vehicles were to be adapted.

The Ordnance Department pointed out that by dint of both solutions, new ground had been broken. As to the Porsche solution, the air-cooled tank engine as well as the petrol electric principle was still not reliable. While it was true that Henschel had been able to gather a wealth of experience about driving and running machines from the 30 tonne vehicles which had been running for two years, further experimental work was necessary. Hitler made it clear once again that both solutions should proceed independently of one another.

Porsche VK 4501 (P)

By exploitation of the experience gained during the construction of the VK 3001 (P), the first prototypes of the VK 4501 vehicles came into being in the Nibelungen works, and it was planned to arm them with the 88mm KwK L/50 tank gun, the upgrading of which was in course. The turret for the VK 4501 was ordered by Porsche directly from Krupps and the two firms developed it in close cooperation with one another. Contrary to previous practice, the Ordnance Department had placed no order with Krupps. Based on 'Special Vehicle No 2', the Porsche type 101, an initial experimental run of ten vehicles was produced. With an all up weight of 59 tonnes, the Mark VI tank — VK 4501 (P) Tiger (P) — had two V-10 carburettor engines of the type 101/1 installed side by side.

The twin-engine arrangement was chosen to get the highest possible engine power out of the restricted space in the engine room. The crankshaft of each engine drive was directly linked to an electric generator of each which in turn had an air blower to cool the engine. The 101 type engine was an air-cooled four-stroke carburettor engine with magneto ignition. The cylinders were in V form at 72 degrees with overhead valves operated by tappets. As was normal, the technical data was tabulated, given in the table on page 26.

The lighting dynamo was installed at the same time as the starter motor and was fed from two 12-volt batteries. The two motors were mounted alongside each other. The air-cooled motors underwent their trials with Simmering-Graz-Pauker AG in Vienna. As starter motor for the subsequent series of thirty-five vehicles, a halved Volkswagen motor (type 141) was used. This produced an output of 9hp at 2,200rpm. Nevertheless, to start a main motor engine, at the least 18hp was needed and it was therefore necessary to fall back on a Bosch inertia starter of the type AL/SED. The firm of Siemens-Schuckert had installed the power transmission unit. The drive was electric through two direct current

25

The full scale wooden mock-up of the VK 4501 developed by Porsche shows the driver's position with the control levers. In the middle of the vehicle are sited the compressed air cylinders which activated the brakes.

Motor Type 101/3A	
Design	Porsche
Manufacturer	Simmering-Graz-Pauker
Maximum output per engine (hp)	320 at 2,500rpm
Fuel consumption (grams/hp/hr)	250–270
Piston speed (m/sec)	12.1 at 2,500rpm
Torque (mKp)	105 at 1,900rpm
Bore and stroke (mm)	115 x 145
Swept volume (cm³)	15,060
Number of cylinders	Ten
Compression ratio	5.9:1
Cylinders	Steel
Cylinder head	Light alloy
Valve arrangement	Overhead, tappets/rocker arms
Crankshaft bearings	Six friction
Engine mountings	Three
Spark plugs	Bosch W 225
Carburettor	Solex 50 JFF II
Cooling	air, via impellers
Weights (Kp)	
Total, engine and generators	1,500
Engine, dry	450
Generator with cooling fans	80
Firing order	1-8-3-10-5-9-4-7-2-6

The omission of the mechanical transmission components and the transfer of the powerplant to the rear gave the forward part of the vehicle an unusually generous appearance. Above left is the driver's observation post, above right the MG 34 operated by the Wireless operator.

A view from the fighting compartment into the turret ring mount.

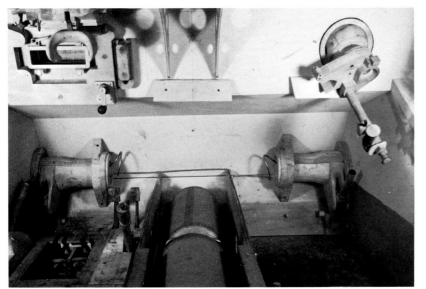

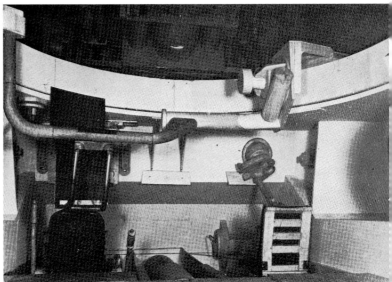

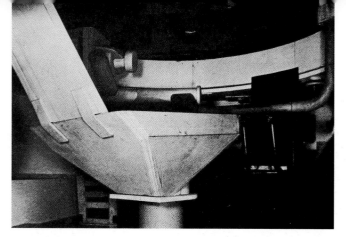

Above and below *Parts of the electrical equipment of the chassis.*

The gunner's position.

Below *View on to the breech mechanism of the dummy gun. Far right in the photograph is the turret machine-gun.*

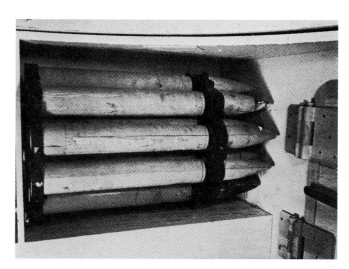

The ammunition storage in the bulge of the upper part of the tank's casing.

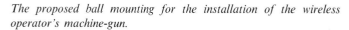

The proposed ball mounting for the installation of the wireless operator's machine-gun.

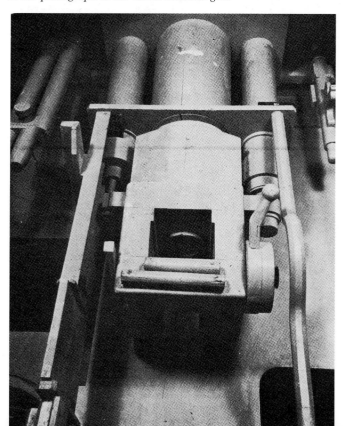

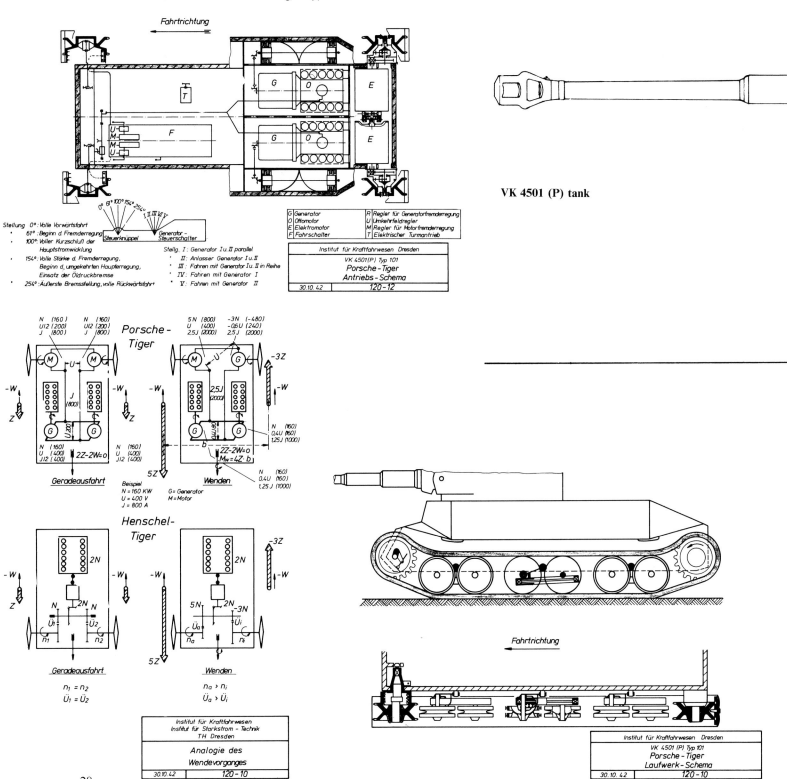

Antriebs-Schema des Porsche-Tiger Typ 101

Fahrtrichtung

Stellung 0° : Volle Vorwärtsfahrt
- 61° : Beginn d. Fremderregung
- 100° : Voller Kurzschluß der
  Hauptstromwicklung
- 154° : Volle Stärke d. Fremderregung,
  Beginn d. umgekehrten Haupterregung,
  Einsatz der Öldruckbremse
- 254° : Äußerste Bremsstellung, volle Rückwärtsfahrt

Steuerknüppel   Generator-Steuerschalter

Stellg. I : Generator I u. II parallel
- II : Anlasser Generator I u. II
- III : Fahren mit Generator I u. II in Reihe
- IV : Fahren mit Generator I
- V : Fahren mit Generator II

G	Generator	R	Regler für Generatorfremderregung
O	Ottomotor	U	Umkehrfeldregler
E	Elektromotor	M	Regler für Motorfremderregung
F	Fahrschalter	T	Elektrischer Turmantrieb

Institut für Kraftfahrwesen Dresden
VK 4501(P) Typ 101
Porsche-Tiger
Antriebs-Schema
30.10.42   120-12

VK 4501 (P) tank

Porsche-Tiger

Geradeausfahrt

Beispiel
N = 160 KW   G = Generator
U = 400 V   M = Motor
J = 800 A

Wenden

Henschel-Tiger

Geradeausfahrt

$n_1 = n_2$
$Ü_1 = Ü_2$

Wenden

$n_a > n_i$
$Ü_a > Ü_i$

Institut für Kraftfahrwesen
Institut für Starkstrom - Technik
TH Dresden
Analogie des
Wendevorganges
30.10.42   120-10

Fahrtrichtung

Institut für Kraftfahrwesen Dresden
VK 4501 (P) Typ 101
Porsche-Tiger
Laufwerk-Schema
30.10.42   120-10

28

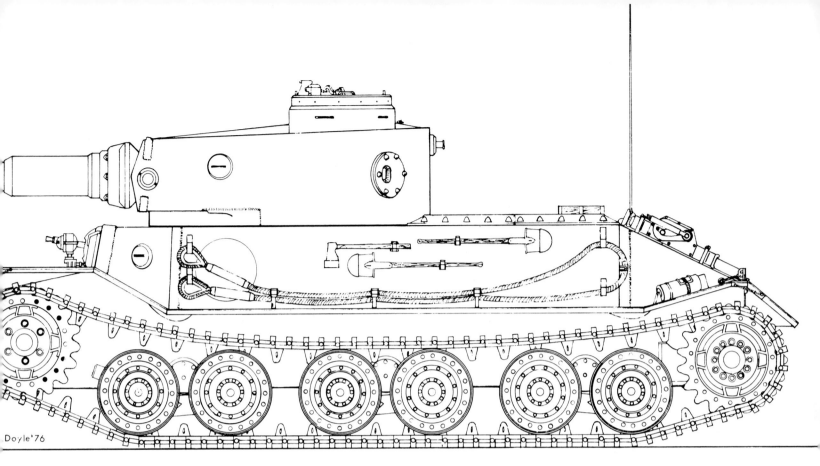

Doyle'76

generators to electric motors which worked directly on the two rear driving sprockets. The transmission ratio was 1:15 and the diameter of the driving sprocket 794mm. A top speed of 35 kilometres per hour was expected.

The running gear consisted of twelve steel double wheels which were suspended in pairs from the lengthwise lying torsion bars. The load per wheel was 4,250Kp. In order to achieve a ground loading of about 1Kp/cm², the tracks, in the course of development, had to be broadened from the original 500mm to 600mm until finally reaching a definitive breadth of 640mm (track type Kgs 62/640/130). The pitch was 130mm.

The main fuel tank, which was sited above the generators, held 520 litres which gave the tank a radius of action of only 50 kilometres. Hitler specially wanted these tanks to be employed in Africa but a radius of action of at least 150 kilometres would be required, and there was no room in the vehicle for that quantity of fuel.

The second series of thirty-five vehicles was to be delivered by January 1943, and the remaining forty-five were expected by the end of April. The last series was to have the type 101/2 engine, now with both oil coolers

The dummy engine shows the transmission-generator assembly. The cooling blower for the engine is above the generator.

29

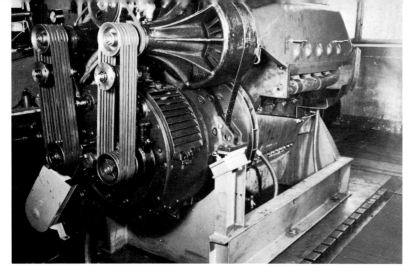

The way in which the V-belt connects engine, generator and cooling blower in the first model of the 101 engine is shown here.

rear-mounted. Likewise, the magneto was housed in the 'V' of the engine.

Besides the type 101 air-cooled engine which could not be put into production because of technical difficulties, Porsche engaged in the development of a water cooled carburettor engine for this vehicle. This type 130, a V-10 engine with a swept volume of 130 x 145mm, was designed for electric drive while the type 131, of similar dimensions, was to be used for a vehicle with hydraulic drive. A rated output of 400hp at 2,500rpm was expected from a swept volume of 19.3 litres. Again, a duplex arrangement of the engines was planned. For vehicle 101, an air-cooled diesel engine fitted with a precombustion chamber was also projected which likewise was to be designed for electric drive. The

The drawings show in plan the assembly of the 101 engine.

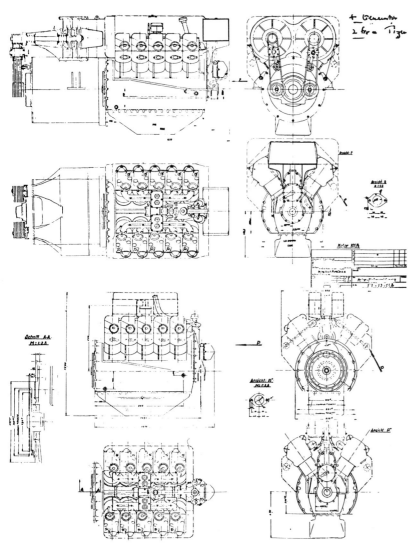

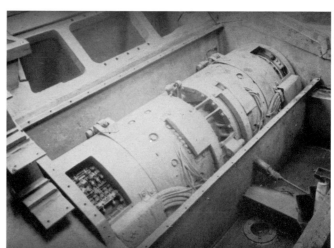

Both electric drive motors lay transverse in the vehicle.

single-cylinder experimental engine type 191 had a cylinder capacity of 120 x 145mm (1.64 litres). The Simmering precombustion chamber fuel system was to be used and much was expected of the V-10 engine 190 with a swept volume of 16.4 litres and an output of 400hp at 2,500rpm. None of these engines was, however, built and all experimentation was stopped in favour of a 16-cylinder 'X' diesel engine.

A few of the prototype vehicles were exclusively armed with the Krupp revolving turret which carried the 88mm L/56 gun — as well as an MG34. A further MG34 was in a ball-mounting (type 80) mounted in front of the wireless operators's position. Seventy rounds of ammunition were

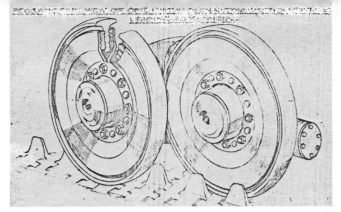

This portrays the Porsche torsion bar-bogie wheel suspension frame which was also used again in the VK 4501.

The photograph shows the first hull for the VK 4501. In front is the turret ring and behind the engine room with, in front, the position for both engines.

The air-cooled engine of this tank was plagued with problems from the start of its development. So that, in the meantime, completed VK 4501 prototypes could be technically tested out, the VK 3001 (P) was used to supply electric power. The photographs show how the VK 3001 (P) supplied the electrical equipment of the VK 4501 (P) with current by cable.

The hull of the second prototype seen from the front. The openings for the driver's vision port and the machine-gun ball mounting are easily recognisable.

carried of which fifty were ready to hand and the rest accommodated directly on the walls of the hull. The usual crew of five manned the vehicle.

For the vehicles which were already in production, 25mm thick bottom armour was ordered. As to main

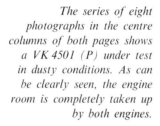

Top, above, below and bottom *The VK 4501 (P) having a rough time testing in difficult terrain. Professor F. Porsche is on the turret.*

The series of eight photographs in the centre columns of both pages shows a VK 4501 (P) under test in dusty conditions. As can be clearly seen, the engine room is completely taken up by both engines.

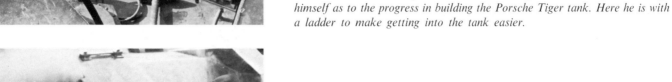

Above *Reichsminister Speer visited the Nibelungenwerk more often to satisfy himself as to the progress in building the Porsche Tiger tank. Here he is with a ladder to make getting into the tank easier.*

Below *Speer tested the vehicle to his own satisfaction. This depicts a first proving run in the factory grounds. In the background is a Panzer IV.*

Above *The inspection of one of the prototypes which already has had a turret mounted on it...*

...and test drive on a hard road.

The high imposed loading of the VK 4501 (P) led time and again to such incidents. Here two further Porsche Tigers were needed to float the bogged down vehicle free.

armament, the alternative of installing a 15cm KwK L/37 or the 10cm L/70 was to be looked into for the future. Professor Porsche promised delivery of the first production vehicle by 12th May 1942.

Henschel VK 4501 (H)

From 1940 to 1941, the installation of new facilities and an expansion of tank production took place at Henschel's in Plant III, Mittelfield. The effect of this expansion first began to make itself really felt in 1942/43. Henschel's production activities included alongside the machining of the tank bodies delivered by the steelworks, the running gear parts, the caterpillar drives, the rear idler wheels with track tension adjuster; and, if scheduled, the track supporting rollers, the steering gear, the turret rack for the turret rotating gear, the driver's position and the operating controls, the munitions store, the motor for the cooling fan, the exhaust system, the entry and service hatches, as well as assembling everything into a ready-for-service vehicle. Subcontractor or Army agencies delivered or fed in the welded and tempered tank bodies, the caterpillar tracks, the ready for service revolving turrets, the optical devices, the rubber tyres for the running gear, complete roller bearings, the drive shafts, water cooling system complete with fans, the electric motors, the transmission gears, the spring suspension items, the shock absorbers and other items needed for fitting out such as tools and measuring instruments.

In the meantime, Henschel had started on vehicle 3601 (officially also entitled the Panzerkampfwagen VI Ausf B). According to the order by the Army Ordnance Department dated 26th May 1941, the chassis was to be built by Henschel's, and the turret by Krupps. The following construction requirements were laid down for it: front armour of 100mm; side armour of 60cm; top speed not to exceed a maximum of 40 kilometres per hour; gun with armour piercing capability of 100mm at 1,400 metres and, in addition, a heavy explosive effect from HE shell. Henschel was tasked with the building in all of one plus six experimental units of this VK 3601 and also with making a delivery date of April 1942. By increasing the weight from 36 to 40 tonnes, the main armament was originally planned to be a type 0725 gun with a tapered bore. The thickness of the turret armour was fixed at 80/60mm. A modified running gear now consisted of large-disc shaped wheels without any convexity made of flat sheet metal discs. These made the return rollers superfluous.

Although it soon transpired that the VK 3601 could only be regarded as an intermediate stage in further development, the Tank Programme for 1941, laid down on 30th May 1941, planned to equip the tank troops with the Mark VI-VK 3601 tank in greater numbers. Initially, 116 were supplied but in all 172 vehicles of the type were to be provided. As variants, these vehicles were also to be prepared as 'Tank command vehicles' as well as 'heaviest concrete cracker'. The turret for this vehicle was developed no further because the Führer had decreed that the tapered bore of the 0725 gun was no longer to be used. Therefore, it was agreed in September 1942 that four of these vehicles, apart from the experimental chassis for Chief Surveyor of Works Kniepkamp, were to be prepared speedily as vehicles for the salvage of Tigers. The vehicle had to be altered to accommodate a 40-tonne cable winch made by the Firm of FAMO-Ursus. As a result, the power take-off from the gearbox was adjusted before anything else. In place of the originally provided Maybach-Motors HL 174, the vehicle was, for the future, to be powered by the HL 210 engine. Unless the production of the Tiger suffered a reduction, the chassis was to be completed by 1942, as Hitler had refused to accept the lack of a salvage vehicle for the Tiger.

The inadequate penetration of the main armament in use up until now required a new solution. On 26th April 1941, Hitler from the Berghof gave the following directive:

'If it emerges that a like penetrative power is possible from a smaller calibre than 8.8cm (for example, 6.0 or 7.5cm), on the grounds of munitions production and turret weight, it should be given priority. The calibre chosen must be fit to take on tanks, ground targets and bunkers.'

After investigation, the Army Ordnance Department ordered an 8.8cm gun with a turret ring diameter of 1,850mm as opposed to one of 1,650mm for the 0725 weapon. The enlarged turret ring alone increased the turret weight by 2.2 tonnes because of the 80mm front and 60mm side armour.

In the middle of 1941, a demand for a capability of penetrating armour 100mm thick at 1,500 metres was made. In the middle of July 1941, the Army Ordnance Department placed an order with the firm of Rheinmetal for a turret, the gun for which had to have penetrative power of 140mm at 1,000 metres, thereby without explicitly ordering the 8.8cm calibre. The order for the 8.8cm gun followed as well in July 1941 and was given to Friedrich Krupp AG which developed the weapon from the 8.8cm anti-aircraft gun. The barrel length was 4,930mm, equivalent to a calibre of L/56, and the weight of the gun was 1,310kp.

Rheinmetal tried to achieve the required penetrative power by using a gun with a cylindrical bore which was justified on the basis of Hitler's ordering the Pak 44. However, the production of such a barrel was heavily dependent on the supply of raw materials. Germany could no longer afford

VK 3601 (H) tank

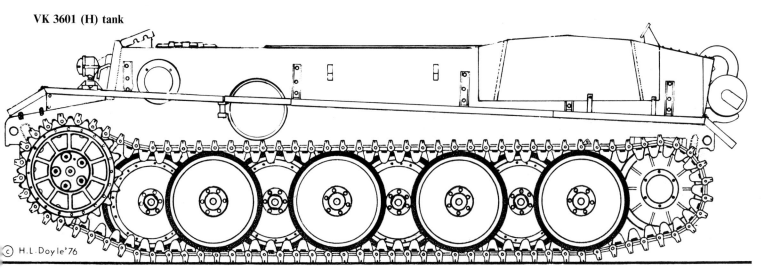

© H.L.Doyle '76

Henschel's VK 3601 remained stuck at an intermediate stage. The photographs below show Minister Speer driving one of the prototypes in country conditions. Professor Porsche is sitting on the side of the hull. Clearly visible is the narrow upper part of the tank's casing which made it impossible to mount an 8.8 cm gun.

to use large quantities of tungsten for the manufacture of guns if as a result the needs of industry for tool making steel were to be endangered. Minister Todt had, at that time, drawn attention to the stock in hand — some 700 tonnes, of which about 260 tonnes was available for the manufacture of munitions. The need of the 0725 gun was specified as about 1kp of tungsten per shell. As long as this supply was insecure, or until an equivalent substitute for industry was found, any development and enhancement of calibre which was not dependent on tungsten had of necessity to be preferred.

A further command from Hitler was to the effect that tapered bores would no longer be used. Accordingly, the turret, developed by Professor Porsche at Krupps for Henschel's 3601 tank, had to be slightly modified since there was no time to find another possible solution. These measures forced Henschel's development into another modification of the chassis so that the Henschel type became a 45-tonne vehicle as well, the VK 4501 (H). Frontal armour of 100mm was considered necessary. Side armour was considered to be adequate at 60mm for both the Porsche and Henschel vehicles. At the same time and above all, track and running gear were to be protected by armour at the front. The order placed with Henschel's on 28th May 1941 was for a redesigned tank with protected tracks and driving sprockets, and the feasibility of producing a turret with the 8.8cm gun. The required protection for the tracks and the driving sprockets ordered by the Führer was to be capable of being raised and lowered.

The hydraulic system which was needed was costly. Its susceptibility to breakdown, as well as the fact that no adequate resistance to penetration by a slanting side shot could be expected anyway, introduced into the task of solving these problems memories of the first demonstrations.

36

The removal of the turret is performed by an 18-tonne half-track truck with a 10-ton crane (SdKfz 9/2). In the right background is a 22-tonne, flat bed trailer (SdAnh 116).

As Henschel had to install the 8.8 cm gun, the VK 4501 (H) came into being so that now the upper part of the tank's casing protruded over the running gear.

The photograph shows the turret after removal with platform and turret turning gear.

Taking the turret off the first VK 4501 experimental vehicle at Henschel's test station at Haustenbeck.

The turret was placed on a ready-made wooden platform.

2. Technical Description — Henschel's Tiger

The VK 4501 (H) consisted of the chassis and a turret capable of training through 360 degrees. The turret, with the tank commander's cupola, armoured manlet and gun, was carried in a vertical ball race bearing on the tank hull. To incorporate the larger turret ring, a new hull with side extensions was necessary, and the cooling system had also been housed in them. The armoured hull was divided by a bulkhead into fighting compartment and engine room, which accommodated the powerplant, power transmission and the running gear bearings.

In the first 250 vehicles, the Maybach HL 210 P 30 engine with 600 to 650hp output was installed. From chassis number 251, the HL 230 P 45 engine of 650 to 700hp was installed. This was a spark ignition V-12 engine, with two banks of cylinders and a dry sump lubrication system.

The pumped circulation cooling system consisted of two radiator cores which were series connected in the system, the ventilator fan casings each with two fans for each radiator, the oil cooler, the centrifugal water pumps as well as the connections and the thermostat. The drive for the fans

The view from above of the complete layout of the tank.

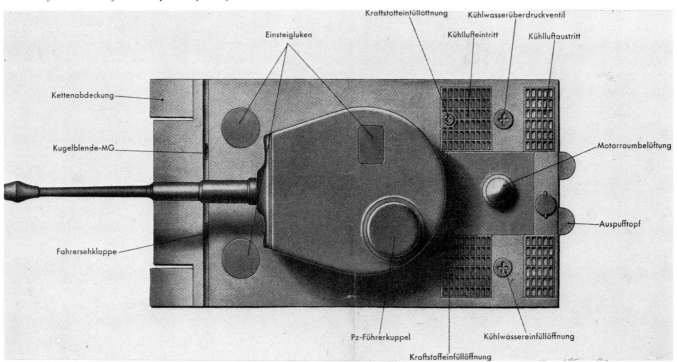

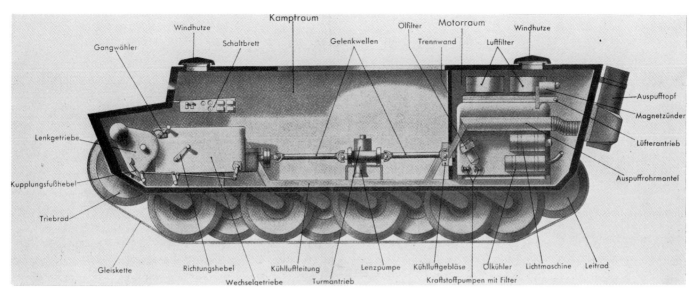

A longitudinal section through the chassis.

View from above and diagram of power transmission.

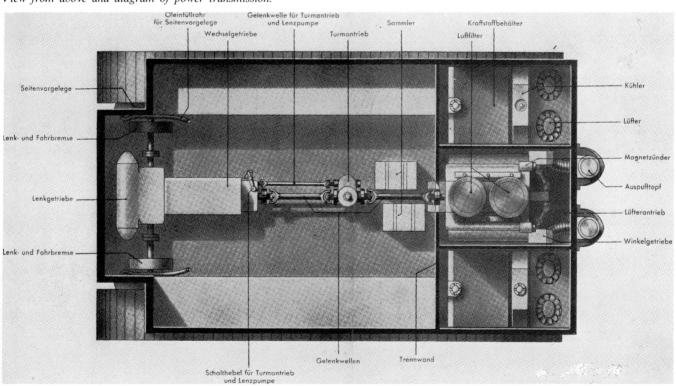

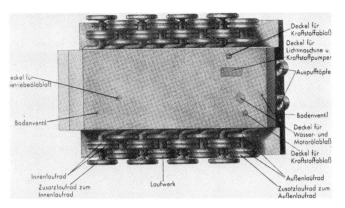

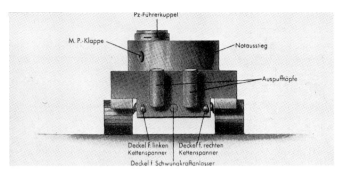

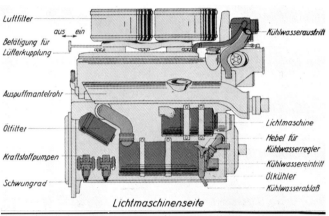

Above *The hull of the tank from below.*

Above right *Diagrammatic rear view of the Tiger tank.*

Right and below right *A diagrammatic representation of the Maybach HL 230 engine.*

Below *The engine room before installation of the power plant.*

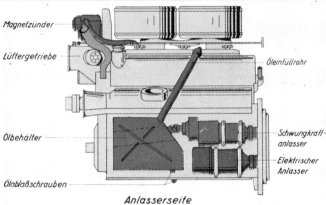

Left *The engine from behind.*

Far left *The engine from the flywheel end.*

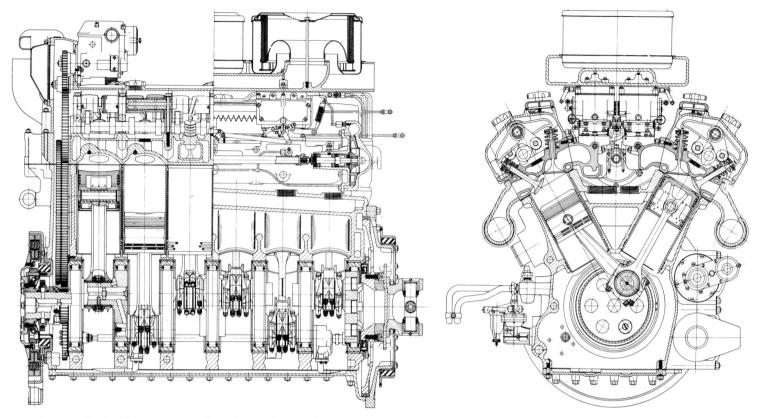

A longitudinal and cross section through the Tiger engine.

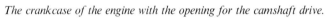

The crankcase of the engine with the opening for the camshaft drive.

The crankcase from below.

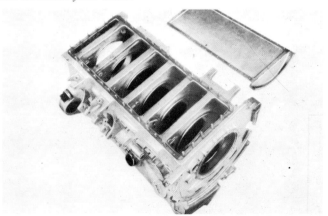

41

The camshaft.

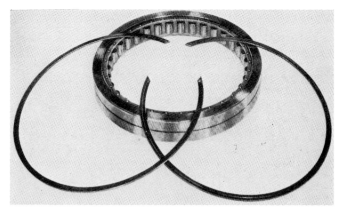

One of the seven roller main bearings.

Pistons and forked connecting rod with gudgeon pins and bearing brasses.

The cylinder head with camshaft rocker arms removed.

The valves and valve springs. One of the sodium-filled exhaust valves is sectioned open.

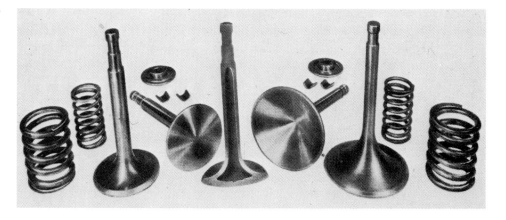

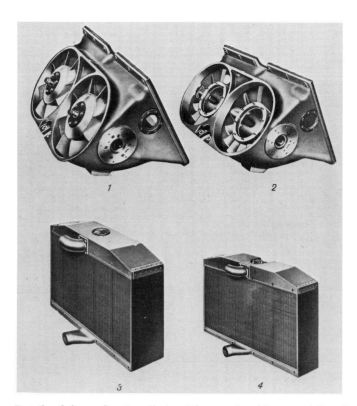

Details of the cooling installation. The complete blower at left and right (1) and (2) and the radiators (3) and (4).

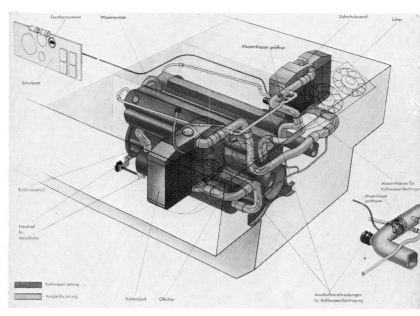

The cooling installation of the Tiger tank.

A diagrammatic layout of the ventilating system.

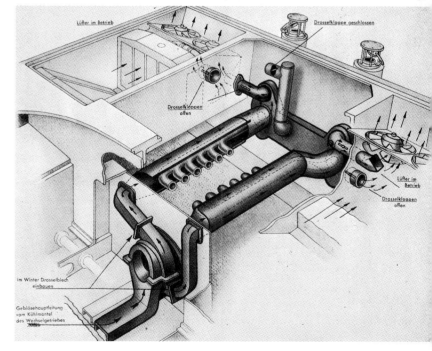

came from the engine through a two-ratio gear, a twin plate clutch, a cone pulley and a bevel gear respectively. In all, nineteen gear wheels were needed. In the first 250 vehicles, a simplified two-stage cooling system was installed. A blower mounted on the partition wall cooled the transmission as well as the exhaust manifold. A centrifugal governor limited the speed to 2,500rpm.

The four in-built fuel tanks held 534 litres in total. The contents of both pairs of fuel tanks were enough for a range of some 30 kilometres. The fuel was delivered by two double Solex mechanical pumps to the carburettors. Four double Solex auxiliary carburettors produced the fuel-air mixture.

The oil-charged air filter was housed on the engine. The use of the vehicle in Africa and in Southern Russia led for some time to the additional installation of a Feifel dry filter as part of the system. These were mounted outside on the rear of the hull and joined to an additional louvre by means of flexible pipes. Fitting this extra filter was discontinued at the beginning of 1944.

43

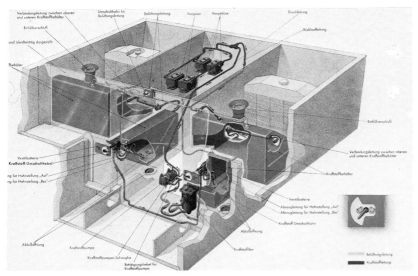

The fuel installation with the four tanks.

Right The fuel tanks with details.

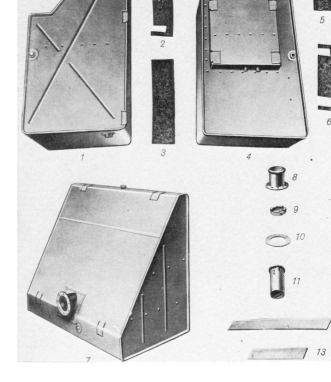

The turret drive with bilge drainage unit.

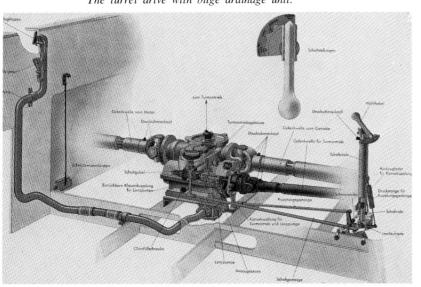

Tiger Ausf E (SdKfz 181)

The engine was connected to the transmission by two drive shafts. They were supported on the turret turning gear housing. The turret turning gear was actuated by power taken off from the gearbox through a drive shaft, a cone friction-clutch and a second pair of bevel gears into the turret turning gear housing. From there, the drive was through a flange coupling to the auxiliary hydraulic transmission and was relayed to the traversing gear through a drive shaft.

The Maybach Olvar gearbox of type OG 40 12 16 worked semi-automatically. It had an eight-speed gearbox with a dog clutch and integral main clutch. Altogether eight forward and four reverse gears were preselected with the selector lever mounted on the gearbox. The hydraulic gear change followed automatically. The main clutch was developed as a wet disc clutch. It was integral to the gearbox and its purpose was to disconnect the transmission of power between the engine and the gearbox. The gears were helically cut and were paired in constant mesh. By operating the preselector lever the channels of the hydraulic system in the gear selector were either opened or closed, whichever was needed for the desired gear to be engaged. Declutching, gear change as well as engaging the clutch was fully automatic. There was allowance for the possibility of an emergency gear change by hand. The overall gear reduction was 1:16.

Both the track and steering brakes were of the disc variety which strengthened the braking effect independently. The brake lining was made from synthetic rubber impregnated with steel wool. Originally, the brakes were to operate hydraulically but because of numerous problems with this arrangement, a mechanical operation was introduced.

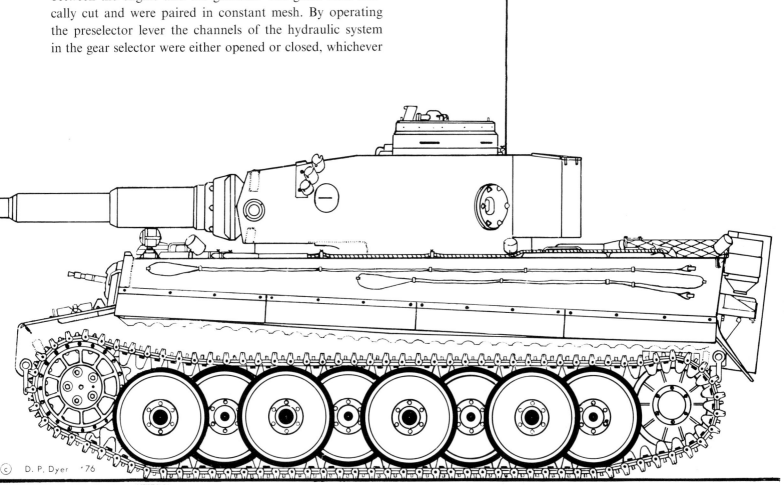

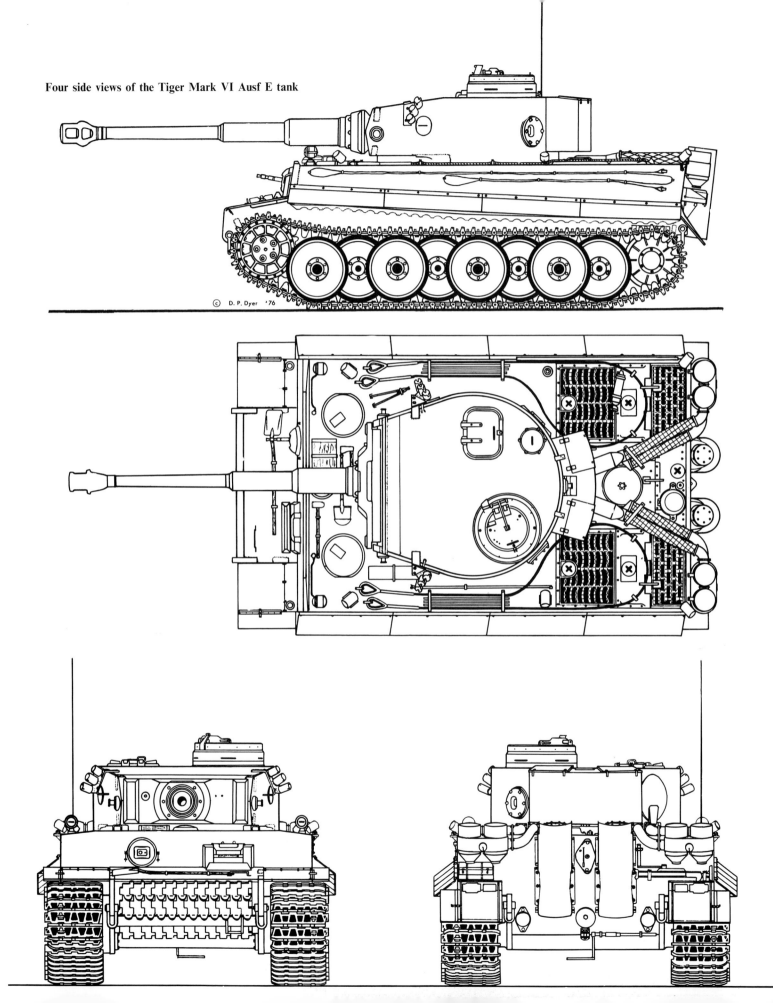

Four side views of the Tiger Mark VI Ausf E tank

© D. P. Dyer '76

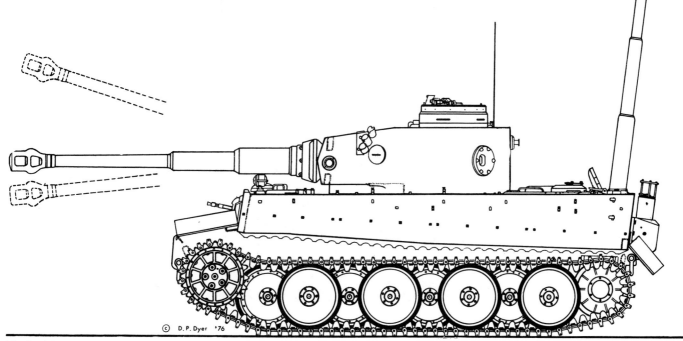

Tank with transportation tracks and air shaft for submerged running

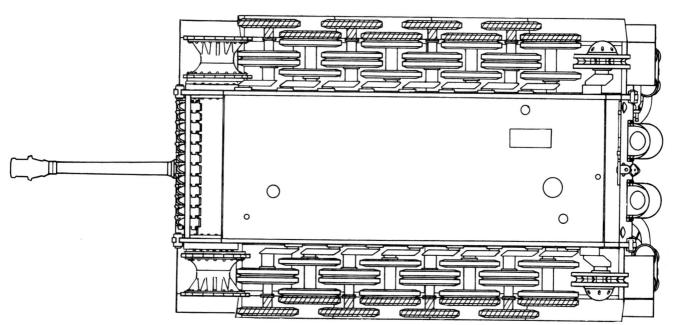

For railway loading, the hatched bogie wheels in the drawing were removed

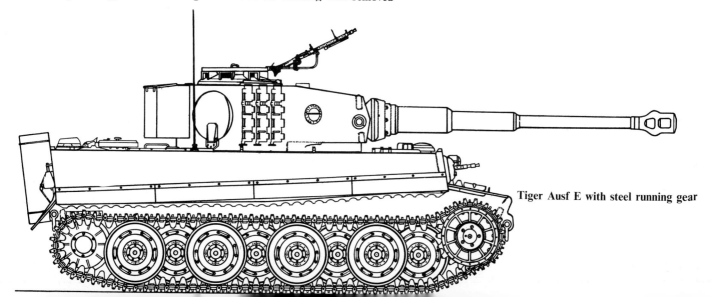

Tiger Ausf E with steel running gear

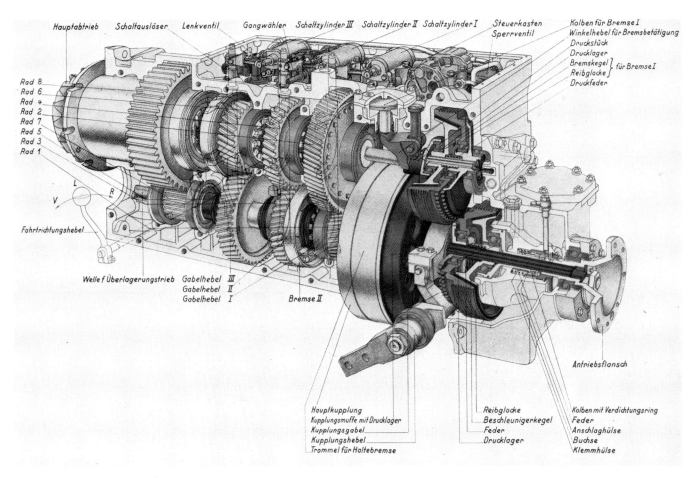

Hauptabtrieb — Schaltauslöser — Lenkventil — Gangwähler — Schaltzylinder III — Schaltzylinder II — Schaltzylinder I — Steuerkasten — Sperrventil — Kolben für Bremse I — Winkelhebel für Bremsbetätigung — Druckstück — Drucklager — Bremskegel } für Bremse I — Reibglocke — Druckfeder

Rad 8
Rad 6
Rad 4
Rad 2
Rad 7
Rad 5
Rad 3
Rad 1

L — R — V
Fahrtrichtungshebel

Welle f. Überlagerungstrieb — Gabelhebel III — Gabelhebel II — Gabelhebel I — Bremse II

Antriebsflansch

Hauptkupplung — Kupplungsmuffe mit Drucklager — Kupplungsgabel — Kupplungshebel — Trommel für Haltebremse — Reibglocke — Beschleunigerkegel — Feder — Drucklager — Kolben mit Verdichtungsring — Feder — Anschlaghülse — Buchse — Klemmhülse

The Maybach OLVAR gearbox.

Both photographs below show the details of the gearbox.

The gearbox with clutch.

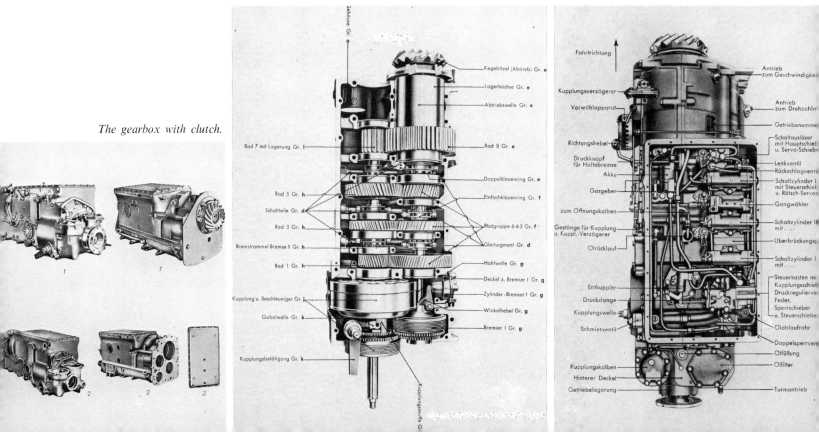

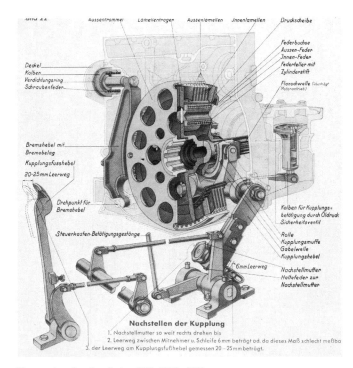

The main clutch of the VK 4501 (H).

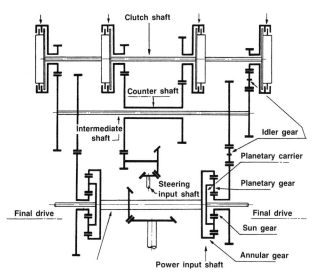

The way in which the Tiger tank's steering operated.

The steering gear dismounted and disassembled.

The steering gear had two turning radii. It was type L 600 C, made by Henschel. It was flanged onto the gearbox. Originally, three radii were planned, but they had to be foregone in favour of the smaller radius because of a weak point in the gearing. As in the L 320 C steering gear of the VK 3001, the different radii were controlled through multiplate hydraulic clutches. For emergency steering of the vehicle, a steering lever was mounted on each of the two brake assemblies. The steering gear itself was actuated by a fixed steering wheel connected to the steering assembly, instead of the normally standard lever link in tanks. In the majority of vehicles, the hydraulic system was originally controlled through a Henschel sleeve valve. Later, for the sake of standardisation, a steering unit from the Südd. Argus factory was used. The steering units were interchangeable one with another. From the steering output, the drive was transmitted through an intermediate shaft to the epicyclic gear in the final drives. The effect was to reduce the rotation of the gear drive.

The final drive, as in the VK 3001, reduced the driving

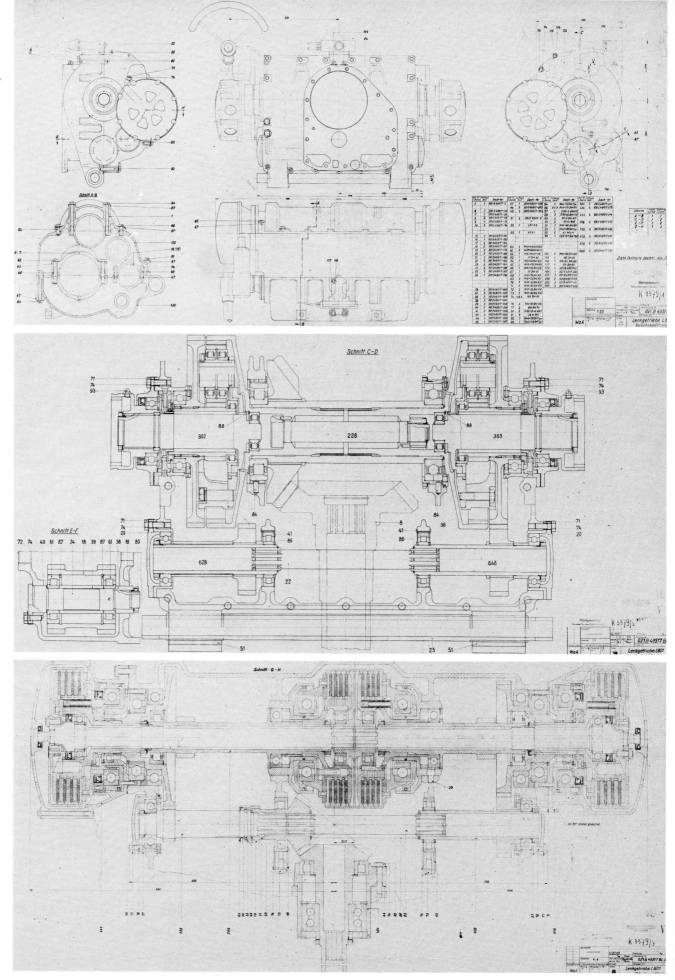

The three drawings show the construction of Henschel's L 801 steering gear.

50

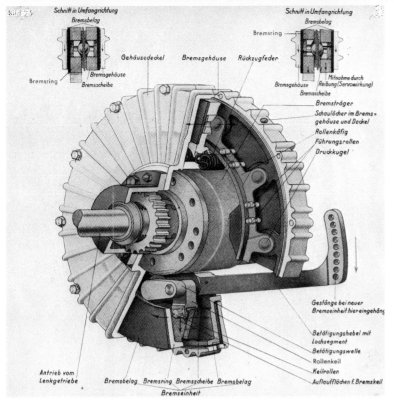

Schnitt in Umfangrichtung
Bremsbelag
Bremsring
Bremsgehäuse
Bremsring
Bremsscheibe

Schnitt in Umfangrichtung
Bremsbelag
Bremsring
Bremsgehäuse
Bremsscheibe
Mitnahme durch
Reibung (Servowirkung)

Gehäusedeckel   Bremsgehäuse   Rückzugfeder

Bremsträger
Schaulöcher im Brems=
gehäuse und Deckel
Rollenkäfig
Führungsrollen
Druckkugel

Antrieb vom
Lenkgetriebe
Bremsbelag Bremsring Bremsscheibe Bremsbelag
Bremseinheit

Gestänge bei neuer
Bremseinheit hier eingehängt

Betätigungshebel mit
Lochsegment
Betätigungswelle
Rollenkeil
Keilrollen
Auflaufflächen f. Bremskeil

Above *The service brake developed by Dr-Ing. Klaue and built by Argus.*

Right *The track drive with components.*

Below *A representation of the final drive.*

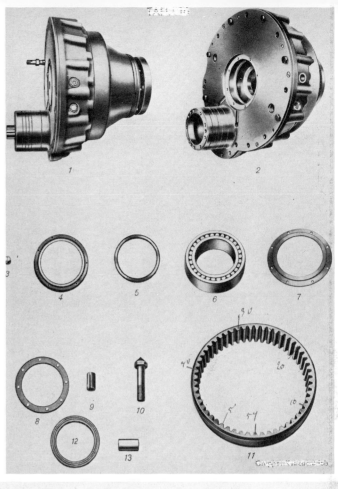

1   2

3   4   5   6   7

8   9   10   11   12   13

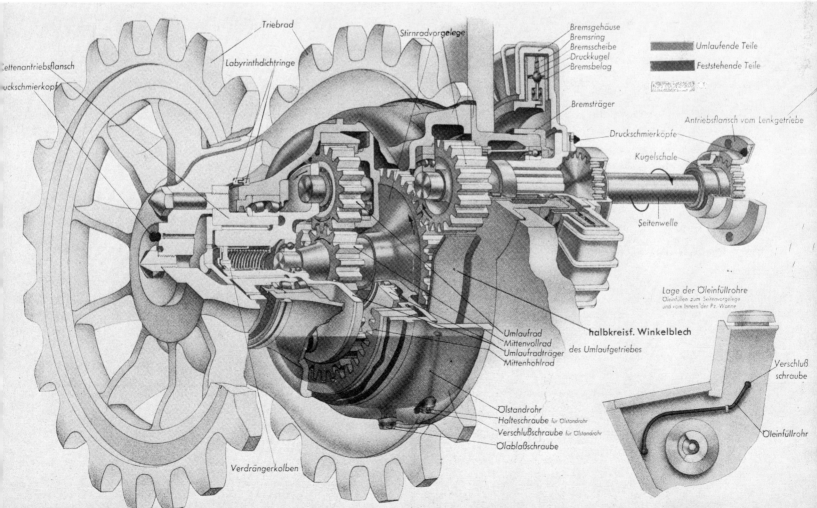

Triebrad   Stirnradvorgelege

Kettenantriebsflansch   Labyrinthdichtringe

Druckschmierkopf

Bremsgehäuse
Bremsring
Bremsscheibe
Druckkugel
Bremsbelag

Umlaufende Teile
Feststehende Teile

Bremsträger

Antriebsflansch vom Lenkgetriebe

Druckschmierköpfe

Kugelschale

Seitenwelle

Lage der Öleinfüllrohre
Oleinfüllen zum Seitenvorgelege
und vom Innern der Pz.-Wanne

halbkreisf. Winkelblech
des Umlaufgetriebes

Umlaufrad
Mittenvollrad
Umlaufradträger
Mittenhohlrad

Ölstandrohr
Halteschraube für Ölstandrohr
Verschlußschraube für Ölstandrohr
Ölablaßschraube

Verdrängerkolben

Verschluß
schraube

Öleinfüllrohr

speed (rpm) in the ratio of 1:10.75 through a spur wheel reduction gearing and a planetary gear. The running gear consisted, on each side of the vehicle, of the driving sprocket, four inner and four outer wheels, eight additional running wheels, the torsion bars, the shock absorbers, the idler wheel with track tension adjuster and the caterpillar track.

The track driving sprocket was attached to the driving flange of the final drive. The toothed gear rims were interchangeable with one another. The bogie wheels were in stacked order. After the beginning of the development work it was discovered that the expected all up weight of the tank by far exceeded the load capacity of the tyres. Therefore, a further running wheel had to be provided on the outside of each existing wheel. The running wheels (size 800 x 95 E) themselves from the VK 3601 were adopted, and were made as disc wheels with rubber tyres. The wheels, with the novel resilient internal rubber spring rims which at this time had not been perfectly developed, created many problems for the troops. The durability of the rubber tyres was too short and there was a constant need to change the wheels. The box formation running gear fell into disfavour as a result. To guide the track teeth, the bogie wheels carried track guide rings. Each pair of bogie wheels, with the additional bogie wheel, were housed in two roller bearings on a suspension arm. These were trailing on the right side and leading on the left side and were carried in two pressed and moulded-material bearings. After about eight hundred VK 4501 vehicles had been produced, the original running wheels were replaced with rubber spring steel bogie wheels made by Deutsche Eisen-Werke (German Iron Works).

The springing of the bogie wheels was by a torsion bar connected to the suspension arm. The heads of the torsion bars were splined and clamped into the suspension arms and into sockets on the opposite wall of the hull of the tank. The first and last suspension arm on each side of the vehicle were furnished with stronger torsion bars. To stabilise

The driving sprocket and other components of the running gear.

The driving sprocket with hub and toothed rim.

Details of the running gear with bogie wheel cranks and torsion bar.

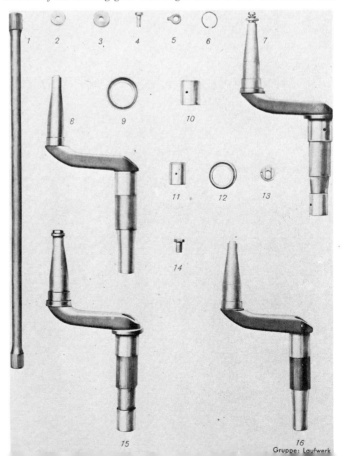

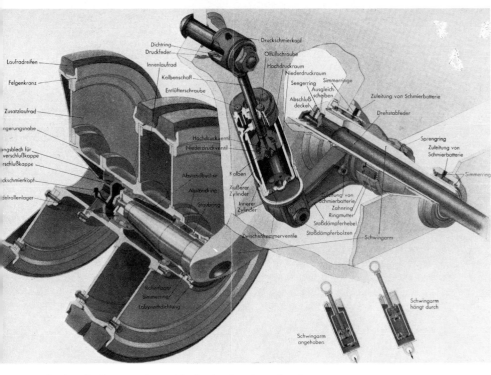

Bogie wheel suspension with shock absorbers fitted.

Right *The shock absorber with full details of the suspension.*

the motion of the tank, unidirectional shock absorbers were attached from inside the tank hull to the first and last suspension arms. The idler wheel with the track tension adjuster ran on two bearings in the hull. To stretch the track, the idler wheel hub was pivoted rearwards.

Originally, a 520mm wide track with a pitch of 130mm was provided. Due to the increase in the all up weight,

The idler wheel with track adjusting device.

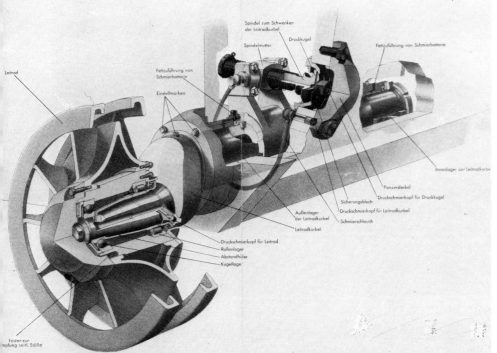

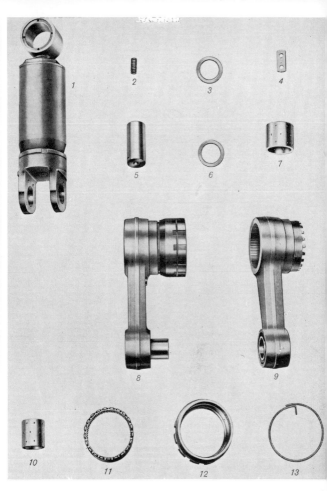

Below *Details of the idler wheel.*

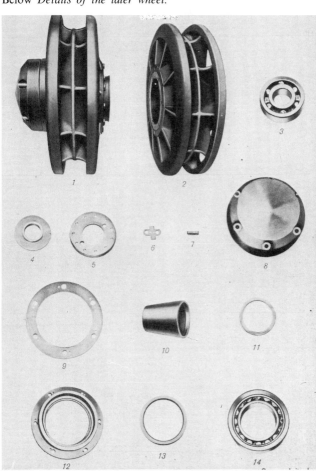

The bogie wheels of the original running gear installation.

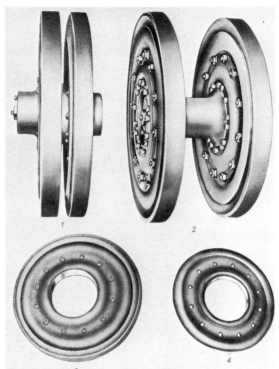

This rubber-spring-rimmed steel running gear was installed later.

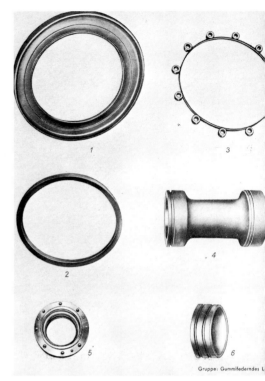

Details of the rubber-spring-rimmed steel running g

broadening of the track to 725mm resulted. As a result, the railway loading gauge was exceeded. Henschel suggested two tracks side by side, but the Army Ordnance Department insisted on two different tracks, namely a ground running (Combat) track and a track for use during rail travel (Transportation). These consisted of ninety-six links which were joined with unlubricated link pins. The Transportation Track was designated Kgs 63/520/130 and the Combat Track Kgs 63/725/130. During the installation of the Transportation Track, the additional outside bogie wheels had to be removed.

In the engine room, an automatic fire extinguishing system was installed. Should the temperature exceed 160 degrees on the electric thermostat, a preset quantity of extinguishing agents was sprayed for some seven seconds on to the specifically endangered locations.

In the future, because of the high all up weight, a submersible depth up to 4.5 metres was required. All openings as well as joints in the vehicle were made watertight with rubber seals. A three-part tube could be put together to form

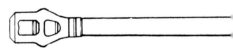

Completed version of the Tiger Ausf E (SdKfz 181)

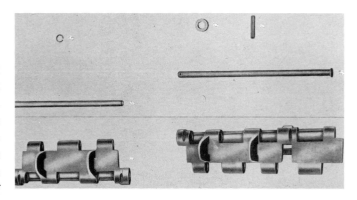

a 3-metre flue pipe for screwing onto the engine room deck plating, guaranteeing intake air for the engine. The exhaust gases were released into the water through non-return hinged flaps. A bilge pump got rid of any water that leaked in. The sealing of the engine room bulkhead was given special attention to reduce the possibility of carbon monoxide gas penetration into the fighting compartment. Experiments lasted for months in order to achieve up to two and a half hours submerged with the engine running. Only the first 495 vehicles were fitted out to some extent with this submersion equipment.

For submersion tests, the Henschel proving ground at Haustenbeck was provided with a concrete basin which gave a submersion depth of up to 6.66 metres. The total volume

Below *Tiger Ausf E with combat tracks.*

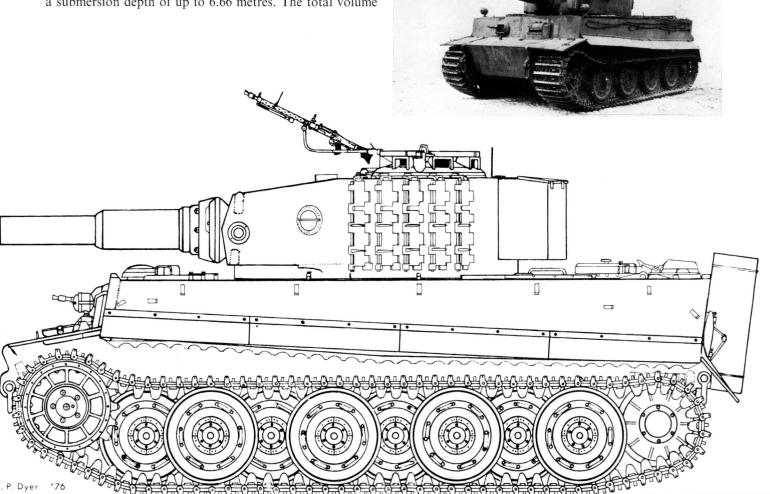

D. P. Dyer '76

55

A Tiger E ready for submersible powerplant run — the air supply pipe is in position.

Henschel submersion basin at Haustenbeck/L for the submersible powerplant experiment with Tiger under construction. The basin was 60 metres long, 18 metres wide and 6.66 metres deep.

The vehicle's engine room with air supply pipe in position for underwater travel.

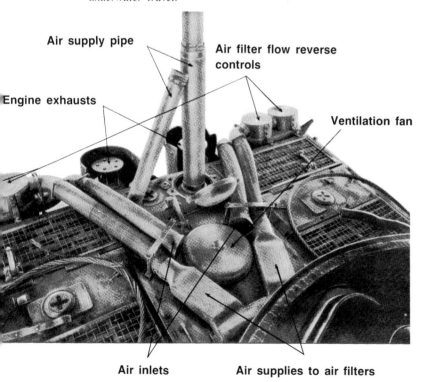

Air supply pipe

Air filter flow reverse controls

Engine exhausts

Ventilation fan

Air inlets

Air supplies to air filters

In case of need, the basin could be emptied in short order.

A Tiger short of the deepest part of the basin.

Left (opposite page) *The underwater powerplant experimental basin with command bridge and observation port. At the bottom on the left can be seen the two heavy duty outlet valves which were installed.*

During the nineteenth underwater test at a depth of 4.1 metres, a thick white smoke suddenly showed above the surface of the water. Both of the basin's valves were flung open. After six minutes twenty seconds the commander's cupola was above water and after nine minutes the basin was empty. For some unknown reason, the automatic fire extinguisher had been activated. The three photographs above and below show the vehicle after the test generating a still greater quantity of smoke.

The crew were equipped with underwater escape gear.

The experimental vehicle V3 rigged out for a submersible power plant run. The ball mounting for the wireless operator's machine-gun was covered by a special cup.

The telescope tube with the direction indicator is discernible, above. The signalling light apparatus was erected in front of the turret.

The vehicle entering the basin, in a depth of water of 4.3 metres.

The exhaust gases cause turbulence on the surface of the water.

The flashing light arrangement served primarily to provide information about the carbon monoxide concentration in the vehicle during the trial.

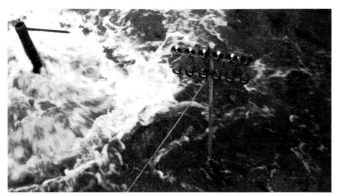

The vehicle emerging from the basin after completing the submersion trial. The steam forming was caused by the hot wet exhaust casing.

On 12th July 1943, the first underwater test in open water (a lake) was undertaken. The three photographs below show the vehicle as it enters and crosses the water. The three shots to the right show the vehicle in the water after repeated trips there and back and as it emerges.

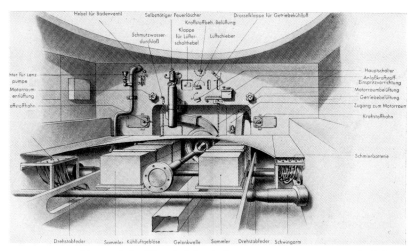

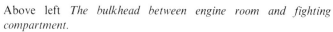

Above left *The bulkhead between engine room and fighting compartment.*

Above right *The instrument board of the Tiger SE.*

Below left *The ball-mounting for the wireless operator's machine-gun housed in the frontal armour.*

Below centre and right *These two photographs show the ammunition bins for the 8.8 cm cartridges.*

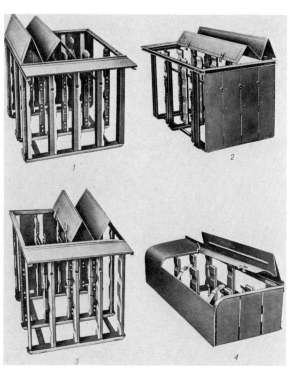

Above left and right: *Both shots show the driver's position in the Tiger. The driver's visor is above the steering wheel; on the left is the directional gyroscope. On the left next to the seat, the front shock absorber is to be seen. Under the instrument board is the preselector lever for gear changing.*

The photograph at left shows the driver's hatch from the outside; the drawing below complements the photograph.

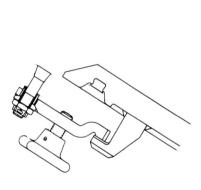

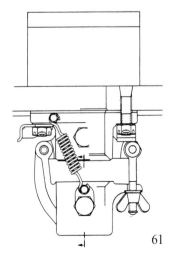

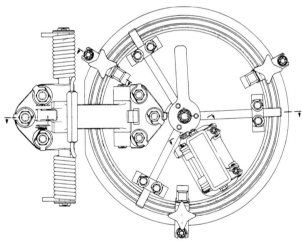

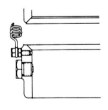

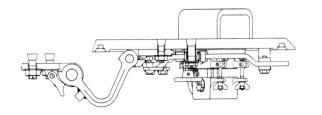

61

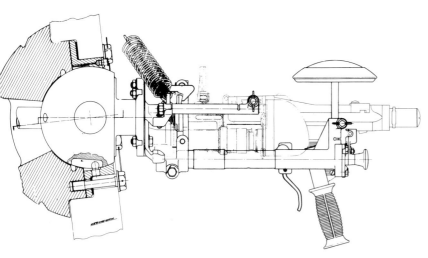

The wireless operator's position with the machine-gun sited in the frontal plate. The entry hatch is visible above. To the right, the machine-gun ammunition is housed in the side extension. The wireless apparatus is positioned to the left of the wireless operator over the gearbox. The right front shock absorber is visible behind the service brake housing.

The illustrations show details of the ball-mounting for the wireless operator's MG 34.

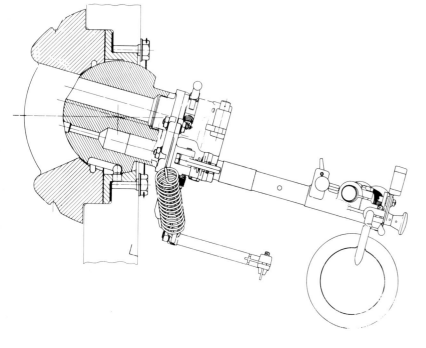

of water in the basin was about 4,400 cubic metres. The inlet and outlet ramps were inclined at 15 degrees. At the deepest part of the basin, two heavy duty outlet valves were installed which could empty the basin of water in between nine

and eleven minutes. A conning bridge was built above the basin and behind that, an observation post which housed, along with measuring gauges, the telephone, radio transmitters and receiving installations. For submersion testing, the vehicle was fitted with a special lamp signalling apparatus which could produce eighteen different signals.

On 12th July 1943, the first submersion test took place in a lake situated in the training ground. A diver was on hand so that in the case of emergency, a tow rope already attached to the vehicle could also be attached to the Panther recovery vehicle. The total submersion time during these tests lasted an hour and 33 minutes. On average, the depth of the water which had leaked into the vehicle was 1.5 to 3cm. The air in the vehicle was good and the temperature was a little lower than outside.

The 360 degree revolving turret stood with its bearing ring on the turret ballrace. It consisted of the turret casing, the turret roof with the commander's cupola and the armoured mantlet with gun and machine-gun. A rotating platform was rigidly fixed to the turret. Beneath it was the sliding contact ring carrier for the electrical controls which rotated the turret. The gun was elevated by an elevating hand gear. Training was through the turret traverse which could be operated either hydraulically or by hand. Using the power traverse, the turret could be turned through 360 degrees in one minute.

The drive for the turret traverse came from the gearbox through a drive shaft to a cone clutch which was engaged, to power the turret, by the radio operator pressing down on the handle. From there the power was led through further spur and bevel gears to the multiplate clutch incorporated into the hydraulic unit. To put these into play, the loader had to swing round. The hydraulic unit, through two bevel gears and the upper drive shaft, propelled the lower worm gear of the turret traversing gear which rotated through a worm wheel and bevel epicyclic type reduction gear to turn the driving pinion meshed into the turret

rotating track. The manual operation of the turret traversing gear was performed through a handwheel in front of the gunners' seat and worked through two bevel gears and a drive shaft to the upper worm gear in the turret traversing gear. This drove the upper bevel gear of the epicyclic gearing through a slipper clutch and, through the planetary carrier, the worm gear of the turret ring gear. An auxiliary drive for the commander turned the upper worm gear of the turret traversing gear in the same way, but, the gunner could prevent this by engaging a pawl in the handwheel. The slipper clutch in the turret turning gear and a relief pressure valve in the hydraulic unit prevented damage to the turret drive were the gun to hit an obstacle.

Right above: The revolving turret of the Tiger E with the new commander's cupola.

Right below: The turret casing without the mantlet.

A schematic explanation of the turret turning gear.

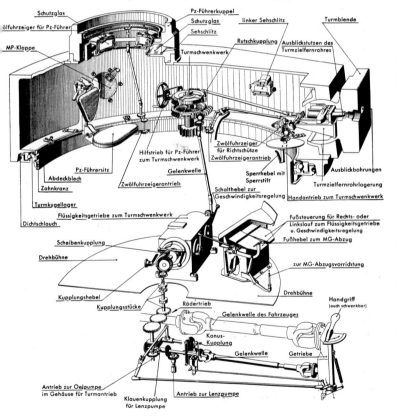

1

2

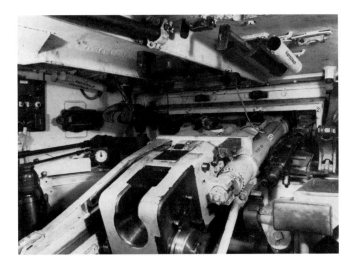

Right *View of the left inside of the turret.*

Left *View of the left front inside of the turret.*

Below left *View of the right front inside of the turret.*

Above *View of the rear bulkhead of the turret. The ventilator is fitted above left in the turret roof.*

Left *The right side of the turret with the emergency escape hatch.*

Right: *View under the breech of the gun. Above left is the eyepiece end of the turret gun sight.*

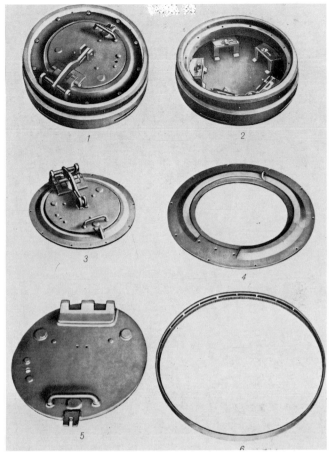

The fully detailed original design of the commander's cupola, above, and below, a cross section of the original commander's cupola.

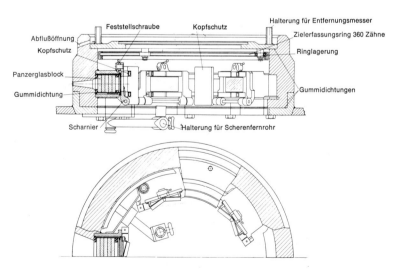

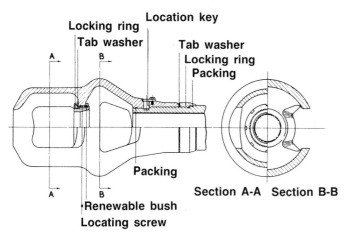

Details of the muzzle brake of the 8.8 cm KwK 36 L/56.

The hydraulic unit (Böhringer-Sturm-Ölgetriebe) consisted of two identical pumps with revolving casings, of

Where items of equipment were housed on the outside of the tank.

External stowage layout

1. Close defence weapons	6. Sledge hammer	16. 15 ton jack
2. Towrope	7. Shovel	17. Track toolbox
3. 15 mm wire rope for pulling tracks (replacement/changing)	8. Jacking pad	18. Towing shackles
	9. Spade	19. Handle for inertia starter
	10. Axe	20. Crowbar
4. Rods for cleaning gun barrel	11. Wire cutters	21. Headlamp(s)
	12. Turret bin	22. Smoke generators
	13. TETRA Fire Extinguisher	23. Openings for screwing in camouflage support (camouflage as lorry or bus)
5. Cover plate for air inlet to engine compartment	14. Wireless aerial protective, stowage slot	
	15. Spare track links	

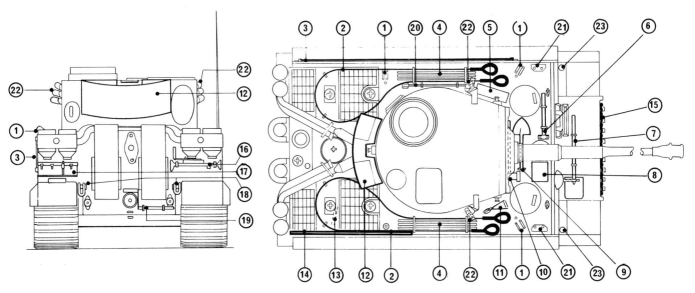

which one was a motor and the other a variable delivery pump. They were incorporated through a lift and delivery duct in a fixed tube into a closed circuit. The control of the driving speed (rpm) was by the variable delivery pump; through it, the speed at which the turret turned was governed by regulating the output of the pump. By adjusting the outer concentricity of the rotating casings, the working space of the pump and at the same time its output was altered, while on the other hand the direction of delivery and thereby the direction of rotation was reversed. The adjustments were made by tilting the gunners' footrest pedal. The greatest speed of rotation from the hydraulic unit was obtained through a lever on the gearbox which altered the output of the hydraulic pump.

Fitting out the Tiger tank for winter consisted of the following:

Cooling water heating apparatus, with blowlamp. The apparatus was installed in the left lower corner of the engine room. It was heated from the outside with the blowlamp; it either thawed out frozen cooling water in winter, or warmed up cooling water to ease starting. The blowlamp was kept in the fighting compartment next to the wireless operator.

Connection and closing valve for the cooling water circulation system (inapplicable in vehicles with permanently installed cooling water heating apparatus).

Arrangement for the use of a petrol-driven crankshaft starting motor.

Primer for the injection pump (priming pump on the bulkhead).

Battery insulating case: by connecting up the hotplate which was mounted on the floor of the battery insulating box, the battery could be kept warm during travel by the lighting dynamo. The illumination of the green control lamp indicated that the heating plate was switched on.

Connecting plate to connect in stray current from extraneous equipment to boost and speed up heating of the battery. The connecting plate had a negative terminal, positive (middle) terminal for charging and a positive terminal for quick heating.

Dr Erwin Aders, who had worked for Henschel's since 1936, designed the tank and was responsible for its technical development. Henschel had planned two versions of the vehicle, in the course of which Krupp armed the turret for the Ausf H1 with the 8.8cm Kwk 36/L56. The Ausf H2 was to carry the revolving turret proposed by Rheinmetal-Borsig and equipped with the 7.5cm Kwk 42/L70. The wooden mock-up of this turret had a ball mounting for an MG34 on the rear. The turret was not manufactured.

On 4th April 1942, Hitler ordered the development of a tank shell 40 with enhanced penetrative power for the 7.5cm and 8.8cm guns for the Tiger. At least ten had to be available in each tank.

Below: *Loading plan and ammunition housing on the right (bottom right) and left (below) sides of tank and turret.*

1.	Kit bin	6.	Cartridge extractor	11.	Spare barrel for turret machine-gun
2.	Butt and bipod for turret machine-gun	7.	Machine-gun tools	12.	Gun balance spring casing
3.	Six belt bags of 150 rounds of machine-gun ammunition	8.	Ammunition bin, 16 rounds	13.	Contact lead for firing smoke generators
4.	Gas mask	9.	Ammunition bin, 4 rounds	14.	Emergency exit
5.	Water bottles	10.	Ammunition bin, 6 rounds	15.	Turret fuse box

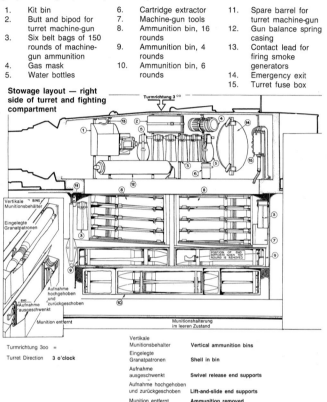

Stowage layout — right side of turret and fighting compartment

Turmrichtung 3oo =
Turret Direction 3 o'clock

Vertikale Munitionsbehalter	Vertical ammunition bins
Eingelegte Granatpatronen	Shell in bin
Aufnahme ausgeschwenkt	Swivel release end supports
Aufnahme hochgehoben und zurückgeschoben	Lift-and-slide end supports
Munition entfernt	Ammunition removed

Below *Where equipment was housed on the turret roof.*

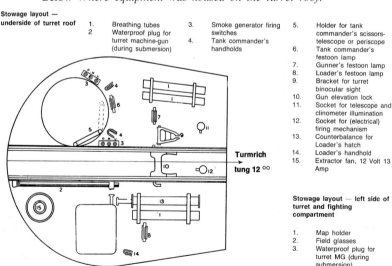

Stowage layout — underside of turret roof

1.	Breathing tubes	3.	Smoke generator firing switches
2	Waterproof plug for turret machine-gun (during submersion)	4.	Tank commander's handholds

5.	Holder for tank commander's scissors-telescope or periscope
6.	Tank commander's festoon lamp
7.	Gunner's festoon lamp
8.	Loader's festoon lamp
9.	Bracket for turret binocular sight
10.	Gun elevation lock
11.	Socket for telescope and clinometer illumination
12.	Socket for (electrical) firing mechanism
13.	Counterbalance for Loader's hatch
14.	Loader's handhold
15.	Extractor fan, 12 Volt 13 Amp

Stowage layout — left side of turret and fighting compartment

1.	Map holder
2.	Field glasses
3.	Waterproof plug for turret MG (during submersion)

4.	Signal pistol
5.	Gas mask
6.	Holder for gun barrel and cradle book
7.	Gunner's personal stowage
8.	Spare prisms
9.	Ammunition bin, 16 rounds
10.	Ammunition bin, 4 rounds
11.	Stowage bin
12.	Wire basket for flags etc
13.	Drive for cupola indicator
14.	Tank commander's hand traversing wheel
15.	Instructions for sealing turret (submersion)
16.	Emergency battery for electrical firing circuit
17.	Emergency switch (changing circuits)
18.	Socket for tank commander's intercom
19.	Socket for gunner's intercom
20.	Turret direction indicator
21.	Contact lead for smoke generator

Turmrichtung 12oo = Turret Direction 12 o'clock

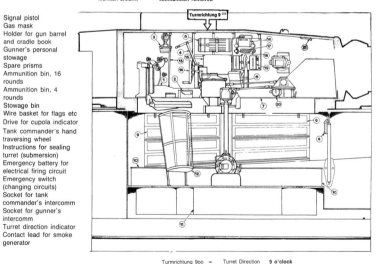

Turmrichtung 9oo = Turret Direction 9 o'clock

67

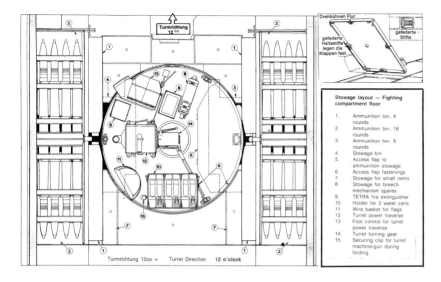

Ammunition storage and details of the fighting compartment's floor.

Drëhbuhnen Flur = turret platform (floor)
gefederte Haltestifte legen die Klappen fest = spring-loaded plungers hold flooring firmly in place
gefederte Stifte = spring-loaded plunger

Stowage layout — Fighting compartment floor

1. Ammunition bin, 4 rounds
2. Ammunition bin, 16 rounds
3. Ammunition bin, 6 rounds
4. Stowage bin
5. Access flap to ammunition stowage
6. Access flap fastenings
7. Stowage for small items
8. Stowage for breech mechanism spares
9. TETRA fire extinguisher
10. Holder for 3 water cans
11. Wire basket for flags
12. Turret power traverse
13. Foot control for turret power traverse
14. Turret turning gear
15. Securing clip for turret machine-gun during fording

Turmrichtung 12oo = Turret Direction 12 o'clock

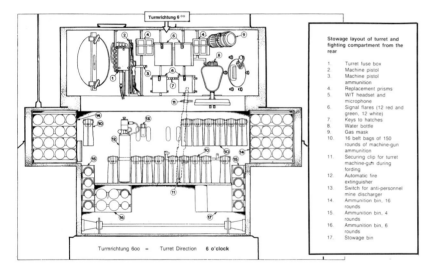

Cross section of storage of items of equipment and ammunition.

Stowage layout of turret and fighting compartment from the rear

1. Turret fuse box
2. Machine pistol
3. Machine pistol ammunition
4. Replacement prisms
5. W/T headset and microphone
6. Signal flares (12 red and green, 12 white)
7. Keys to hatches
8. Water bottle
9. Gas mask
10. 16 belt bags of 150 rounds of machine-gun ammunition
11. Securing clip for turret machine-gun during fording
12. Automatic fire extinguisher
13. Switch for anti-personnel mine discharger
14. Ammunition bin, 16 rounds
15. Ammunition bin, 4 rounds
16. Ammunition bin, 6 rounds
17. Stowage bin

Turmrichtung 6oo = Turret Direction 6 o'clock

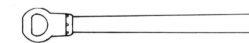

Tiger Ausf H2 (proposal)

Housing of equipment and ammunition in the driver's and wireless operator's areas.

Turmrichtung 12oo = Turret Direction 12 o'clock

Turmrichtung 12oo = Turret Direction 12 o'clock

Turmrichtung 12°°

Turmrichtung 12°°

Stowage layout — driver's compartment

1. Breathing tube
2. Replacement prism
3. Water bottle
4. 'Magnet' inspection lamp
5. Headlamp
6. Ammunition bin for 6 rounds
7. Gyro direction indicator
8. Telescope accessories
9. Gas mask
10. Oil can holder
11. W/T headset and microphone
12. Small compartment for adjusting tools

Stowage layout — wireless operator's compartment

1. Replacement prisms
2. Water bottle
3. 16 belt bags of 150 rounds of machine-gun ammunition
4. First Aid box
5. Machine-gun accessories (belt boxes)
6. Machine-gun butt and bipd
7. Headlamp
8. Machine-gun spares
9. Breathing tube
10. 2 spare machine-gun barrels
11. Gas mask
12. Toolbox

While Henschel fitted the turret with the 8.8 cm KwK 36 L/56, Rheinmetal-Borsig designed a turret with the 7.5 cm KwK 42 L/70. The Tiger tank with this turret was to be designated model H2. The turret was not built.

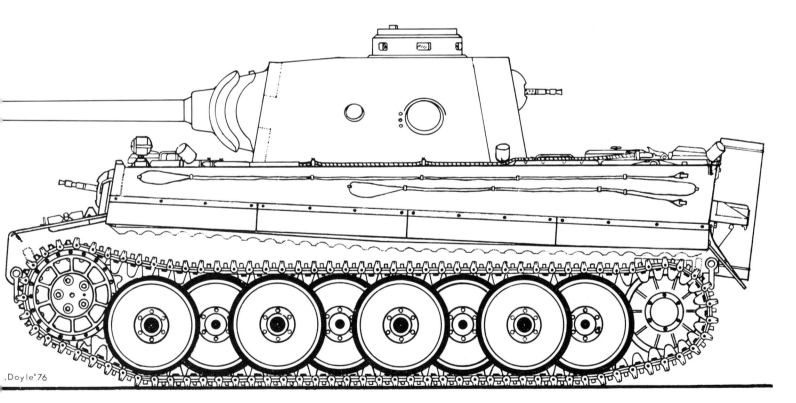

.Doyle'76

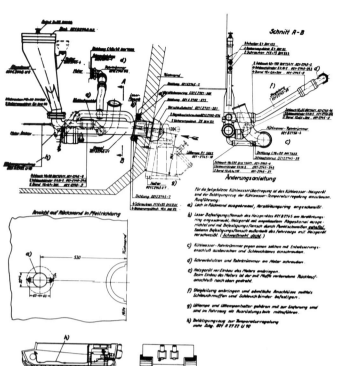

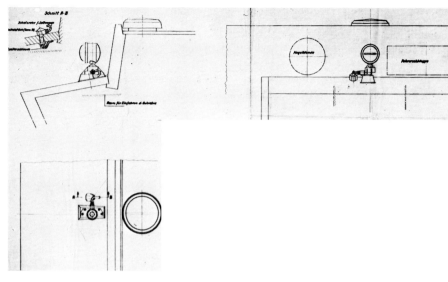

The sketch shows the searchlight arrangement for the last model of the Tiger E.

After the omission of the cooling water transfer arrangement, a cooling water-heating apparatus could be fitted additionally. The sketch shows the method of installation.

Tank transporter (Porsche type 142)

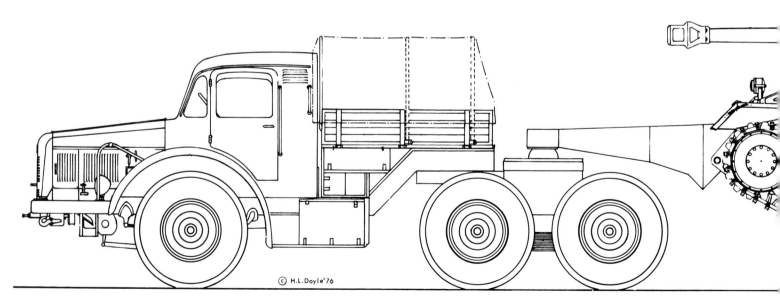

70

Tiger Tank Transporter (72)«npo»

On 26th October 1941, a design for a tank transporter and recovery equipment for the VK 3601 was requested from Kämper-Motoren AG by the Official Motor Vehicle section of the Office of Inspectorate 6 of the Army High Command. The firm of Kämper was to be responsible for the diesel engine and the assembly of the vehicle while the electric motor was to be supplied by the firm of Brown-Bouverie and Company. The hydraulic system came from the firm of A. Teves.

The tractor as well as the trailer had all-wheel drive in the form of identical pairs of synchronised driving wheels, each wheel having its own electric motor. Two 150hp Kämper diesel engines type 6 D 13 E (six cylinders, 13.5 litres capacity) were linked with the BBC generators. A top speed of 40 kilometres per hour was made possible. The weight of the tractor was 20 tonnes, that of the trailer about 18 tonnes. The vehicle was equipped with solid rubber tyres. A four to six-man crew was envisaged. Two experimental vehicles were being assembled in 1942 and a one-off run of thirty was in the preparatory stages.

Hitler stressed on 25th May 1942, that it was not necessary in the case of the Tiger for exactly as many heavy transporters as tanks to be made. He considered that about sixty to eighty of these vehicles would be sufficient. Later, he stressed that a ratio of one to two was reasonable throughout. Otherwise he took the view that these transporters must be suitable for other heavy loads.

Independently of these solutions, Porsche was trying to solve the problem of a heavy transport vehicle for tanks and the carriage of matériel. The Porsche Model 142 comprised a five-axle transporter with diesel-electric all-wheel drive. The tractor had three axles. Basically, the load was carried by being suspended between the tractor and a twin-axled trailer. For that reason, standardised suspension equipment was necessary on all future armoured vehicles for this mode of conveyance. Accordingly, the clearance between the tractor and trailer could be varied, which was of special importance where various heavy armoured vehicles were involved. A steering arrangement on the tractor operated, through two levers, an electric steering facility similar to the tank's itself. The two axles of the trailers were electrically driven. The total length of a load was 17.4 metres.

On 9th October 1942, it was pointed out by Daimler Benz AG that a test engine of the prototype MB 819 for the project on the transport of heavy loads was to be delivered in 1941. As a result of a favourable outcome to the

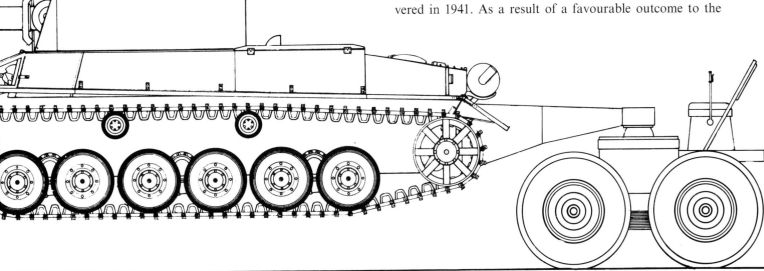

A flat bed trailer with a payload of 10 tonnes for the movement of tanks of the Tiger class, manufactured by Karl Kässbohrer, Ulm. It had forty-eight solid rubber 670 x 170 tyres.

first trial, it was possible that a steady requirement for the series could ensue. The 12-cylinder 450hp diesel engine had originally been developed for use in tanks.

As late as 3rd December 1942, it was confirmed that a heavy transporter was found to be under development for the Todt Organisation at the Polytechnic at Berlin Charlottenburg for whose generator drive two experimental MB 819 engines were for the time being available. A future need was, as before, dependent upon the outcome of the tests. However, the project was not completed. As transport for

the VK 4501, an exclusive and special trailer was produced which had a load carrying capacity of up to 60 tonnes.

Henschel and Porsche (in the Nibelungenwerk) worked day and night to complete a Tiger each so that they could be paraded in front of Hitler on his birthday on 20th April 1942. The photographs show the first tank in the Nibelungenwerk.

3. Tiger E — Production

As a result of the urgent need for vehicles like the VK 4501 — above all at the beginning of the Russian campaign — both the Porsche (P) and Henschel (H) VK 4501 tanks were to be put into multiple production without previous trials. In the middle of 1941, Henschel was scheduled for sixty vehicles in two models. Component parts for a hundred were ordered. Before even a single vehicle had been built or test run, there arrived both a components parts order and the tool procurement to cover mass production of at least one thousand three hundred vehicles, not to mention the need for any attrition replacements.

Henschel versus Porsche

In March 1942, Hitler emphatically declared his interest in getting the first Tiger to the front immediately. Testing could take place at the same time as commitment to the front. The new vehicle was to be made available in the greatest numbers yet possible by May 1942. The potential of committing the vehicle operationally in these numbers was of the greatest importance.

On 19th March 1942, Hitler took notice of the number of Tigers which would be available by October 1942 and by March 1943. It was on a purely theoretical basis that he was promised sixty Porsche and twenty-five Henschel Tigers by the end of September 1942, and a further 135 from Porsche and Henschel by the end of February 1943. As a result it had to be decided as quickly as possible whether the Porsche or the Henschel model should be built, so that only one model would be turned out in quantity. In the circumstances, a preliminary decision was possible provided that the Porsche solution was outstandingly satisfactory.

On 22nd March 1942, Hitler asked about additional cooling in connection with the tank's use in deserts but at the same time also asked about heating for the vehicle. Professor Porsche confirmed that these problems were too vast and that he already had found a solution for his vehicle.

Dr Aders described the demonstration of the first Tiger in the following manner in his literary bequest, which we shall not withhold from our readers:

While work proceeded with all available and attainable energy and preparations for the completion of already more than a hundred tanks had been made, Hauptamsleiter [Secretary of State in the Reichs Office for Supplies and Munitions] Otto Saur had the bright idea — in those days alarming — of presenting the first tank to the Führer on 20th April 1942 as a birthday gift. With enhanced numbers in the work force, with more shiftwork and by disregarding all considerations of good management, the realization of the bold intention was finally achieved, but there was no more time for testing. The vehicle had to travel 500 metres before it would be resting on a platform car. That was 18th April. The tracks extended 50mm on each side over the railway loading gauge. The railway management thereupon closed the line from Kassel to Rastenburg (East Prussia) to all other traffic to avoid collisions. The transport left from a station near the Headquarters on 19th April. A 70-tonne crane of the State Railway was already under steam at 9 o'clock. We did not dare to travel immediately over an open road into the Headquarters but had to wait to use the cleared road along with our rivals (Porsche).

'Professor Dr Porsche had also received an order, that is from Hitler (by-passing Ordnance Department), and apparently did not want to turn it down. For his

The first tank before transportation to Rastenburg. To the front left on the side of the hull is still visible the welded-up round opening which was originally for an exit hatch.

For the Henschel Tiger, railway transportation had to be on duplex working since the tank exceeded the railway loading gauge.

50-tonne vehicle, which was to have the same Krupp turret as Henschel's, he proposed two engines, air-cooled diesels of course, together with electric power transmission through two rear-mounted electric motors. The steering was also to be electrically operated.

'We had an hour to wait and used it for test running and adjustments and also to give explanations to a group of officers from Headquarters, of whom the younger in particular were very enthusiastic.

'The transport from St Valentin (Nibelungenwerk) came in about 10 o'clock. A platform wagon with an emergency power unit was on board — obviously welding had still been going on while en route. The tracks lay spread out nearby and the vehicle was set upon them. Accidentally and unfortunately, it now stood diagonally across the railway line. Its first journey under its own power had also to start with a right-angled turn. It could not make it and through persistent and repeated efforts, the tracks dug themselves in deeper and deeper until after

an hour they rested on the sub-base of the road. Design Engineer Remspiess sought our help but his colleague from Electrical Planning (Zadnig) stopped him. Porsche stood by and let all this happen.

'We then received orders to move to the entrance of Headquarters and park our vehicle in the wood. Later we moved off first and after we went the steam crane was called up once again and the Porsche menace was hooked up to the crane and turned into the correct direction of travel. It came up to requirements on a surfaced road and also reached its parking place in the wood.

'Next morning, 20th April 1942, both tanks drove into Headquarters. Towards 10.30am, the great ones of the Third Reich and the Army foregathered. Gœbbels and Göring were absent. When Hitler appeared towards 11 o'clock, the representatives of industry were presented in the order Krupp, Niebelungenwerk and Henschel. Porsche was then awarded the War Service Cross First Class. Hitler then allowed himself half an hour for an

The photographs of comparative plastic models show the difference between the Henschel (light) and Porsche (dark) production models of the Tiger.

The following photographs give an insight into the production of a Tiger Ausf E. (seen here, right).

Right middle: *The complete view of the manufacture of the bulky parts.*

Right bottom: *The swing arm shop of the mechanical section.*

explanation of the construction of the Porsche vehicle and the revolving turret (Chief Engineer Heerlein of Krupps). It was pretty obvious that everything was already prejudiced in Porsche's favour. As for Henschel, Hitler had only two or three minutes to spare. For all that, he also got up on to the Henschel tank, squeezed a question out touching upon the cooling system (because he saw the grating for the inlet of fresh air on the top of the tank) and climbed down again. I already had the feeling on this occasion that Hitler sensed my cold personal attitude and had his style well cramped by it.

'In the forenoon, the actual demonstration took place with a straight run by the tanks along the well-surfaced highway which led to the "Wolf's Lair"; both tanks disappeared quickly in the distance but neither returned immediately. Henschel first had to put the untested brakes right; nothing was heard about what Porsche had to do. While we then waited at Headquarters again for further orders, we heard that a second demonstration was to take place for Göring.

'The Reichsmarshal arrived towards 3 o'clock with great pomp and circumstance in nothing short of a close-fitting comic opera get up. He handed his Marshal's baton along with his sword of honour to a disreputable chum from St Valentin to hold and as Hitler had done, climbed up on to the Porsche tank. Again it was made clear that Henschel was disfavoured and no notice at all was taken of the Henschel tank. As the Porsche tank was going off on a driving session, Secretary of State Otto Saur, to my dismay, drove into the Henschel tank so that it frisked about on the fallow land at the side of the road. I was quite prepared for a disastrous breakdown but I was to be disabused of the idea in a so to speak triumphant way. It so happened that when the demonstration was over and done with, our tank drove away and without any hesitation crossed a country lane with a light stony surface as if it were a matter of course and regained the highway in the distance.'

Turning the turret seating during processing of the hull.

Recessing the grooves with a special piece of equipment during processing of the hull.

Boring with the eight-spindle boring mill during processing of the hull.

Processing the steering gear housing.

Boring the hull under the roof boring mill.

Inspecting the steering gear housing.

The manufacturing shop of the final drive housing.

Cleaning off a swing arm in the swing arm shop.

The precision boring of the epicyclic unit in the final drive.

Right: *Boring a swing arm in the swing arm shop.*

Below: *Inspection of the epicyclic unit.*

Boring a swing arm on the four-spindle horizontal boring mill.

Finished swing arms are arranged for production.

The installation of the idler wheel crank in the assembly shop.

Bogie wheels being put together in the pre-assembly shop.

The installation of the swing arms in the assembly shop.

Maybach engines were prepared in the pre-assembly shop.

The torsion bars were introduced into the swing arms.

Mounting the bogie wheels on the swing arms.

Above and below: *Subsequently, the chassis was run-in on liquid gas.*

The tracks were fitted on in the eighth work cycle.

A completed chassis in the assembly shop.

Individual vehicles weighted with heavy rings were taken for test running during completion.

The turret supplied by Wegmann was fitted by Henschel on to the chassis.

Finally, the Tiger was completely fitted out.

Completed vehicles before hand-over. Far right are two Panther tanks also manufactured by Henschel.

Four shots show a newly-manufactured vehicle being taken over by a tank crew. It is rigged with Transportation Tracks.

This shows the contrast between the vehicle with Transportation Tracks in the foreground and the other with Combat Tracks.

Top and bottom right *A Tiger and a Panther being loaded into a SSyms railway flat wagon in Henschel's factory railway station.*

Critical Testing: Porsche versus Henschel

On 23rd June 1942, Hitler was told that up to 12th May 1943, 285 Tigers in all would be available. He indicated he was content.

Minister Speer drew attention to the susceptibility of the vehicle to failure as revealed by the results of testing, whereupon Hitler gave the following order:

'The Tiger must this year, and in fact no later than September, be fit for the front.

'Just because a gentle driving style is to be provided does not mean that each vehicle can be otherwise unserviceable.

'It may, to begin with, be used in France so that the difficult Russian conditions can be determined there but the less rigorous test conditions should also be taken into account. The heavy Russian Mark VII tank is undergoing prolonged trials under the same constraints. It will subsequently be obvious that the materials of which the Russian tank is made will also fail under maximum stress.

'Even heavy tanks must be driven with sensitivity.

Four views of a newly completed Tiger Ausf E.

'Accordingly, both Tiger tanks are to be checked out after being through the less rigorous test conditions.

In June 1942, an investigation was ordered into whether the Tiger's frontal armour could be upgraded to a thickness of 120mm.

Continuing difficulties with the engines delayed the completion of the Porsche tanks which were in the meantime laid up in the Nibelungenwerk.

In August 1942, Henschel commenced mass production of the Tiger Tank Ausf E Mark VI (SdKfz 181). The serial numbers allocated to the chassis ran from 250,001 to 252,000. The numbers completed by Henschel as the sole manufacturer and the details of the order are shown in the accompanying tables on page 90.

The test vehicle in Kummersdorf had run 320 kilometres by 9th July 1942. Engine faults showed up and the axles of the first front bogie wheels were badly bent and had to be replaced. The gearbox would only change up to the sixth gear. The fuel consumption was 5.5 litres per kilometre. At this time Henschel was still pressing on with transferring tank production in favour of locomotive production from the Cassel factory to Berlin-Falkenberg.

At a meeting of the Tank Commission on 14th July 1942, it was decided that a further two of each of the Henschel and Porsche tanks should be subjected to testing forthwith at Kummersdorf. Under this arrangement one of each was to be tested under easy conditions and the others under rigorous conditions. In this connection, it was made known that none of the highest stress chrome alloy sprung steel was

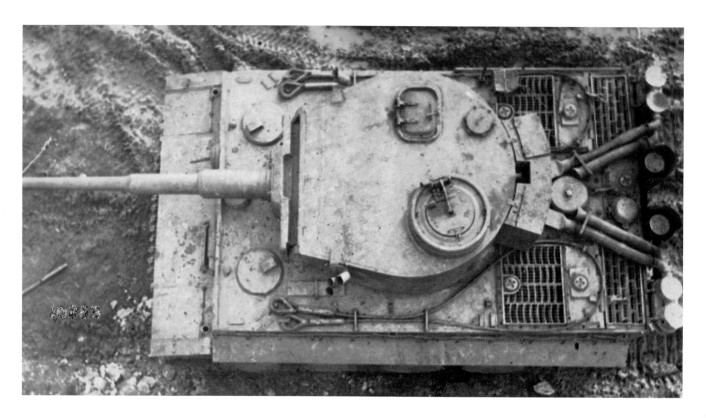

A Tiger Ausf E seen from above with closed and open hatches.

Above and below: A Tiger with snow plough, July 1942.

A Tiger E being tested under snow conditions in the Grossglocken area under the direction of Major (Ing.) Dipl.-Ing. Th. Icken.

Above left and right: *Changing the track was thoroughly practised during training. Since tracks weighed about 3 tonnes, it was no easy matter and took twenty-five minutes.*

Below: *This photograph shows the beginning of the regular job of exchanging Transportation Tracks for road tracks after unloading at the railhead.*

The shots above show the difference in width — 400 mm — between the Transportation (above) and road tracks (above right).

Right: *Recovery was also thoroughly practised.*

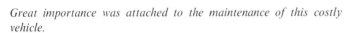

Bottom right: *The special 18-tonne half-tracked truck used for tank recovery work which in some cases, as SdKfz 9/6, was fitted with a 40-tonne cable winch.*

Great importance was attached to the maintenance of this costly vehicle.

Details of Henschel Order

	Number of Items	Sale Order	Army Order
Test	2	424 047	SS006-6307/41
Vehicles	1	424 048	SS006-6307/41
Series	30	420 437	SS4911-210-5904/41
Series	30	420 438	SS4911-210-5904/41
Series	40	420 439	SS4911-210-5904/41
Series	200	420 442	SS4911-210-5910/41/42
Series	124	420 480	SS4911-210-5910/41/42
Series	250	420 520	SS4911-210-5910/41/42
Series	490	420 560	SS4911-210-5910/41/42[1]
Series	128	420 660	SS4911-210-5910/41/42[2]
Series– Supplement	45	420 750	SS

[1] Chassis No 250675-251 164
[2] Chassis No 251165-251 292

Henschel Production

	1942	1943	1944
January	–	35	93
February	–	32	95
March	–	41	86
April	1	46	104
May	–	50	100
June	–	60	75
July	–	65	64
August	8	60	6
September	3	85	
October	11	50	
November	25	60	
December	30	65	
Totals	78	649	623

to be used except on the Tiger's suspension. On 15th July 1942, it had been agreed to equip the second series of Henschel Tigers with the 8.8cm L/56 tank gun. Up to 1st May 1942, a minimum production of 145 units was planned which had by that date not only to be manufactured but to be in good working order, that is to say, run in, fitted out, equipped and acceptance tested.

On 16th July 1942, the test vehicle was given a day's testing of 209 kilometres in the country. Colonel Thomale, who drove it himself, said he was content. Up to 22nd July 1942, 960 kilometres in all had been driven at a combat weight of 56.7 tonnes. In reasonably rough country the average speed was 18 kilometres per hour while the fuel consumption was 430 litres per 100 kilometres. The tank was not yet ready for the front in its present state. The provision of a squadron of twenty-five or so tanks in good working order was not expected before 1st October 1942.

During a similar journey at Kummersdorf on 27th July 1942 — over rough country and sand — the Porsche tank was a complete failure. The Henschel tank fulfilled all requirements. A further three months was thereupon conceded to Porsche for further trialling. As a result, the reduction gearing of the final drive was to be changed from 1:15 to 1:19 and the diameter of the sprocket and idler wheels was to be reduced in size. Only each second track link was to be fitted with a driving cog. Because of the failure of the Porsche Tiger, Henschel was directed to build no fewer than 210 of its tanks by 1st May 1943.

Henschel's Success.

An order from the Führer demanded that a Tiger Company of nine tanks, completely finished, acceptance-tested and ready for service, was to emerge from Henschel's Cassel factory on 26th August 1942. Accordingly, the Henschel Tiger was to be clearly fit for operation in the West and the East at a cruising speed of between 15 and 20 kilometres per hour.

Leaky engines increased oil wastage to 15 litres per 100 kilometres but this was regarded as reasonable on take-over. Damage to the tyres of the bogie wheels caused Colonel Thomale to order a new improved running gear from tank number 101 inclusive. This was not easy to develop. For winter running, Henschel were, in cooperation with Wegmann, to fit out nine Mark III tanks with coupling flanges

These original shots of the first Tiger action are by Colonel a.D. Dip-Ing. Th. Icken. Of the four tanks committed to action, all were stricken; it was possible to recover three but the fourth was blown up.

The first four Tigers of 502 Tank Battalion were in action at Mga on 29th August 1942. Here, one is salvaged by two 18-tonne half-tracked trucks.

The replacement engines had to be flown in straight to the combat area by Junkers 52 to restore the Tigers to combat worthiness. Here, an engine is unloaded.

This photograph shows replenishment of ammunition on the battlefield from an armoured personnel carrier (SdKfz 251).

for the transfer of cooling water. To begin with, each Tiger was to be accompanied during action by a ZW vehicle. At Fallingbostel (where 501 and 502 Tiger Battalions were stationed) a period of gunnery trials took place. Crew training took place at the Kassel-Wilhelmstat driving school.

Colonel Thomale explained that the Porsche tank had to be turned down because its radius of action was too short, its engine leaked oil, causing serious impairment of the cooling system, and it had fundamental running gear defects.

The nine Henschel tanks provided for the troops had front suspension arms made of improved material and the V belt for the fan-drive was different. For driving underwater, valves were arranged between the engine room and ventilation compartment as well as intake couplings for exchange of cooling water from the accompanying ZW vehicle. These were not supplied by Wegmann (on account of the defective 5cm KwK L/60) but by Alkett or Daimler-Benz.

Amongst ourselves the Henschel Tiger was identified as C10 while the improved model was identified as C11. The latter was to commence production with five units in January 1943. The C10 production provided for 185 units. At the beginning of September 1942, the Henschel's production norm was fixed as fifty C11 and thirty C10.

On 19th August 1942, General of Artillery Lieb, as Head of the Ordnance Department, expressed his thanks to Henschel's for meeting the output of the Tiger which Hitler had so urgently demanded. The order to install the Panther tank's engine in the Tiger as well caused Maybach to recommend building a model intermediate between the VK 4501 and the projected VK 4503 so that as from vehicle number 200, a VK 4502 could be fitted with the Panther engine, including the Panther cooling system. According to Maybach, all that was necessary was to incline the rear wall of the hull about 22 degrees off perpendicular. Henschel initiated a corresponding investigation. For the first nine C10 units the hot water transfer system leaked. They had to be installed later.

The appointed day for the delivery of the first four production Tigers was advanced to 18th August 1942. Numbers 5 and 6 went to Fallingbostel on 27th August. As had happened before, considerable difficulty was experienced with the Maybach Olvar system, mainly through failure of the hydraulic pumps and the bursting of the pressure cylinders in the upper part of the gear unit. In addition, there was a continuous clogging of the oil pressure regulator valve.

Reichsminister Speer decreed late in August 1942 that Henschel be given a follow-up order for over three hundred Tigers. Upon enquiry as to the type to be produced, it was stated that Tigers 1 to 140 were to be in the current mode while Tigers 141 to 300 were to be unaltered except for the fitting of a slanted front. The proposal by Maybach for an intermediate model with the Panther stern, engine, ventilation and cooling system was rejected. On 10th September, orders were given for the Tiger's fighting compartment also to have heating.

The gear wheel factory at Friedrichshafen had in the meantime developed an electric transmission. Lieutenant Schreiben was to conduct tests on the transmission beginning on 2nd September, first in type VK 3601 and secondly on type VK 4501.

These jacking-up trials, with a hydraulic telescopic jack of the Hydrovis type with a lifting capacity of 15/30 tonnes, provide a clear view of the details of the running gear and track of the Henschel Tiger.

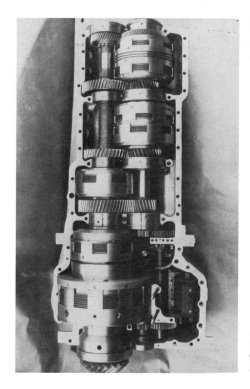

Left: *The experimental type 12E170 2 x 6 gear (twelve-gear) Electro-clutch gearbox.*

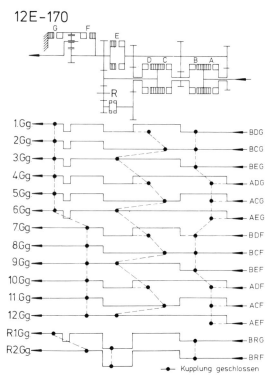

Right: *The circuit diagram for the experimental type 12 E170 electro-clutch gearbox.*

The first action by Tiger tanks made by Henschel took place on 29th August 1942 in the neighbourhood of Leningrad. The badly prepared offensive foundered on unsuitable terrain and led to the premature revelation of secrets.

In the middle of September 1942, the first reports from the Front of damage to the gearbox and steering wheel came in: Colonel Thomale took the view that the Tiger had to be rejected as unfit for use by front line fighting men. He asked for an investigation into whether the ZF dogclutch constant mesh gearbox used in the Panther could not also be used in the Tiger. Colonel Thomale did not mince his words, saying 'he refused to send German men into battle in such a tank'. A representative of Maybach strongly opposed the allegation that ' consistently the vehicles were wanting and absolutely unserviceable', and said it was their exclusive aim to send to the front what could there be proved to be up to field service standards. The Maybach gearbox was also produced by the firm of Adler. On 21st September, Henschel informed Chief Designer Kniepkamp that the ZF constant mesh gearbox could be installed in the Tiger. On 23rd September, two ZF electric 12 E 170 gearboxes were completed and ready for installation in the Tiger. The new

steering gear, which was under test at the end of September 1942, was in mass production by the firms of AVOG, Holland and Mühlschlegel, Bühlerthal/Baden.

Pre-empting this, at the beginning of September 1942, Hitler had wanted the first series of the still unavailable Porsche Tiger to be sent to Africa immediately, since he believed that they would be specially suitable in that zone because of the air-cooled engines.

Out of the October 1942 production, three vehicles were to be made available for experimental purposes. Chassis number 250,017 was to be sent on 12th October to Döllersheim/Niederöstereich for comparison running with the Porsche Tiger. Tank number 6 chassis number 250,018, which was successfully run in on 6th October, was fitted out with the ZF electric gearbox and, without turret and equipment, was likewise shipped to Döllersheim. The vehicle with chassis number 250,019 was delivered for winter trials with the service. In addition, a vehicle was ordered for UK-trials (Unterwasserfahrten: submerged running).

At the beginning of October 1942, the delivery schedule for the VK 4503 was proposed. The volume of production starts arising from the schedule, taken together with the

94

During trialling with the VK 4501/V3, the track wound itself off the driving sprocket while reversing and turning.

As a result, the left track detached itself from the sprocket wheel.

The final drive was wrenched out some 5 cm to one side (see next page also).

Continuing the sequence of illustrations of the trialling from the previous page, here the track, detached from the outer sprocket wheel, can be clearly seen.

The track had to be cut through with an oxy-acetylene burner after the first outer bogie wheel had been removed.

large number of Tigers of the first model on order, 424, was explained to be intolerable. Transferring of 170 vehicles to the VK 4502 and increasing the Series 1 to 2 to a total of five hundred was recommended so that from vehicle 501 the type 3 could be built. Colonel Thomale rejected the plan which involved a manipulation of the VK 4502 production. He conceded the Serial run of the VK 4503 for September and approved of the approximately one hundred Tiger 3s which would thereupon be available for the 1944 New Year offensive. The VK 4502s still remaining were to have a sloping forefront of something under 40 degrees.

In October 1942, Speer set up a Tiger Commission which was to come to a conclusion about the definitive choice of a model. Colonel Thomale expected that Henschel as well as Porsche, two of the best and competing exponents of the Tiger, would be asked to appear before the Commission. All aspects were scrutinised during a period of about six days and analysed without the presence of the manufacturers. At the end, the presiding gentlemen 'as the lawful advocates of their product' had occasion to indicate their particular preference for construction.

All tanks which were run in until the middle of October suffered from gearbox failure. The carburettor adjustment was criticised. The VK 4501 was, because of the unreliability of the Maybach gearboxes, absolutely unsafe for service or operation. On 12th October 1942, it was ruled in connection with this situation that the Tiger would for the first time be fitted out with the Panther engine. From 15th October no further vehicle was allowed to be delivered without winter oil. Also in October 1942, an order was given for the fitting out of the Tiger for tropical use.

On 12th October, Henschel intimated that as from vehicle number 170 the Panther engine was to be installed in the Tiger. This interim solution made the installation of a so-called Zig-Zag gearbox with spiral-toothed bevel gears a pre-requisite. The gearbox was completed by mid-November. The commission set up to appraise the Tiger tank convened at Eisenach (a garrison training area) between 26th and 31st October (whose composition is shown on page 98.).

The result of the trial comparison was that the Henschel model was unequivocally superior — and a decision was made in its favour. Of the Henschel Tigers ordered up to 10th October 1942, 424 were to be delivered in Design 1 and the remaining 176 in Design 3.

Both batteries were accommodated in heating boxes made by the firm of Flender. The driveshaft ran between the batteries.

The photograph shows one of the boxes with the inlaid heating plate to pre-heat the batteries lying loosely in it — 'oben' signifies 'This Way Up'.

Both batteries covered up. The turret turning gear is in the lower centre part of the photograph.

The heating plate with connecting cables.

Here, a battery is removed from the heating box.

97

Tiger Tank Commission

Technical President Prof Dr-Ing. Eberan von Eberhorst	Dresden Polythenic
Military President Colonel Thomale	Head of Army Armament sand Reserve Army Staff
Colonel Dipl.-Ing. Esser } Colonel von Wilcke	Ordnance Inspectorate Branch 6
Senior Ministerial Counsellor Dipl.-Ing. Baier	Ordnance Branch Armaments Inspectorate - Projectiles
Lt Colonel Dipl.-Ing. Bolbrinker } Lt Colonel Dr Körbler	General Army Branch/Inspectorate of Transport Troops
Captain Ohrolff	Head of Army Armaments and Staff of Reserve Army
Senior Controlling Surveyor Röver } Controlling Surveyor Grosser	Ordnance Department Head of Engineers 4
Dr Dipl-Ing. Freyberg Consulting Engineer } Rosenfeld	Alkett
Senior Controlling Surveyor Knönagel Consulting Engineer } Wittman Dipl.-Ing. Mann	Ordnance Department Head Engineers
Director Dipl.-Ing. Welge } Dr Aureden, Krupp	Tank Commission
Lt Colonel Post Major Lueder	CO 503 Panzer Battalion CO 501 Panzer Battalion

The C10 with ZF electric transmission left the factory on the evening of 20th October 1942, after it had done only 10 kilometres of trial running. This journey had an impressively agreeable outcome.

The next few weeks were packed with work and discovery. No spare parts were made for the steering gear of tanks 1 to 10 so none was in stock. Repair was only possible by the substitution of a new unit. In the middle of November, the underwater testing of the Tiger was started. It was suggested that the exhaust pipes should be capped on account of the development of large jets of flame from the exhaust. Further investigations were started on how to accommodate the additional fuel needed for some 50 to 60 kilometres. Most difficulties during November, in addition to installation problems, were caused by unforeseen breakdowns. Engine fires, repeated leaks from the cooling water system, short circuits in the electrical wiring as well as defective gearboxes, all happened. Moreover, it was becoming quite clear that the higher incidence of installation failures was due to the great stress and strain on the labour force.

At a conference on 20th November it was laid down that the designed upgrading of the VK 4501 was to run alongside the introduction of the VK 4503. According to the current output schedule the production of the 424 (plus three) VK 4501s on order was to come to an end in September 1943. The building of the VK 4503 was to start with one vehicle in the same month and the full production of fifty per month was to be reached by May 1944. Thereby there was likely to be a shortage of about two hundred and fifty tanks over the months of September 1943 to April 1944. Therefore, it was agreed that Henschel's would be given yet another additional order for around two hundred and fifty VK 4501s. Thereafter, Henschel's had 242, plus 250, totalling 674 VK 4501 chassis and 176 VK 4503s on their order book. Added to this were three experimental VK 4501s for Weapons Testing Branch 6.

As previously related, an electric gearbox was fitted in vehicle 018 and it was back again at the gear wheel factory in Friedrichshafen. It was no longer known as experimental vehicle number 2. Instead, this V2 experimental vehicle, which was delivered to the 501 Tank Battalion, became number 250, 018.

The cranks for the track adjustment were changed from vehicle 26. From vehicle 37, an improved eight-gear gearbox, which incorporated numerous modifications, came to hand for installation. Up to fifty vehicles were fitted with a 'sea cock' in the hull.

In the middle of December 1942, a suggestion was made that the tank run on liquid gas; Alketts had already started work on the idea. At this Meister Schlickenrieder developed a similar unit with a motor lorry application which was immediately successful. So far road testing (120 kilometres) used up between 800 and 900 litres of petrol. It was accordingly calculated that no fewer than 500 litres could be saved if road testing alone were done on liquid gas and the acceptance testing (about 25 to 30 kilometres) were done exclusively on petrol. With a production of eighty vehicles in a month, a saving in petrol of about 40,000 litres was achieved.

Production

Designation	Weight (metric tonnes)	Armament
Mark II tank (Fox)	12	2cm KwK 38
Mark III tank Ausf M	23	5cm KwK 39 L/60
Mark IV tank	23	7.5cm KwK 40 L/43
Panther tank	45	7.5cm KwK 42 L/70
Tiger tank (H1)	57	8.8cm KwK 36 L/56
Tiger tank (H3)	65	8.8cm KwK 43 L/71
7.5cm self-propelled assault gun 40	23	7.5cm StuK 40 L/48
8.8cm self-propelled assault gun 42	40	8.8cm StuK 42 L/71
Ferdinand self-propelled assault gun	65/70	8.8cm StuK 42 L/71
Light self-propelled gun	11	7.5cm PaK 40 L/46
Light field howitzer 18 on Mark II tank	11	10.5cm lFH/2 18 L/28
Heavy close support gun 33 on 38/(t) tank	11	15cm heavy close support gun 33 L/11
8.8cm Heavy self-propelled gun on Mark III and IV tanks (Hornet)	24	8.8cm PaK 43 L/71
Heavy self-propelled gun on Mark III and IV tanks (Bee)	21	15cm heavy field howitzer 18 ML/28
Heavy self-propelled gun on Panther tank	40	15cm heavy field howitzer 43 or 12.8cm K

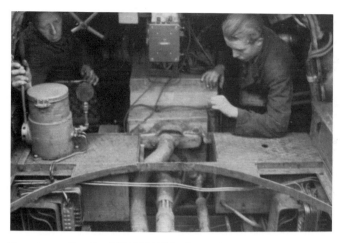

Experimentally, the VK 4501/V3 had a Helios automatic hydraulic high pressure control lubrication system of the HA type installed behind the driver's position as shown in the photograph.

The feeder pipes are visible at the left and right close by the fire wall and also next to the batteries under the floor of the fighting compartment.

Towards the end of 1943, the 'Adolf Hitler' programme of the Central Tank Committee was published which planned the tank production shown in the accompanying table.

Henschel was to build the 8.8cm self-propelled assault gun 42 as well as the Tiger Tank. These vehicles were identified internally in the factory as 'ssSfl' (super heavy self-propelled gun).

There were continuous modifications during the production of the Tiger and these were channelled into the manufacturing process. Accordingly, the track support for the track brakes as well as the complete brake linings from vehicle 151 on were fundamentally modified. As already mentioned, the Maybach HL 230 P 45 engine became available for installation. As a result, the left and right fans of the cooling system were also modified. As many as two hundred and eighty vehicles had their transmission shaft exchanged during repairs to the steering mechanism. From vehicle 301, the forward shock absorber mounting bracket was altered. The seating and mounting of the fuel tanks were re-designed from chassis 250,351. The finishing of the turret

For winter running, grouser bars, which projected from 20 to 24 mm over the actual track tread, were produced.

After about eight hundred vehicles had been built, the running gear was changed to rubber-saving steel running wheels.

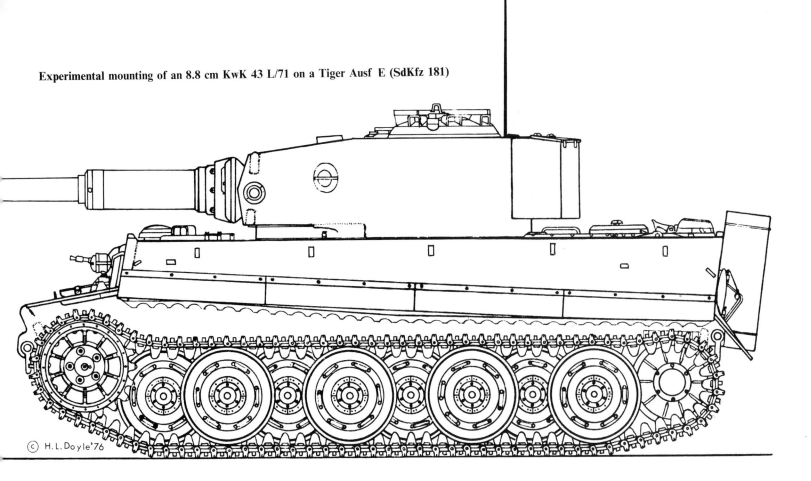

Experimental mounting of an 8.8 cm KwK 43 L/71 on a Tiger Ausf E (SdKfz 181)

© H.L.Doyle '76

casing for the Tiger I was also carried out by the Siemens-Schuckert factory in Mülheim/Ruhr. The revolving turret was fundamentally modified as from vehicle 391 and the result was a new commander's cupola, copied from the Panther tank. In addition, the escape hatch was modified, as well as the firing gear, the turret ball race, the prismatic reflector mounting and the clamp of the gun barrel. Also modified was the mounting of the turret machine-gun, the twelve-hour azimuth indicator drive, the turret position dial indicator, the seating for the turret crew, the cylinder-housed coil spring arrangement balancing the gun as well as the turret accessories and mountings. From June 1943, an improved MG34 anti-aircraft installation was mounted on the Commander's cupola.

In a letter of 11th June 1943, the firm of turbine manufacturers Unna/Westphalen submitted a diagram for a traversable smoke shell projector. Whether this projector could be mounted in the Tiger's turret behind the loader had to be investigated. In addition to the investigation into what space was available, a crude wooden model was prepared by 23rd June. The projector was to be installed in the Tiger B turret as a standard item.

On 6th July, Head Official Saur demanded that Henschel comply with the scheduled output of sixty-five tanks monthly laid down in the programme. A third Tiger manufacturing establishment next to the Dortmund-Hoerder Associated Foundry and Krupps had to be found. Witkowitz was to be responsible for the delivery of smelted steel, the rolling and the heat treatment, while the Skoda factory finished the mechanical treatment and the assembly of the casing.

In the middle of 1943, Krupp made 13,600 tonnes of unwrought steel available each month. At maximum, the following was needed:

140 Tigers Mark II = 95 tonnes each = 13,300 tonnes
120 BW (Panzer IV) = 23 tonnes each = 2,750 tonnes
Five Maus   = 280 tonnes each = 1,400 tonnes

On the orders of Head Official Saur Wegmann was to

expedite provision of an H1 turret with an 8.8cm KwK L/71. The turret was delivered by Krupps late in September. From tank number 391 protection was fitted to cover the shell trap between the bottom of the turret and the hull to eliminate penetration of direct hits in this area. In October 1943, eleven Tiger Command tanks stored at Magdeburg were reconstructed into normal tanks. The completion of the H1 experimental turret with the L/71 gun was delayed. The barrel earmarked for it was despatched from the experimental establishment at Kummersdorf to Unterluss. It was due to arrive there on 10th October. For the October production only four command tank turrets were required.

The housing for the L 600c steering gear was modified as from vehicle 425. From chassis 250,501 the engine room bulkhead was re-designed. As already mentioned, after the manufacture of about eight hundred vehicles, wheels with resilient internal rubber spring rims replaced the rubber tyres on the running gear. Finally, from chassis number 250,201, the vehicle was given modified upper left and upper right fuel tanks.

On 10th May 1944, the following was the final position on orders for the Tiger 1: three experimental vehicles for the Ordnance Testing Department; 1,292 production tanks for Ordnance Battle-readiness Department; and fifty-four further production tanks for the same headquarters. The three experimental vehicles were also delivered by Henschel; their modified Krupp turrets came from Wegmann.

By 31st May, Henschel had delivered vehicles for the series up to their number 1,201 and needed turrets for them until 24th May. Henschel required a further eighteen turrets for the June output which ended at vehicle number 1,219. In June, Henschel's delivery was of vehicles up to number 1,276 and in July, the remainder up to number 1,292. No definite day of delivery was laid down for the fifty-four newly ordered vehicles and they were scheduled for the month of July 1944.

Already at the beginning of December 1944 Speer had drawn Hitler's attention to the fact that the result of using the Tiger in penny numbers would cause heavy losses. By combining into larger formations, new vehicles could gain a much better exchange of experience about the elimination or avoidance of faults, more effective use of workshop facilities and the better workmanship of the resident foreman. Otherwise, the supply of spare parts was for the time being too small. There was only one spare steering unit and one spare gearbox for every ten tanks, since it was not desired

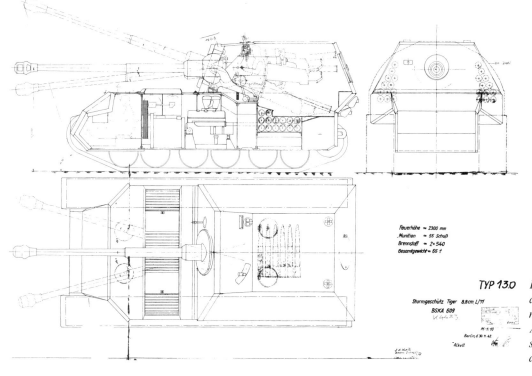

TYP 130

Sturmgeschütz Tiger 8,8cm L/71
BSKA 609

In September 1942, Hitler demanded the conversion of a number of Porsche Tigers to Assault Guns. The drawing shows ALKETT's original design for this vehicle.

endanger the output of new vehicles. The result of using tanks in penny numbers led to a shortage in the supply of spare parts along with a complete breakdown in the repair of battle damaged tanks. In spite of all of this, Hitler ordered that the tanks had to be strengthened for an offensive in the East while a concentrated attack was planned in Africa.

At last the German tank crews had a tank which could engage all other enemy tanks in battle with good prospects of success. The outstanding main armament manufactured by the firms of R. Wolf, Madgeburg-Buckau and United Dortmund-Hoerder Foundry was a major factor. The repeatedly reorganised ammunition storage was arranged in four parts, to the front and rear as well as to the right and left. In addition, there was another storage space under the turret floor next to ammunition containers 1 and 2. Altogether ninety-two rounds of 8.8cm ammunition were carried.

The cooling water circulation system was redundant after the fitting of the Fuchs engine heating apparatus (invented by War Administration Official Fuchs).

The designation 'Mark VI tank' ('PanzerKampfwagen VI') was banned by order of the Führer on 27th February 1944. The official designation was from now on Tiger Tank Ausf E. The last vehicle of this class left Henschel's assembly line in August 1944. The cost of each vehicle was 250,000 Reichsmarks.

Originally, the firm of Wegmann-Wagonfabrik AG in Kassel was to assemble the Tiger as well but this work needed too much space and they devoted themselves to the assembly of Tiger turrets instead. The turrets were delivered to Henschel in completed form.

Porsche had, at the beginning of the development of the Tiger, already voiced doubts whether the use of a mechanical gearbox was still defensible for such a heavy vehicle. The result of these considerations was the Porsche type 102 which was to be fitted with a hydraulic gear unit supplied by the firm of Voith of Heidenheim. Compared with type 101, the vehicle itself remained unchanged. Originally, fifty of these gearboxes were ordered but only one was actually delivered. It required rather a lot of space and was, as opposed to a mechanical transmission, of fundamentally lower efficiency. It was expected, however, that its output would be similar to that of an electric gearbox which was under test at the same time. For each gearbox, two hydraulic torque converters were provided.

The steering gear of the type 102 consisted of a superim-posed gear unit with only two differentials. Their operation was hydraulic. It was planned to fit out vehicles 91 to 100 with this gear unit. The first installation took place in March 1942 at the Niebelungenwerk where it was driven up to 2,000 kilometres experimentally. As a result of persistent engine problems, the transfer of the vehicle to Kummersdorf was delayed until March 1944. A variant of type 102 came into being through the use of Voith's NITA gearbox in the course of which the engines of the vehicle, now designated type 103, were equipped with two cooling air blowers. Neither of these developments was taken further.

On 22nd September 1942, Hitler had ordered the conversion of a number of Porsche Tigers into assault guns armed with the 8.8cm L/71 gun and with 200mm frontal armour. In addition, the possibility of the installation of a captured French 21cm mortar was to be looked into. Hull and top were to be strengthened accordingly. Hitler agreed that the tank armour was to be taken out of naval stocks. The order for the modifications into an assault gun without a turret was officially given to Porsche on 26th September 1942 by the High Command of the Army. On 14th October 1942, Hitler stated that if the heavy infantry gun were to be mounted on the Mark IV tank chassis, the need for an assault gun based on the Porsche Tiger with the long 8.8cm gun or the 21cm mortar would no longer be needed in the numbers previously foreseen. Accordingly, a specifically constructive proposal was to be drawn up before anything else was done.

On 5th January 1943, Hitler wanted to know about the trials of the Porsche Tigers with an 8.8cm L/100 gun — the shortage of spare parts for Henschel Tigers caused grave difficulties at this time. A requirement to up-gun the Tiger had existed for some time. On 23rd July 1941, Colonel Fichtner as representative of the Ordnance Department had told Professor Porsche that he was not happy with the Krupp turret and that he should aim at a better long term solution. Now, under a written order of 21st June 1942, Porsche was to investigate whether the Flak 41 could be fitted in the Tiger turret instead of the 8.8cm KwK L/56. Again in writing on 10th September 1942, the firm was told that provisionally only the L/56 gun was suitable for VK 4501. In the same month however, the firms of Krupp and Rheinmetal were ordered to put forward a plan for a revolving turret armed with the 8.8cm Flak 41 for installation on the VK 4501 tank (Porsche and Henschel). In August 1942,

Hitler demanded prompt information on how short a time it would take to fit the long 8.8cm gun in the Tiger. It was required to have a capability of penetrating 200mm of armour.

In the meantime, the Model E (Ausf E) of the Tiger, earlier known as 'Tiger 1', proved useful because of its outstanding size and weight. In addition, the technical shortcomings had abated to a tolerable extent after the replacement of the rubber-tyred running wheels. A further larger production of the series was therefore to be hoped for, but the Ordnance Department insisted on a new development.

In the spring of 1942, Henschel tried to persuade the Department to accept an interim solution. Under it, the Model E Tiger would be fitted with a convex front plate. With the retention of the present L 600 steering gear, an interim solution would have to be devised between the stepped hull and the proposed hull for the Tiger II. This solution was rejected.

For the sake of completeness, the Model F of the Tiger tank has still to be mentioned. However, all further details about it are missing.

Tiger Ausf E for Japan

On 19th May 1943, Ordnance Inspection Department 6 informed Henschel that Japan had plans afoot to bring its armaments into line with Germany's by copying its arms, equipment and munitions. As to tanks, the Tiger 1 and the Panther were planned. Henschel was asked to send two complete sets of design and construction blueprints to Japan. The blueprints were to be sent as microfilm.

On 19th September 1943, Henschel was informed by the AGK (the Export Union for War Equipment of the Reichs Industry Group) that it had been notified by the High Command that a Tiger 1 tank — complete with munitions — was to be delivered to Japan out of Army stocks. The vehicle destined for Japan was taken to the Army Tank Ordnance Dept at Madgeburg/Königsborn.

It was then pointed out that the vehicle was to be sent to Japan probably on 10th October 1943 from Bordeaux together with a Panther tank to be supplied by MAN. Concomitant with pricing policy, exhaustive discussions ensued about the contractual position of construction under licence, and of the copyright of creator and inventor. Further, they wanted the despatch entrusted to German and Japanese commercial houses so that the commission due to them would not be lost.

Late in September 1943, the Japanese pressed for delivery of the tanks forthwith. Consideration was given to how the vehicles could be shipped in disassembled form. For the Tiger the following possibilities emerged:

Hull with all contents and running gear but without the turret and tracks — 36 tonnes;

Hull as above but without running gear and driving wheels — 29 tonnes;

Turret with gun loaded separately (gun could be separated from the turret) — 11 tons;

Supposing the running gear and driving wheels were separated from the hull, weight of running gear without track — about 7 tonnes, driving wheel about 1 tonne;

Weight of both combat tracks 6 tonnes, of the transportation tracks — 5 tonnes.

On 1st October 1943, the AGK informed Henschel that the established armed services price for a complete Tiger tank Model E fitted out with the following items — ninety-two rounds of 8.8cm ammunition, 4,500 rounds of machine-gun ammunition, 192 rounds of machine pistol ammunition, wireless equipment Fu2 or Fu5 and optical system, came to 300,000 Reichsmarks. An export price of 645,000 Reichsmarks was suggested. On 7th October, this amount was charged to the account of the Japanese (see Appendix K).

On 14th October the Army Tank Ordnance Depot, Königsborn, produced a Tiger tank (chassis number 250,455) for delivery to Japan via Bordeaux railway station. The vehicle arrived at Bordeaux on 27th October after it had been held up for several days because it exceeded the railway loading gauge.

Henschel confirmed the receipt of the purchase price of 645,000 Reichsmarks on 28th February 1944. It is interesting in this connection to break down the price into the costs of individual items (given in Reichsmarks): engine 13,000, gear change mechanism 8,300, hull 54,000, turret (with commander's cupola and mantlet) 26,000; turret assembly 20,000, chassis assembly 12,4000, tracks 7,000, gun 22,000, ammunition 9,000, optical system 2,900, radio equipment

3,000, two MG34s 1,100 and a machine pistol 75. Thus, from the selling price after deduction of the armed service price of 300,000 Reichsmarks and the outlays for packing, shipment and commissions amounting to 33,166 Reichsmarks, there remained 311,834 Reichsmarks (to be distributed).

Of this residual sum, the armed services received 80 per cent (249,467), and Henschel for their trouble over the transaction 2.5 per cent (7,795.85). A further 17.5 per cent went to the three development firms of Henschel, Krupp and Maybach (54,570.95); out of the share for the development Maybach received 7.1 per cent, Krupp 22.7 per cent and Henschel 70.2 per cent.

According to notification from the High Command head of Army Armaments and Commander in Chief of the Reserve Army General Army Branch Staff 1b (2) No 11646/44 of 21st September 1944, the Tiger destined for Japan was no longer to be delivered. The vehicle would be put at the disposal of the German Army by way of loan.

4. Tiger B — King Tiger: Production

In January 1943, Hitler decreed that the new Tiger which was in the course of planning was to be equipped with the long 8.8cm gun and from the outset was to be fitted with 150mm frontal armour and 80mm side armour. By sloping the front armour plate 35 per cent and the side armour plate 65, a vehicle resembling the Panther emerged. The armour plate was interlocked.

A new track was developed with a breadth of 800mm and a pitch of 130mm. It was comparatively light — 2.8 tonnes per track — and consisted of cast steel links and forged steel intermediate links. An improved track was developed by the firms of MIAG and Skoda which was availa-

The new hull layout for the Tiger Ausf B. Below to the right the revised engine room cover is visible which was still being used in the last production run of these vehicles.

ble from July 1944. As a result, the connecting links (without the guide tooth) were cast as one piece. The rigidity against component force was thereby considerably increased, although the weight per track was of course increased to 3.2 tonnes. For loading on a railway flat truck, a 600mm wide transportation track had to be fitted; the width of the vehicle was then 3,300mm.

The whole running gear with bogie wheels and driving sprocket had to be produced in a new form. For the first time, a 'Staffel' (square box formation) running gear with two by nine pairs of bogie wheels with resilient internal rubber spring rims of 800mm diameter were installed. These rubber-saving wheels were a development of the German Iron Factory. Each consisted of two strong steel-sheet-metal wheel rims which clamped a steel rim between two rubber

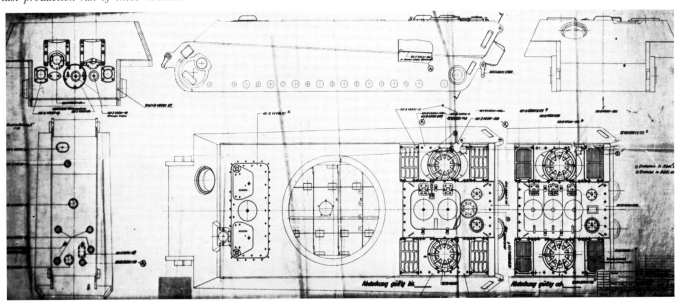

The presentation of the wooden mock-up of the Tiger B and 8.8 cm ammunition to Hitler and Speer. Ammunition was not interchangeable between the two models of the Tiger.

tant mesh. From there, the power was transmitted to theMaybach OLVAR EG 40 12 16 B gearbox; the driving bevel gear was now no longer housed in the gearbox. A new steering mechanism, type L 801, had also to be developed by Henschel. Originally, dry clutches had been provided for the steering while only the clutches for the control of the steering radii were to be oil-bathed. These designs were discontinued. Both driving bevel gears were housed in the steering mechanism. Matching gear 1 and gear 8 resulted in a smaller turning radius of 2.4 metres as well as a larger of 114 metres.

The OLVAR gearbox needed a gear operating sequence

A cross section of the 8.8 cm KwK 43 L/71 planned for the Tiger B. It could destroy any enemy tank at 2,000 metres.

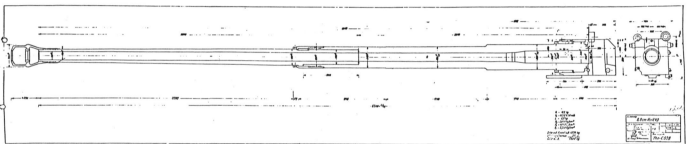

bands under considerable pressure. The driving sprocket was similar to that of the Tiger E but of heavier gauge. The bogie wheel cranked axles were drop forged in one piece and substantially strengthened. The crank stop resembled the Panther's without rubber but with a conical stack of bellville washers; four stops were provided. Compared with the Tiger E, the suspension emerged strengthened and provided with torsion bars with splined heads. They were, however, no longer different in diameter so that the fine adjustment was lost.

The Maybach HL 230 P 30 engine — already used in the Panther — was installed; at 3,000rpm, it was to have an output of 700hp. The Panther cooling system was also adopted; under this, four fans were arranged in pairs left and right. In addition, there was a horizontally lying fan wheel at each side.

The turret gear was actuated by bevel gears in cons-

which was like one of the hand-controlled gearboxes with a power breaker. Accordingly, trouble-free operation depended largely upon the skill and imperturbability of the tank driver (even in battle). Defects occurred more extensively in the overriding clutches and the accelerator as well as in the brake couplings. In the course of development they could, it is true, be reduced but not completely eliminated. Thus the gearbox, which, from its conception onwards, had worked well under the simpler operating conditions of the motor car and which needed a good calm driver to make the best of its indispensable function, was only of very limited suitability in the difficult technical and human circumstances of a very heavy tank. Still, the light controllable OLVAR transmission gear and the light steerable twin radius steering gear were a quite decisive improvement for the driver.

It was possible for both Tiger models to turn on the

The inside of the hull of the VK 4503 shows the housing for the torsion bars. The turret turning gear with its connecting flange for the drive-shaft lies in the middle. The pipe lines to the left and right are components of the multiple lubrication system for the running gear.240

Here, all the cranks on one side of a chassis are installed, as well as the movable spindle of the track adjuster on the idler wheel. The cranks trailed in opposite directions on either side of the chassis.

Now the bogie wheels are attached, likewise the driving sprocket at the front and the idler wheel at the rear.

This photograph shows the running gear cranks (swing arms) with the heads of the torsion bar suspension. The seating of the torsion bar inserted from the other side of the hull lay between the opposite swing arms.

The driving sprocket is bolted on.

The cap of the track adjuster was securely fixed with four nuts.

The large maintenance cover in the rear armour was constructed in two pieces.

The track adjusting equipment could be reached after removal of the cap.

Here one of the two towing shackles is firmly fixed to the rear plating.

The opening for the inertia starter.

The track for the Tiger B was fundamentally altered. The photograph shows the first type.

This series of photographs on this page shows the fitting of the track from beginning to end.

A track pin is driven home.

The completed running gear without the track cover.

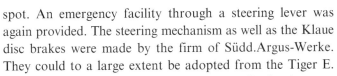

The photograph gives details of the running gear of the Tiger B.

spot. An emergency facility through a steering lever was again provided. The steering mechanism as well as the Klaue disc brakes were made by the firm of Südd.Argus-Werke. They could to a large extent be adopted from the Tiger E.

In February 1943, an extensive standardisation between the Tiger B (VK 4503) and the improved Panther II was ordered by the Weapons Inspectorate Department 6/111. As a result, it was provided that essential components should be compatible so as to facilitate the provision of spare parts. These endeavours held back Henschel's development work for several months before the Panther II eventually came out of the experimental stage.

The engine room and cooling system were the same in each vehicle. The driving shafts from the Tiger E were adopted but so designed that they could also be telescoped for use in the Panther II. The Panther's engine compartment cover proved to be unsuitable and had to be developed afresh. The engine covers were now designed in three parts to improve accessibility to the engine. The Panther's style of driver's and wireless operator's hatch covers which were compensated by springs and swung out sideways were also adopted. This occasioned representations by the Ordnance Department that these arrangements, above all in view of the sloping profile of the vehicle, brought considerable disadvantages with them and it insisted on spring loaded and, in the event of need, hinged hatch covers which could be

released and dumped. This was not taken further. The driver's vision slit was completely abolished. The driver's view was assured through a tilting and rotating periscope developed by Henschel. For the driver, a seat which could be elevated was installed so that during travel the driver could sit with his head out of his entry hatch and have an unrestricted view.

The photograph shows the fighting compartment seen through the turret ring with a view of the firewall between the fighting compartment and engine room. In the middle, the drive-shaft with the interposed turret turning gear. Both batteries are to the left and right of the shaft.

Above right: *Details of the turret turning gear. The turret platform is visible at the top of the photographs.*

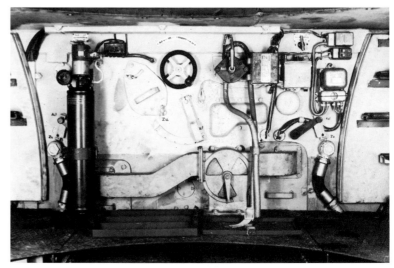

Middle right: *The firewall separates the fighting compartment and the engine room.*

The photograph shows the forward part of the hull with the driver's and wireless operator's positions. Between them lies the gearbox which is linked through a drive-shaft to the rear-lying engine.

Tiger Ausf B (SdKfz 182)

Tiger Ausf E (SdKfz 181)

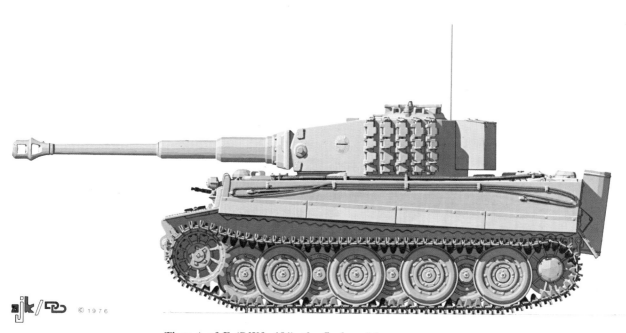

Tiger Ausf E (SdKfz 181), the final model

VK 4501 (P) tank

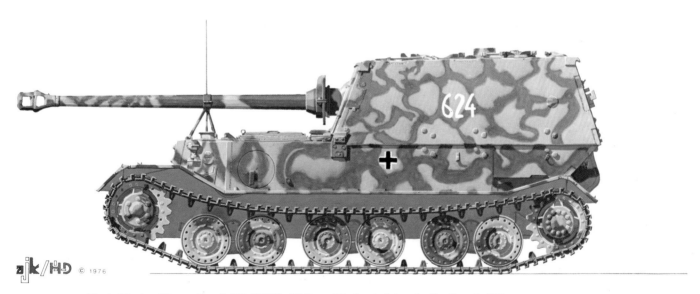

Tank Hunter (Panzerjäger) (P) (SdKfz 184) — Elephant, formerly Ferdinand *263*

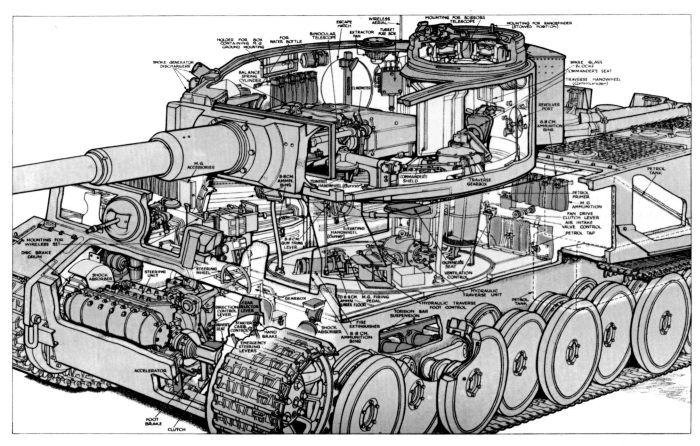

Cutaway illustration for the British Intelligence Report prepared on the Tiger tank

The driver's and wireless operator's positions are clearly visible here. To the left is the steering wheel and the driver's periscope. Above the gearbox is the accommodation for the wireless. The back rest of the driver's seat is folded backwards.

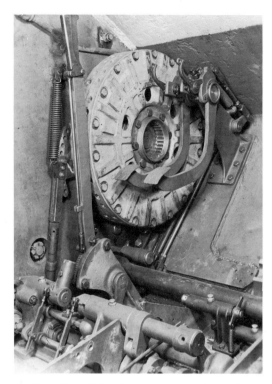

Another shot of the driver's position shows the left disc brake and the foot pedal.

At the wireless operator's side, the disc brake is uncovered; the suspension of the forward shock absorber is clearly visible.

The detailed shot of the driver's position shows the emergency lever, the foot pedal and, below left, the forward shock absorber. To the right on the gearbox is the preselector lever.

117

The steering gear of the Tiger B.

Both these shots show the installation of the gear unit through the entry hatch above the driver and wireless operator.

The vehicle's gearbox; the drive is at the right.

The detachable headlamp was secured on the front of the glacis panel.

The air filter unit is installed on the engine.

The photograph shows the first Tiger B tank with the Porsche turret.

Left and middlle left: *The front and rear views of the Tiger Ausf B.*

The turret shows the entry hatch in the roof as well as the open driver's and wireless operator's hatches.

Details of the turret roof with a clear view of the commander's cupola and ventilator. The close defence weapon is at the rear of the loader's hatch.

Right: Driver's and wireless operator's entry hatches seen from the turret.

Left: The engine cover shows the adaptor piece for the submersion installation.

The photographs show the close defence weapon both open and closed from the inside of the turret.

The close defence weapon which could also be used as a smoke discharger, shown both closed and open.

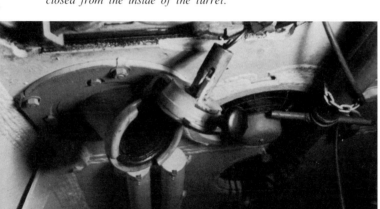

Comparison between the Tiger B with the Porsche turret (above) and the production turret.

As main armament for this vehicle, the successor to the 8.8cm KwK 36, the 8.8cm KwK 41, was planned. The development order for it was given to the firm of Friedrich Krupp AG of Essen in November 1941. The mass production of this gun, now brought up to calibre length of L/71, was planned for October 1942. As the 8.8cm KwK 43 (L/71), it was principally manufactured by the firm of Fr. Garny at Frankfurt am Main.

The turret, armed with this gun and an MG34, was positioned in the middle of the tank. The barrel with recoil gear and hydro-pneumatic recuperator, and the MG34 as well as the telescopic sight (TZF 9b/1) were mounted on the cradle. This was moved manually by the handwheel of the elevating gear (to the elevating pinion via a bevel gear and a worm and worm wheel). The depression and elevation ranged from -8 degrees through to +15 degrees. The turret could be traversed through its traversing mechanism either from the engine via a hydraulic unit or by a handwheel operated by the gunner. The turret was carried on a crowded ball race. The front plate of the turret was convex and the side plating, like the rear, was sloped at an angle of 60 degrees to the horizontal and bellied out at the ball machine-gun mounting as well as at the tank commander's cupola. The roof of the turret was sloped some 12 degrees towards the front and the rear. The turret ring mount had an inner rack with 208 teeth and the load-carrying ball bearings of the turret ball race had a diameter of 45mm. The spacer balls between the load-carrying balls measured about 43mm in diameter. A watertight rubber tube in the annular groove on the outside of the stationary ball race kept the turret sealed against water penetration during submerged running. The firing mechanism for the gun was mounted on the elevating hand wheel and the machine-gun firing mechanism was operated by pressure on a foot pedal.

The commander's cupola was situated centrally in the left half of the top of the turret. It served the tank commander as entry hatch and observation cupola. The hatch in the turret roof was the access for the remainder of turret crew. In the rear wall of the turret there was a hatch through which the gun was mounted and dismounted. In addition there was also a machine-pistol port which was closed off with a stopper. On the roof of the turret, close defence weapons were installed which discharged Nbk 39 90mm smoke generators, anti-personnel mines and type 160 orange smoke markers as well as star shell. Since the Porsche

122

The optical opening for the turret telescopic aiming sight was to the right of the turret while the turret machine-gun was left of the gun.

The wireless operator's machine-gun in its ball-mounting. The Zimmerit protective coating was to prevent magnetic anti-tank charges from adhering to the tank.

In the first experimental Tiger B, no idler wheel stop was installed. As a result, the idler wheel's hub could rub against the outer rim of the last bogie wheel.

The open cover for the telescopic shaft for the underwater powerplant installation. It was still only provided on a few vehicles.

The forward towing shackle at rest.

Above and below: The photographs show a section of the underwater air supply shaft.

Above and below: The photographs show the driver's hatch and the driver in his raised seat while under way.

The vehicle from behind with Transportation Tracks; the track guards have been removed.

In the last production runs, the engine room cover was constructed in three parts and as a result the opening was enlarged.

At the front beside the wireless operator there was an emergency exit hatch in the turret roof. The adjacent photograph shows the position of the hatch; the one below shows the hatch itself.

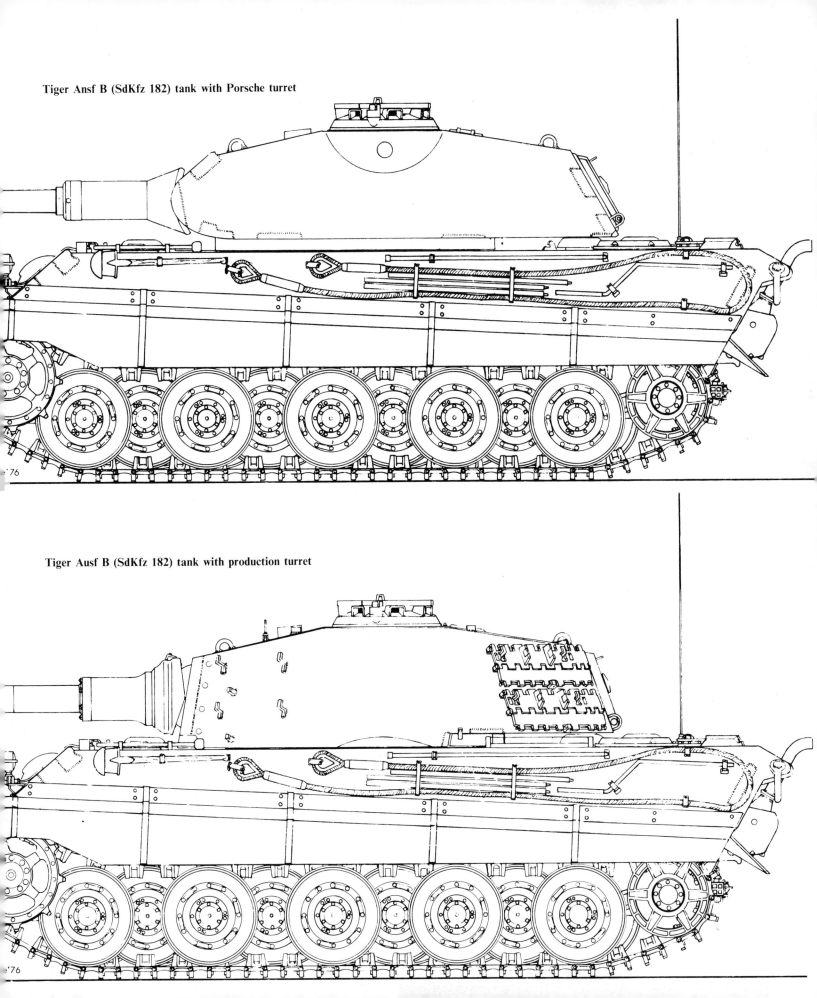

Tiger Ansf B (SdKfz 182) tank with Porsche turret

Tiger Ausf B (SdKfz 182) tank with production turret

Production

	Number	Selling Order	Army Order	Chassis Nos
Experimental	3	424 056	SS 066 6362/42	
Series	176	420 500	SS4911-210-5910/42	280001-280176
Series	350	420 530	SS4911-210-5910/42	280177-280526
Series	379	420 590	SS4911-210-5910/42	280527-280905
Series	329	420 680	SS4911-210-5910/42	280906-281234

VK 4502 which was under development at the same time had not emerged from the planning stages, the fifty turrets planned for it (of which a description is given above) and which had been manufactured were used for the Henschel VK 4503.

The table shows the number of items put in hand. The whole order therefore amounted to 1237 units of which three were for experimental use. The presentation of the wooden mock-up took place on 20th October 1943.

In January 1943, Hitler had already ordered that new developments must not be revealed to the enemy through sending tanks into action too soon. Superiority in war could only be assured for a limited period, at the most a year. Superiority in 1944 had therefore to be planned even then. The Tiger I and the Panther would assure the position in 1943. It should be guaranteed in 1944 by the Maus and the new Tiger with the 8.8cm L/71 gun.

In spite of extreme pressures, above all through the Ministry of Munitions, which absolutely insisted on output

of the first production models of the Tiger 3 Ausf B in July 1943, Henschel had to promise to start building the new series in September. As a result, Speers was already aware in February 1943 of the decision that standardisation of the assembly of the Panther II and the Tiger II had to be brought about. On 3rd May 1943, Henschel made it clear

The heavy wear on the teeth of the driving sprocket is clearly seen in this photograph. However, only every second tooth showed this wear. The reason was an uneven pitch in the track.

Above and below *The Dräger protective ventilation system was to be installed in the Tiger B, but it stayed at the experimental stage. The photographs show how bulky this installation was.*

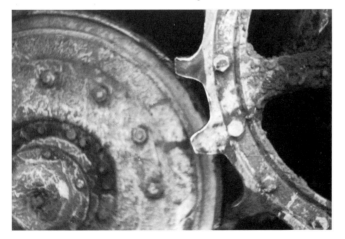

Triple-pronged hooks were produced experimentally for towing tanks. They were fitted with a securing device.

Above and below *The effectiveness of the protective ventilation system was tested by enveloping the tank in smoke. The equipment produced a maximum super pressure in the fighting compartment of 7.4 mm above normal at 2,500. The duration of the test was about forty minutes. The equipment prevented the entry of any smoke into the fighting compartment.*

that it did not expect to make a start on the Tiger 3 before January or February 1944. It was in the course of these interchanges — the subject still being a Tiger Assault Gun on the model 2 chassis which was to become so ponderous — that it became apparent that Henschel's crane facility was no longer adequate. The Tiger 2 Assault Gun, in contrast to the Assault Gun 1, was to be constructed with a movable superstructure. Henschel confirmed that they had no lathes capable of turning from 4,000 to 4,500mm.

On 5th July 1943, the order was given that foreign workers without clearance were not to be employed on the manufacture of the Tiger II. On 18th November 1943, the first turrets produced by Wegmann for the Tiger II (type 180, designed by Porsche) were examined. Defects were found in a number of these but at first these were in the main remedied by patching them up. The first prototype of the new Tiger ran in October 1943. Two further vehicles were also delivered in December of the same year. Mass production began hesitantly in January 1944, with larger numbers first coming in May 1944.

After the tapering off of the production of the Ausf E in August 1944, a monthly output of one hundred of the Ausf B (Tiger B) was planned. The production figures shown in the table on page 132 were those actually reached by Henschel at Kassel. The new vehicle was designated Tiger Tank, Ausf B (SdKfz 182).

The photographs on these pages show trials of a Jagdtiger towing a broken-down Tiger B.

128

A towrope eyelet (above) was provided so that a vehicle under tow could be pulled sideways.

During testing of an existing Tiger B, the foremost bogie wheel crank broke on chassis number 280,009 after running 1,400 kilometres.

To prevent damage to the ventilator fans through being shot up by fighter-bombers, the front and rear ventilation gratings were covered with steel plates.

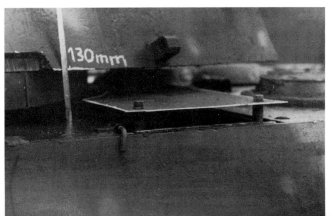

The Henschel factory at Kassel was heavily bombed on 7th October 1944. The photograph shows railway trucks, laden with tracks, which were destroyed.

A Tiger B chassis alongside destroyed buildings.

Destroyed vehicles in the final fitting and shop. The damage to parked vehicles was heavy.

Above and below *Partly-prepared hulls for the Tiger B lie outside the bombed out workshops.*

Henschel's assembly line after the attack.

Above and below Fifty Tigers had to be fitted out with the turret which had been manufactured for the Porsche-Tiger II.

Henschel Tiger Monthly Production			
	1943	**1944**	**1945**
January		3	40
February		5	42
March		6	18
April		6	
May		15	
June		32	
July		45	
August		84	
September		73	
October	1	26	
November	–	22	
December	2	60	
Totals	**3**	**377**	**100**

Already in December 1943, Hitler had made it known that it was most important that the shell trap which existed on each side of the gun under the front panel of the turret had to be eliminated. It had to be investigated forthwith how a deflector plate could be welded on to improve the situation. The 180 turrets of the Porsche design which were taken over required further intensive work on them, principally the application of convex armour of greater strength. In May 1944, the first Krupp-developed and Wegmann-built turret for the Tiger II made its appearance and it was used from vehicle 51 on. It had a smaller frontal area and considerably strengthened frontal armour. The ammunition store in the tank was also increased from seventy-two to eighty-four rounds. The rear part of the side walls of the turret were cleared by Weapons Experimental Department 6 for the attachment of spare track.

On 5th June 1944, the High Command of the Army, Weapons Inspectorate Tanks III c, in the person of Dipl. -Ing. Stollberg, communicated to Henschel that under no circumstances whatsoever was the present lubricating system of the Tiger to be changed to a central lubrication system. A central lubrication system was being built experimentally at Haustenbeck. The firm of Gebr.Böhringer of Göppingen had difficulties with the turret power transmission of types L3SI and L4SI. It came back again to oil leaks, also indicating that the housing was permeable.

The original turret for the Tiger II was also manufactured by the Skoda factory at Königgrätz. Eleven had been delivered to Wegmann's plant by 10th August 1944.

In 1944, the Armaments Department demanded the installation of anti-gas protection into the Tiger B and Panther. It was a question of taking up a lot of room to accommodate a clumsy piece of equipment which consisted of a filter case, a selector switch and a centrifugal fan for the creation inside the fighting compartment of air pressure exceeding air pressure outside. The fan was driven by gearing through a separate shaft. The equipment, which was manufactured by the Drägerwerke in Lubeck was only built by way of experiment.

As of August 1944, a change over from roller bearings to plain bearings was required. The firm of PAN-metallgesellschaft of Mannheim offered to Henschel a Radiax plain bearing of brass alloy PAN-So-Ms-3a of the metal grade 355. Its finely porous die cast structure retained lubricant and, compared with a uniform homogeneous structure, afforded better lubrication.

On 28th July 1944, it was decided to send Experimental Tiger E, chassis number 250 018, to Kummersdorf. There, consideration was being given to changing the Tiger B bogie wheel construction so that it operated on greased lubrication instead of on standard roller bearings. Henschel intimated on 28th August 1944 that plain bearings with grease lubrication were already being researched. A plain bearing model for the production line hubs and cranks was ready by the end of August. In the final analysis, these efforts produced no useful improvement.

On 19th August 1944, the Army High Command Ordnance Branch Armaments Inspectorate 6/VIII ordered that, forthwith, all tanks had to have additional camouflage treatment. In addition to the yellow first coat, the surface had to be painted olive green (RAL 6003) and reddish brown (RAL 8017) (RAL: Reichs Board for Supplies and Standards). This was to be a matter of decisive importance in the field: every effort was to be made to provide a part of the August output with the new camouflage.

The tank, which was also known by the enemy as the King Tiger, entered active service in August 1944.

In September 1944, further orders followed concerning substitutions for ball bearings. A proposal was made by MIAG to replace the central roller bearings in the planetary gears on the Tiger's steering gear and final drive. Similar experiments had been successful in the Panzer III. A further attempt was made to reduce the stress and strain on the steering gear of the Tiger B by enlarging the small radius in the first gear from 1.78 to 2.5 metres. Corresponding specifications for the necessary number of teeth for gear wheels 12 and 13 (40/60 for 2.5 metres instead of 45/50) had already been proposed in May 1944. The proposition was made that the series 2 and 3 of the Tiger B should be delivered with the revised small radius. In the steering gear, however, the large sun driving wheel was sited directly next to the sun wheel. The central roller bearings in the planetary gear had therefore to absorb about half of the tooth pressure of these gears and for that reason these bearings could not be interfered with. Standard plain bearings were introduced for the hand lever and foot pedal mechanism.

As a matter of interest, a communication of 23rd September 1944 spoke of a 2-tonne emergency crane in quick assembly order for the Tiger B of which any further details are missing. The crane was developed for the removal and installation of engine, gearbox and running gear and was to be mounted on the turret. The attachments for the crane were to be provided on all turrets so that crews could remove and replace the necessary parts.

In November 1944, means of reducing the weight of the

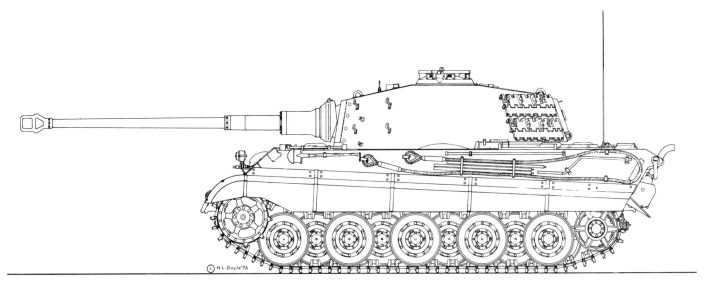

Views from four sides of the Tiger Ausf B (SdKfz 182) with the
production turret

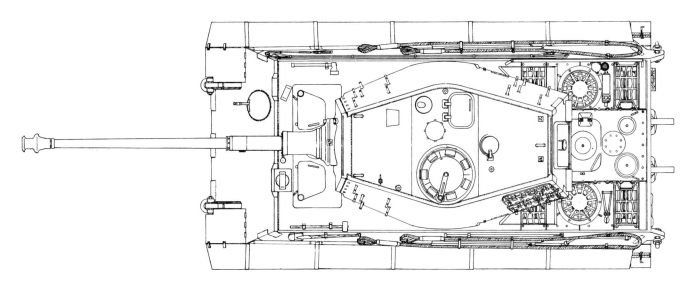

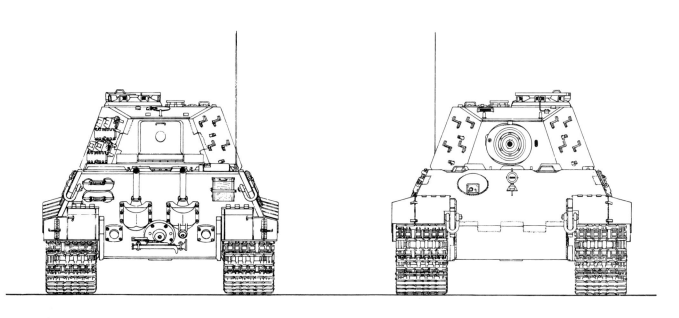

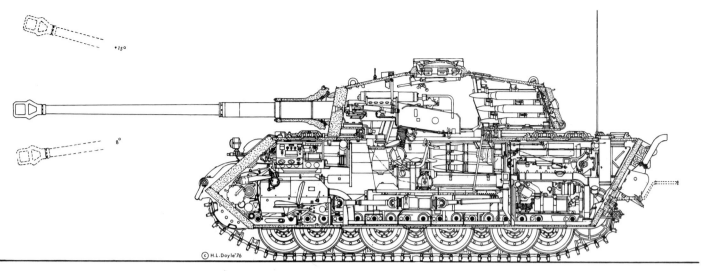

Longitudinal section and cross sections of the Tiger Ausf B with the production turret

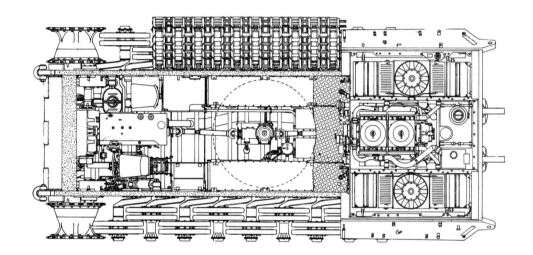

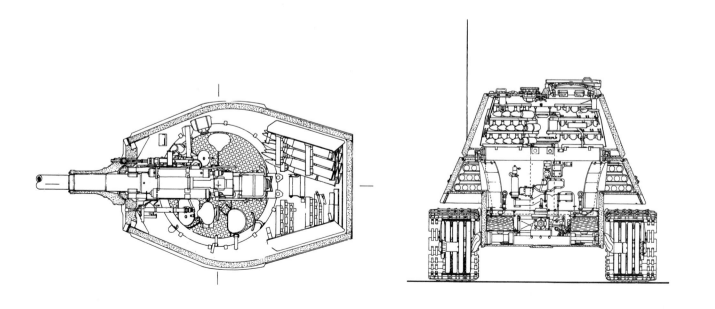

These comparisons show the old production turret for the Tiger II on the left and the final turret on the right.

The first presentation of the Tiger B with the production turret (chassis number 280,100). In the background, the full-scale mock-up of the Panther II is visible.

Tiger B were investigated. As a result, economies of up to 10 tonnes were achieved, principally by a reduction in the thickness of the sides of the Tiger E's hull.

During November 1944, several changes were made in production. On 18th November, the installation of flares simulating fire was required. The idea was that if a tank came under enemy shell-fire the crew could use the flare to make it appear that they had been hit and were 'brewing up'. The facility for raising and lowering the driver's seat had badly needed to be improved. Late in November, the new caterpillar track for the Tiger B, type Kgs 73/800/152, was introduced. Five hooks for attaching camouflage netting were welded on to the sides of the turret.

Late in November, further instructions were given about the painting of the exterior surfaces. The outer coat of variegated colours was to remain as before but all parts of the tank's casing were to be given a single coat of dark green (RAL 6003) by the manufacturer before delivery. This had to be overcoated with the additional reddish brown or dark yellow colours in accordance with prescribed camouflage patterns. Three different camouflage patterns were produced which were notified from time to time by Ordnance Materials Branch 5. The colours were sprayed on in the most

The details of the turret show that the area of the frontal armour has been reduced but strengthened and also shows the long gun carried in a mantlet resembling a sow's head.

This model of the Tiger B was built until the end of the war.

One of the last models of the Tiger B in action in Budapest.

sharply defined demarcations possible.

Under pressure, further changes were made. Extremely heavy losses were sustained by tanks being transported to the front from the guns of Allied fighter-bombers. Principally, engine room vents suffered damage from gunfire and splinters. Guard plates were produced for the inlet and outlet vents of the engine room cover which did not obstruct the flow of fresh and hot air. Shortage of real leather for the seats in the tank led to canvas or canvas upholstered with paper being prescribed. The anti-aircraft equipment mounted on the commander's cupola was dropped in March 1945 in favour of a twin-barrelled model.

From March/April 1945, a compressionless barrel exhaust taking the form of a pneumatic recuperator cylinder was introduced as a means of controlling the recoil of the gun. At the same time, the MG34 was replaced by the MG42, because of which a completely new machine-gun mounting had to be produced. The machine-gun ball-mounting beside the wireless operator was replaced by a machine pistol port. Armoured caps to the torsion bars were dropped. After drastic reductions in stocks interior painting had also to be dropped.

By late in January 1945, a total of 417 Tiger IIs had been delivered. The production programme for this tank was forty-five in February, fifty in both March and April, sixty in each of May, June, July and August, and in September forty-five.

Considerable difficulties were again experienced with the final drive of the Tiger II. As far on as November 1944, Hitler had ordered that drastic measures be taken to make sure that an improved final drive was provided. In fact, the configuration of the final drive was a technical success. Considering the given weight of the tank, the high torque of the caterpillar track could be handled by only one planetary gear. The Panther — in accordance with the way it was designed — had a rear-wheel drive, and what is more, a particularly highly-stressed final drive which led to repeated failures. Despite the carefully assessed dimensions of the Tiger's final drive, more failures occurred than were foreseen. It was notable that failures were still more numerous in the Jagdtiger. The smaller traverse of the Jagdtiger's gun meant that the tank had to be repeatedly slewed during a shoot and this stressed the final drive more than in the combat Tiger. The problems were, despite everything, largely overcome.

137

The guide teeth of the track had only 2mm play at each side of the bogie wheels whereas in the Tiger E they had 4mm play. The inaccuracy in the manufacture of the rubber-spring-rimmed bogie wheels and their mounting on the hub was too great to accommodate such a small play. From this arose the introduction of the 'echelon formation' of the bogie wheels instead of the 'square box formation'. The axles would not be rhythmically stressed and would thus differ one from another in their working and slewing. Through the one-sided stress on the inside of the track, the link pins were bent and were no longer free to rotate. Thus, the flexibility of the track was considerably reduced. A product of the rubber-spring-rimmed bogie wheels was axial displacement resulting in a distorted seating so that the disc wheels wobbled. A definitive remedy for these problems had still not been found by the end of the war.

Henschel employed the same synchronised system of work in its construction of the Tiger B as on the Model E and had put nine cycles of work into operation in each period of six hours. On average, fourteen days were needed to complete a vehicle. Eighteen to twenty-two tanks were on the hull production line while ten were on the assembly line. As to the requirements of basic materials (excluding weaponry) the following different items emerged by comparison for the Panther 1:

	Panther I	Panther II
Iron, unalloyed (kp)	33,409	44,009
Iron, alloyed (kp)	44,060	75,789
Total (kp)	777,469	119,798
Of which heavy and		
medium plate (kp)	30,735	62,976
Thin gauge plate (kp)	1,888	2,248

Only a few of the Tiger II tanks were still provided with a submersion capability.

The Tiger IIs were the heaviest in service in the German Army up to the end of the war, serving in eleven independent heavy Army tank battalions and also in four tank regiments. Its size and the small weight per horse power did not always allow its outstanding armament and armour protection to come to bear. They represented nonetheless an important peak in weapon development. In terms of supply and support, they were almost always a strain. When the tanks were in action, aggravating defects continued to show up in the Maybach engine and these, in many cases, led to the total loss of the tank.

A specially set up Committee of Engineering of the Tank Commission visited the Maybach factory on 23rd and 24th November 1943 to make themselves familiar with the problems on the spot. In particular, defects in the connecting rod bearing led to engine failure. The Commission had directed that an immediate programme to eradicate this defect be commenced with the intention of making the engine safe for use for at least 2,000 kilometres, something like a hundred running hours. Furthermore, proposals were to be made for the redesigning of the HL 230 engine until such time as a new tank engine was produced.

Dr Maybach undertook that the first experimental engine would be on the test bed in April 1943, at the same time as the launch of the series. The engine was to be a further development of the HL 210 which had to some extent proved useful. Under test conditions, the new engine had already shown that it had a leaky cylinder head gasket which caused water shock as well as sticking of the connecting rod bearing. The oil level was difficult to ascertain and the cooling water could only be replenished with difficulty. Backfiring caused engine room fires. Carbonization, iron oxide formation as well as pitting and shrinkage appeared on the connecting rod bearings. Added to this were complaints about the composition of the lead bronze — with too little lead and too much phosphorous. The introduction of Glyco bearings on 1st November 1943 to replace the previous plain bearings brought no improvement. Excessive flexural vibration at the free end of the crankshaft was assumed to be the reason and the incorporation of an eighth main bearing next to the torsional vibration damper was planned. Five of these engines were actually running at this time at Kummersdorf and one already, after 1,076 kilometres, showed a defect in the fifth connecting rod bearing and another, after 2,647 kilometres, showed seizing marks at the sixth. The three other engines had covered over 2,000 kilometres without trouble.

At a subsequent review, twenty-eight engines of the HL 230 type were demonstrated of which twenty-six were dismantled. It was determined that insufficient ventilation was provided for the cooling system which led to formation of air locks. Of the twenty-six dismantled engines, twenty-three showed connecting rod scuffing. Of these, the number

5 and 6 crankshaft pins were mainly affected. It was noticed that the gap between the connecting rod shells on the side facing the connecting rod measured only 1.5mm from face to face. As a result, the leading edge starved the oil film from the half of the bush on the rod side which was deflected inwards by the combustion pressure. Each of them, almost without exception, showed scuffing at this point.

In addition, it was established that the crankshaft pins had been inadequately tempered. Criticism was also levelled at the proposed modification of the cylinder head gasket with a copper collar and a Reinz gasket sealing washer (Dichtung). In the long run this combination resulted in no great improvement.

The following recommendations were submitted:

File down leading edges of the connecting brasses by 0.02 to 0.03mm.

Future provision to be made for the exchange of the forked and blade connecting rods so that the leading edge of the adjacent rod which was stressed through combustion pressure was aligned with the trailing half of the bush.

Recommendation for an oil compensator after the Daimler-Benz model.

Immediate experiments with an oiliness dope such as 1.G.891 or the like, all the more so when the total running time of the engine during production amounted to only two to three hours and, consequently, the danger of piston rings sticking would not be apparent to Maybach. Moreover, the bad quality of the standard Wehrmacht oil was to be blamed.

Improve the oil cleaning filter at the inlet since so many bearings were scored. Alteration to the filters so that the whole of the debris would not be expelled by the operation of the relief pressure valve.

Alteration of the crankshaft oilways to 90 degrees leading and 90 lagging. This had already been incorporated by Maybach in four experimental engines and had so far proved successful.

Torquing up the bolts to correct the inadequacy of the torque wrench (an inspection revealed only from 0.13 to 0.16 instead of 0.17).

Special review of the thickness of the bearing bushes. Inspection of one half of a bush revealed a deviation of up to 0.07.

Inasmuch as it was accepted that the continuous scuffing of numbers 5 and 6 connecting rod bearings arose not only from the flexural vibration of the shaft end but also from insufficient oil feed due to foaming (the inlet of the oil was from the rear into the crankshaft) it appeared that measurement of foam using a graduated measuring glass over a parallel duct was an urgent necessity.

It was further established that the 25 litres of oil circulating at a rate of 96 litres per minute was totally insufficient since foam testing had shown that it was some minutes before the foam had dispersed. A considerable enlargement of the oil tanks was therefore necessary.

All these difficulties had still not by any means been overcome by the end of the war. Only the further development of these basic models for the French Army reached the otherwise high reliability of Maybach engines. In 1961, a Tiger B came back to Germany as a present from the US Army to the Bundeswehr and was mounted at Combat Troops School 2 at Munster.

The 'VK 4502' which Dr-Ing. hcF. Porsche KG only realised as a drawing also had a newly-developed hull with sloping sides. The Porsche model 180 had a similar but strengthened running gear to the model 101 which at this stage had a wheel loading of 4,650kp. The total weight was estimated at about 64 tonnes. Yet again a double engine installation of model 101/3 was planned. However, the engines were to be provided with a new cylinder head. As before, they drove two generators which in turn drove two electric motors. The breadth of the track was, as before, 640mm with a pitch of 130mm and the ground loading had been increased to 1.15kp/cm². As to the ammunition storage for the 8.8cm KwK L/71, sixteen rounds were stored in the turret, and forty-two in the hull and about ten were stowed away over the floor of the hull. A second proposal for the model 180 planned the use of two engines of the model 101/4. That produced only an insignificant difference.

While the model 180 had a petrol electric drive, the model 181 was designed for hydraulic drive. New track, 700mm wide, was planned and, as a result, the ground loading was reduced to 1.06kp/cm². Equally, the wheel loading

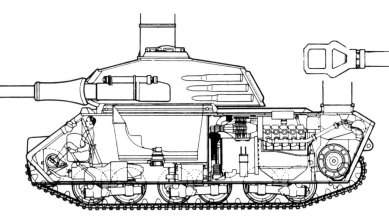

Above and below *Comparative views of the Porsche design 180/181, with front (above) and rear (below) positioned turrets, which got no further than the drawing board. This was Porsche's proposal for the Tiger II, Porsche type 180/181).*

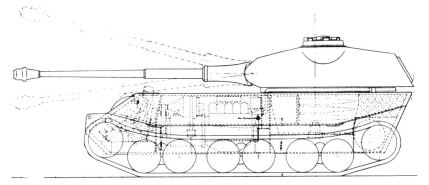

Bottom of page *A view from three sides of the VK 4502 (P) with the fighting compartment at the rear.*

was reduced to 4,520kp. The gear reduction was altered although the running gear otherwise remained the same. The first design of the 181 was again planned with two engines of the type 101/4 while for the second design, two Porsche-Deutz diesel engines were planned. These diesel engines had sixteen cylinders in 'X' configuration with 110mm bore, 130mm stroke and swept volume of 19.6 litres. The maximum output per engine was to be 370hp at 2,000rpm. The weight per horse power of the vehicle rose as a result from 8.5 to 10.4hp per tonne. For the third design of the type 181, a Porsche diesel engine was to be used which, similarly designed as a sixteen-cylinder 'X' engine, was to produce a rated output of 700hp at 2,000rpm. With a bore of 135mm and a stroke of 160mm, the swept volume was 37 litres yet only one engine was built. It got no nearer to manufacture. Designs were drawn up also to explore building the 'Special Vehicle III' as the Porsche types 180 and 181 were otherwise known, with a rear fighting compartment which meant that the powerplant would have had to be in the middle of the vehicle. Not counting the revolving turret, which was later installed on Henschel's first VK 4503 production vehicle, none of these vehicles was built.

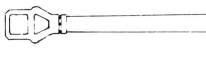

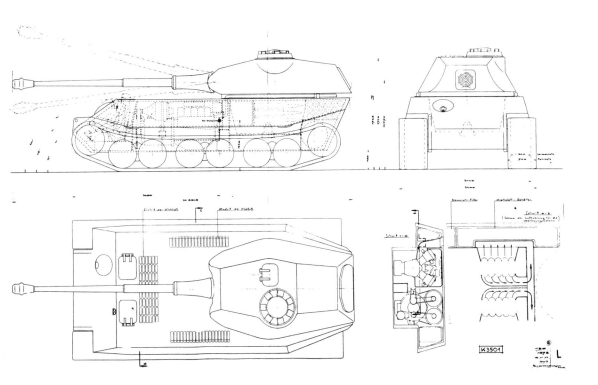

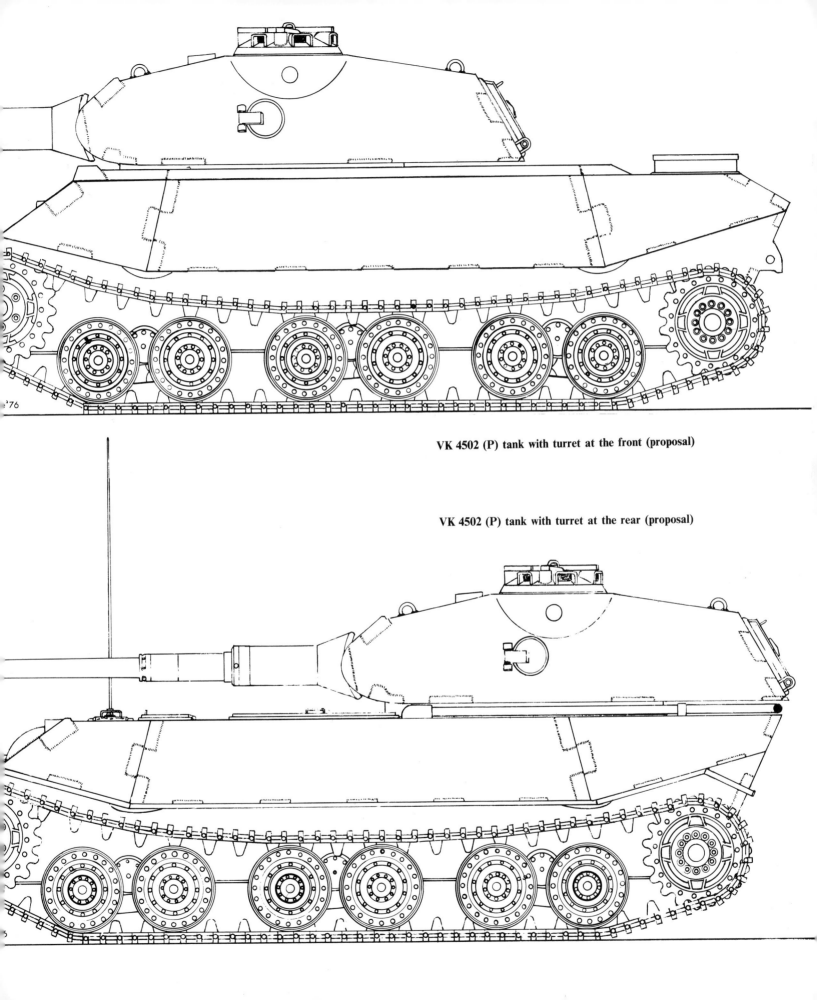

VK 4502 (P) tank with turret at the front (proposal)

VK 4502 (P) tank with turret at the rear (proposal)

5. VARIANTS

Tankhunter Tiger (Panzerjäger) Elephant

The modification of the Tiger tank into a turretless assault gun which had been ordered on 26th September 1942 was started in cooperation with Altmarkirchen KettenWerk GmbH (Alkett). On 7th February 1943 — in spite of being advised about continuing defects in running gear and simply quite inadequate test running — Hitler ordered all available means to be used to complete ninety Panzerjäger (Tank Hunters) on the chassis of the Porsche Tiger with the long 8.8cm gun and 200mm frontal armour, the Ferdinand. The required testing and completion was to be given priority so that within the shortest possible time, tank after tank could be brought to the Front.

Since the manufacture of the air-cooled engines originally planned for this vehicle had still not begun, the chassis was fitted with twin Maybach water-cooled engines of the HL 120 type. The engine room was sited in the middle of the vehicle. The electric power transmission assembly was delivered by Siemens-Schuckert. The frontal armour of the hull was doubled in strength to 200mm by the addition of 100mm of plate. The solid tank assembly had armour of 200mm at the front and 80mm at the sides and rear. The traverse of the 8.8cm Pak 43/2 L/71 (Maker-Dortmund-Hoerder Hüttenverein, Werk Lippstadt) was 28 degrees and the depression/elevation from –8 to +14 degrees. The distance from the ground to the axis of the gun barrel was 2,310mm. Fifty rounds of new ammunition were carried. The crew consisted of five men. At a fighting weight of 65 tonnes, a maximum speed of 20 kilometres per hour was possible. The fuel reserves of 950 litres gave a potential cruising radius of 150 kilometres.

The vehicle's official designation ran 'Panzerjäger Tiger (P) — Elefant — für 8.8cm Pak 43 L/71 (SdKfz 184).'

Chassis numbers ran from 150 001 to 150 100). The modification of the chassis and the construction of the armoured housing for the gun at the Niebelungenwerk were completed on 8th May 1943.

The vehicle first saw action in July 1943 in Operation CITADEL in service with a Panzer Regiment made up of two battalions. The technical failure rate was high and the small ammunition reserve and the absence of anything like means of close defence (there was only an unmounted machine-gun which had been brought along) showed up disadvantageously. The vehicles were lost either through enemy action or were brought to a standstill by virtue of the technically expensive petrol electric engines. The fifty vehicles still remaining were provided with a ball-mounted MG34 beside the wireless operator during overhauling at home. In addition, the hitherto unprotected mantlet was covered in with a sheet of armour fixed in place where the barrel projected from the turret. The tank commander was also given the so badly needed cupola. Some of the vehicles later saw action in Italy.

The Porsche chassis was the subject of other proposals. Five were modified as recovery tanks, and construction of three Ramm-Panzer was proposed: see pages 150-1.

The 'Adolf Hitler Tank Programme' also planned the production of an Assault Gun with the 8.8cm KwK L/71 on the Tiger I chassis. The vehicle was designated 'superheavy self-propelled gun' (SS Sfl) and was included in the planning stage early in 1943, yet the thought was in mind that it would possibly be armed with the 12.8cm Pak L/61. The production was to start in October 1943 and by December 1943, fifty were to have been turned out. In August 1943, the decision was dropped, however, and instead of the SS Sfl normal Tiger Is were to be delivered.

The order to convert the Porsche Tiger into a Tank Hunter involved, in part, considerable alterations to the hull. The photograph on the left shows the hull of the tank with the engine room at the rear, and that on the right shows the modified hull with the engine room now in the middle. It was separated from the new fighting compartment by a firewall at its rear.

The last chassis of the Porsche Tiger range on the Nibelungenwerk production line.

This series of shots on these two pages shows the assembly of the Tank Hunter (Panzerjäger) Tiger (P) at different stages of construction.

144

145

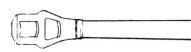

Panzerjäger Tiger (P) for the 8.8 cm PaK L/71 (SdKfz 184) Elephant

Panzerjäger Tiger (P) for the 8.8 cm PaK 43 L/71 (SdKfz 184) Elephant — after general restoration

Top *After completion, the vehicle was road-tested.*

Centre and bottom *The last vehicle with chassis number 150,100 was completed on 8th May 1943. Note the front positioned cogged idler wheel.*

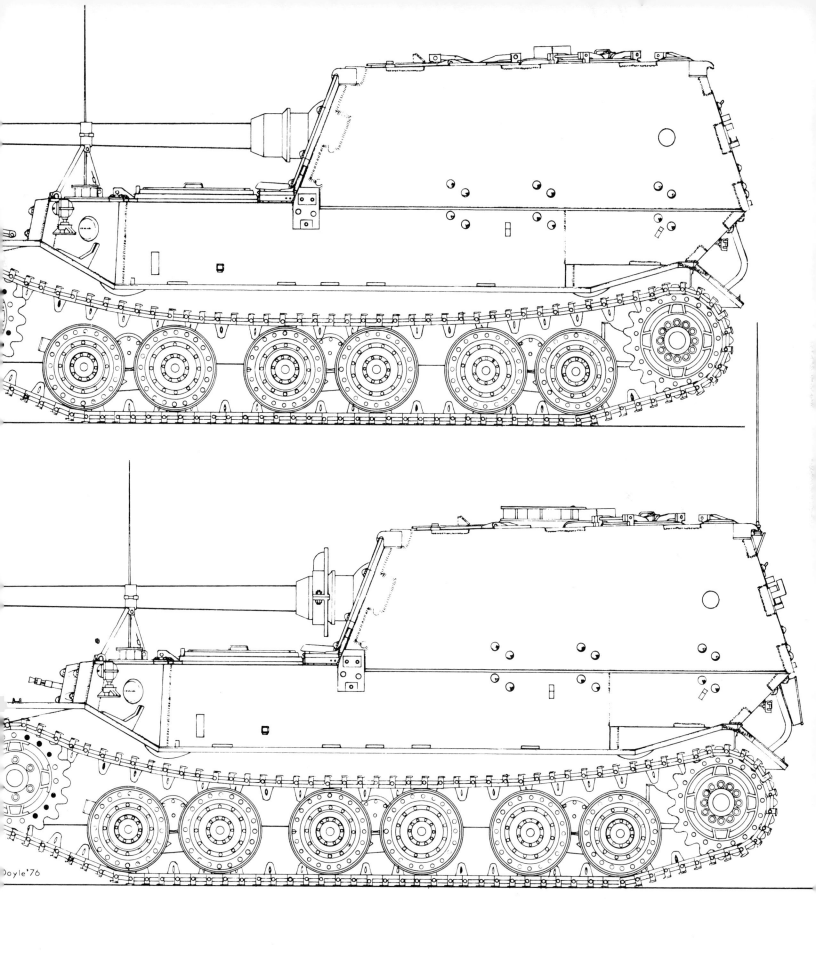

Doyle '76

Four views of the original production model of the SdKfz 184.

Covered by tarpaulins, the Ferdinand, later named the Elephant, goes to the front.

The ninety Ferdinand (Jagdpanzer) Hunting Tanks comprising the 656 Jagdpanzer Regiment suffered heavy casualties in the Kursk Offensive (Operation CITADEL) which started in July 1943. Here are two stricken Tigers in Russian hands.

Right, below right and bottom right *Details of the Porsche running gear with the bogie wheel suspension frame exposed.*

Below and bottom left *The remaining serviceable vehicles were released to the Nibelungenwerk and were generally overhauled there. They were then equipped with a machine-gun for the wireless operator, protective armour for the gun and a commander's cupola.*

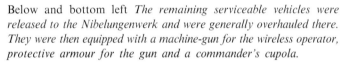

Above and top *A front and rear view of the final model of the Elephant.*

The series of photographs on the left shows both Tiger (P) and Panzerjäger battalions received Rescue and Recovery vehicles of similar construction, but they had no strengthened armour. An MG 34 was available for close defence.

Opposite page For street fighting in towns, a vehicle with a ram for demolishing houses was to be built on a Porsche Tiger chassis. Photographs of both models amplify the design sketch.

© H.L.Doyle

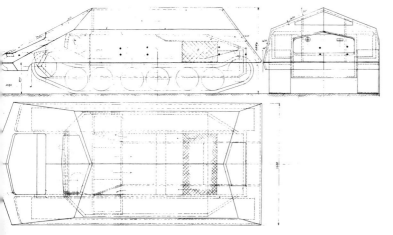

Five Porsche Tiger chassis were fitted up and used as salvage and recovery vehicles. They were not equipped with the Panzerjäger's additional armour and carried in the rearward part of the vehicle a humble armoured erection with a ball mounting for an MG34 as a self-defence weapon.

On 5th January 1943, Hitler declared himself to be in agreement with the proposed construction of three 'Ram' Tigers on Porsche chassis. The concept originated from impressions left by street fighting in Stalingrad. The chassis was to carry a ram extension for the demolition of buildings and such like and to carry fuel in a trailer. These plans were not realised.

Tiger (P) Rescue and Recovery tank

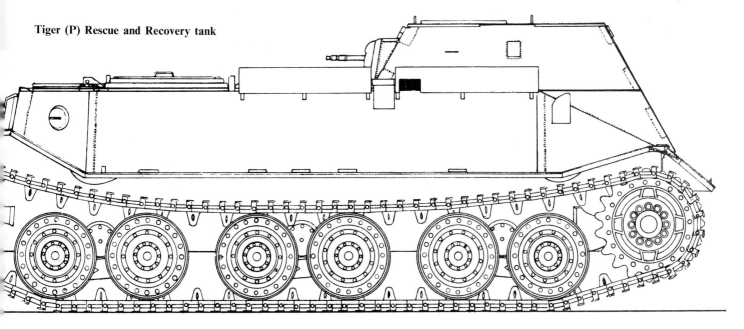

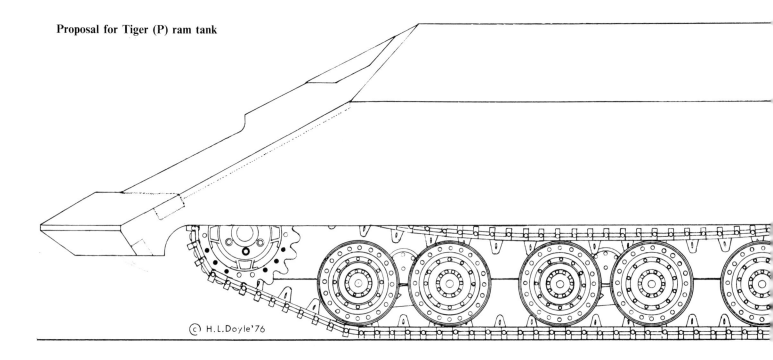

Proposal for Tiger (P) ram tank

© H.L.Doyle'76

Hunting Tiger (Jagdtiger)

While design work was still going on at Henschel on the Tiger B, the plan for a Hunting Tiger Assault Gun had to be taken in hand. In cooperation with Krupps, this vehicle was to carry a 12.8cm gun on a solid mounting. The chassis had to be extended some 260mm rearwards and the two-fold rear opening doors had to be designed as gastight and shot proof. A new ammunition store was designed because the 12.8cm gun required separated ammunition. Since the overhang of the barrel was much larger, an additional barrel brace proved to be necessary.

The wooden mock-up of the Jagdtiger was introduced on 20th October 1942 on the occasion of a demonstration before the Führer at Arys, a troop training area in East Prussia. On 7th April 1944, it was possible to deliver the first photographs of the Panzerjäger Tiger Ausf B (SdKfz 186) to Hitler. The demonstration of the first production model followed on 20th April.

The fighting weight, with a six-man crew, forty rounds of ammunition and 860 litres of petrol came to 75.2 tonnes. It was thus, of its time, the heaviest tank used in service by any nation. The solidly-built armoured body had a frontal

The presentation of the full-scale wooden mock-up of the Jagdtiger (Hunting Tiger) in front of Hitler on 20th October 1943. In the background are the mock-ups of the Tiger B and the Jagdpanther (Hunting Panther). In the foreground is an Italian Type P40 tank.

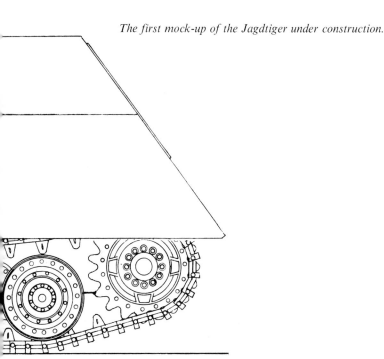

armour of 250mm sloped at 75 degrees. The sides and rear were protected with 80mm armour. The main armament, manufactured in Breslau by the Krupp Bertha-Werk was mounted in a mantlet resembling a sow's head. The 12.8cm Pak 44 (also Pak 80) L/55 with a muzzle velocity of 920 metres per second was one of the most powerful anti-tank weapons of the Second World War. The height of the axis of the barrel from the ground was 2,165mm. An MG34 was sited beside the wireless operator in a ball mounting on the frontal plate.

On 12th September 1944, Henschel suggested a price of 140,000 Reichsmarks to the Nibelungenwerk for the first one hundred Tiger-Jäger which was considerably under the accepted price for a tank. On 12th October 1944, a proposal was put to Hitler that, to begin with, an unprecedented run of 150 Jagdtigers be produced so that they were available to the Inspector General of Tank Troops to use for special purposes. The scheduled continuous production of fifty Jagdtigers per month was slowed down, so that its greater individual requirement for materials was diverted to the output of a possibly higher pro rata number of Panthers. Hitler wanted to speak once again with Guderian and Buhle on this score before a final decision.

Above and below *A comparison between the Tiger B and the Jagdtiger shows (above) the tank with revolving turret and 8.8 cm KwK 43 L/71 and (below) the Jagdpanzer with the 12.8 cm PaK 44 L/55.*

Jagdtiger tank bodies damaged by bombing in the Nibelungenwerk.

Above and below *Stages in the production of the Jagdtiger in the Nibelungenwerk.*

On 5th December 1944, Hitler ordered that alongside the existing experiments with the design of a flamethrower tank the solutions to two further developments of that kind had to be urgently resolved. First, it was proposed that a heavy tank, as effective as the Tiger, was to carry a flamethrowing device of the greatest range behind heavy armour protection so that it could act as a spearpoint vehicle. Secondly, on 29th December 1944 Hitler thought of using the Jagdtiger especially, if 'a jet 200 metres long could be produced'. Both had to be resolved.

On 5th January 1945, Hitler emphatically laid down that under no circumstances had the production of the Jagdtiger to be slowed down at the end of the first run of 150 vehicles. Every effort had to be made, having regard of course to the capacity of the steel rolling mills, to produce the highest possible numbers.

Again on 26th February 1945, Hitler ordered the immediate and drastic measures to increase the output of

Panzerjäger (Tank Hunter) Tiger Ausf B Jagdtiger (SdKfz 186).

View on to the top of the superstructure of the Jagdtiger showing the entry hatch and the kidney-shaped opening housing the optical system.

The photograph shows the open driver's hatch with the periscope in front of it.

A view from above shows the wireless operator's entry hatch open and to its right front the ventilation cap and to the left beside that the periscope with its arched steel shield.

In this photograph, the wireless operator's hatch is closed.

The right rear of the Jagdtiger with recessed starting crank under the right exhaust silencer.

The bow of the Jagdtiger with machine-gun mantlet and headlamp.

The sow's head mantlet with lifting point.

The engine room cover with inlet and outlet gratings. The fuel filler neck can be seen at the left of the photograph and that for cooling water to the right. The arched protective shield for the loader's periscope is at the bottom right.

The inside of the fighting compartment with gun and its armour.

The rubber inset in the mantlet which sealed the front of the fighting compartment is at the top of the photograph.

The top of the superstructure has been removed.

A close-up view of the gunner's position. To the left in the photograph are the charge holders.

The gunner's position is to the left of the gun and the commander's to the right.

The breech of the gun with recoil mechanism and loading tray as well as the counterweight mounted at the left side.

A view over the left side of the superstructure with laying and training gear visible.

A view through the double doors at the rear of the superstructure shows, to the right, the ammunition holders.

View from the firewall on to the commander's position, with charge holders. The accommodation for shells is visible in the middle of the photograph.

The view on to the firewall shows details of the automatic fire extinguisher. Above right is the Sum-priming pump for the fuel system.

Shells and charges were stored separately.

The breech block opened (left) and closed (right). The counterweights are mounted at the left.

Panzerjäger (Tank Hunter) Tiger Ausf B (SdKfz 186) Jagdtiger (Hunting Tiger)

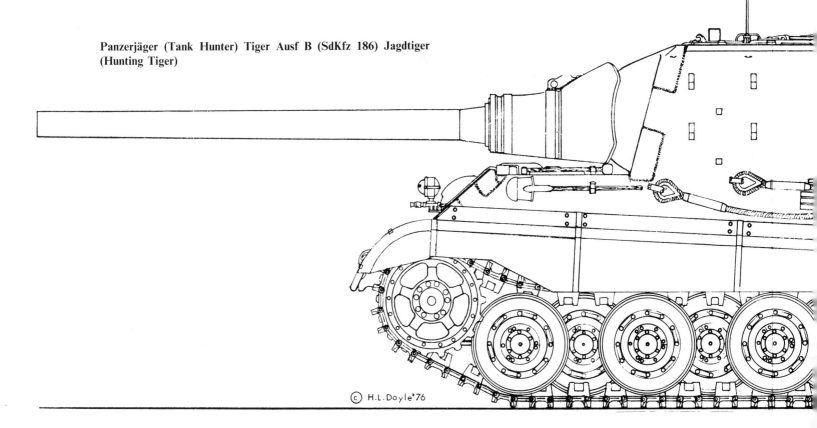

© H.L.Doyle'76

Above and below *Details of the shell storage are discernible here.*

The breech operating handle is at the left in the picture. The commander's position is visible above right.

A view from above on to the gunner's position with the training gear.

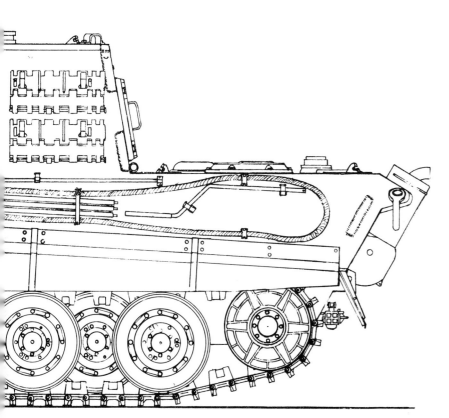

The left wall of the superstructure with housing for shells and charges.

Jagdtigers to the maximum in the shortest time. As from March of that year, against the background of the first action by 512 Jagdtiger battalion at Remagen on 10th March 1945, there was a bottleneck in the supply of 12.8cm guns and Hitler ordered that it was to be ascertained immediately where such guns were still available and that if necessary any 12.8cm guns which had been installed in captured gun carriages were to be recovered. Should this turn out to be impossible, the Jagdtiger was to be equipped with the 8.8cm Pak 43/4. A series of at the least twenty- five, at the most fifty was planned. To that end, the Jagdpanther gun made by the Halle'schen Maschinenfabrik was redesigned for installation in the Jagdtiger. It was designated Pak 43/3 Ausfuhrung D. The weapon was to be delivered from Lippstadt

Centre left and bottom left *These shots taken through the driver's entry hatch show the accommodation for the wireless apparatus. An entry hatch was provided in the floor of the hull beneath the wireless operator's position.*

Bottom right *The wireless operator's position seen from behind. The sheet-metal casing of the gearbox is at the left in the photograph.*

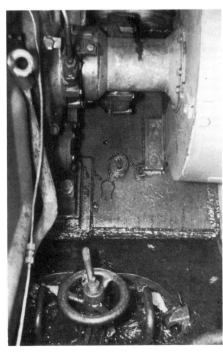

© H.L.Doyle '76

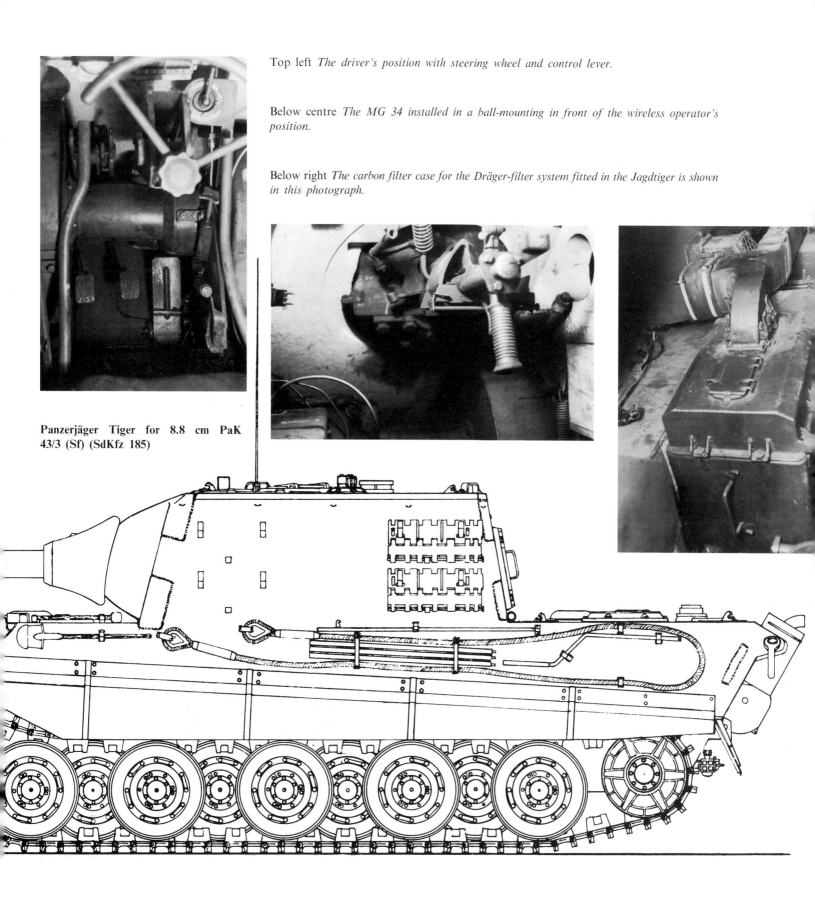

Top left *The driver's position with steering wheel and control lever.*

Below centre *The MG 34 installed in a ball-mounting in front of the wireless operator's position.*

Below right *The carbon filter case for the Dräger-filter system fitted in the Jagdtiger is shown in this photograph.*

Panzerjäger Tiger for 8.8 cm PaK 43/3 (Sf) (SdKfz 185)

Top and mid right *As the Tiger was manufactured in the Nibelungenwerk, strenuous efforts followed to fit the vehicle with a simplified running gear. The new running gear was developed by Porsche. The upper plate in this comparison shows the track drive with the original running gear whereas in that below the Porsche running gear is shown.*

ready for installation, and test fired. The recess in the front wall of the tank superstructure was altered by the Eisenwerke Oberdonau. The vehicle equipped with the 8.8cm Pak was designated Panzerjäger Tiger with 8.8cm Pak 43/3 (Sf) (Sd Kfz 185).

Actually, forty-eight Jagdtigers were built by the Steyr-Daimler-Puch AG Werk Nibelungen GmbH at St Valentin in 1944. By the end of January 1945, sixty of these vehicles altogether were delivered. The final programme for Jagdtiger output provided for the following numbers in 1945: none in January, thirteen in February, forty in March, thirty-seven in April, and twenty-five in each of May, June, July and August. (As a substitute, the vehicles of the E range were planned.) The armoured superstructure was assembled by the Eisenwerk Oberdonau in Linz. The cast front panel, of which 133 were already available by the end of August 1944, was delivered by the firms of Bergische Stahlindustrie Remscheid-Bochumer Verein Bochum, Friedrich Krupp AG, Eisen, and Oberhutten, Malapane. By order of the Führer on 27th February 1944, the suggestive designation Jagdtiger was confirmed. The chassis numbers ran from 305,001. Altogether up to the end of the war about seventy Jagdtigers were made.

Considerable influence was exerted by interested parties to have not only the Jagdtiger, which Henschel was having to construct at the Nibelungenwerk, but also tanks under construction with the Porsche running gear. The result of that was War Contract 258 in favour of Porsche which was to lead to a standard running gear for the Tiger and the Panther involving the use of the minimum of high priority materials. Accordingly, a running gear was produced which consisted of a supporting pylon pivoted on its inner side in a bracket attached to the hull of the tank. One end of the supporting pylon carried a bogie wheel; and from the same end, a second pylon was flexibly attached, elbow fashion, below and parallel to the first. The end of the second pylon carried the second bogie wheel. The two bogie wheels were of the rubber- rimmed spring steel variety and

Panzerjäger Tiger Ausf B (SdKfz 186) Jagdtiger, an experimental vehicle with Porsche running gear. The new running gear was developed by Porsche

© H.L.Doyle'76

The Henschel suspension required precise boring from both sides of the hull with a comparatively high expenditure of time on the mechanical treatment of the hull.

With the Porsche suspension, the time consuming precise boring was no longer needed. Likewise the installation did not need to correspond exactly on both sides. The elastic quality had deteriorated, producing more limited play.

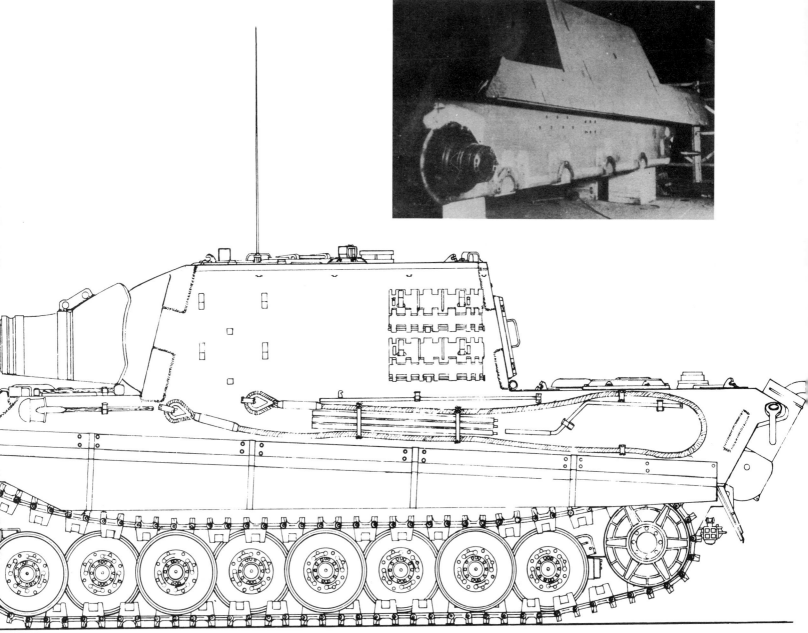

The Porsche bogie wheel suspension frame with lengthwise lying torsion bar suspension seen from inside.

Driving sprocket and foremost running wheel of the Porsche running gear.

The Jagdtiger on chassis numbers 305,001 and 304,004 were equipped with Porsche running gear. The photograph shows one of the vehicles with a shortened gun.

The idler wheel arrangement of the Porsche running gear.

The vehicle ready to run seen from the left side.

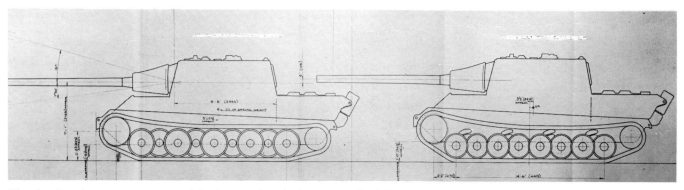

The drawing shows a comparison of the layout of each chassis. To the left is the Henschel running gear, and Porsche's to the right.

Diagrammatic Comparison of Each Suspension System

HENSCHEL

Time taken on processing hull	360 hours
Cost of necessary machine tools	RM 866,000
Weight of raw material for suspension parts and shock absorbers	17,200 Kp
Net weight after machining these parts	9,480 Kp
Time expended on machining these parts including shock absorbers	460 hours

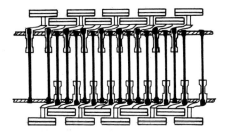

To remove a crank arm it is also necessary to dismantle the adjacent bogie wheel.
Eighteen torsion bars each 1,960 mm long with a finished weight of 887 Kp.
Central lubrication for thirty-six swing arm bearings.

Heaviest forging (swing arm)   200 Kp

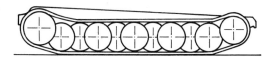

PORSCHE

Time taken on processing hull	140 hours
Cost of necessary machine tools	RM 462,000
Weight of raw material for suspension parts and shock absorbers	12,000 Kp
Net weight after machining these parts	6,800 Kp
Time expended on machining these parts including shock absorbers	230 hours
Saving in weight	2680 Kp
Saving in cost of machine tools	RM 40,4000

It is possible to dismantle a bogie wheel suspension frame without also having to disturb other parts. In addition, no need for lifting gear. All bolted joints are accessible from the outside.

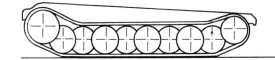

165

The photograph shows details of the vehicle's rear.

springing element of the suspension consisted of a single longitudinal torsion bar which served both bogie wheels within the main supporting pylon. The scissor-like working of the two pylons was converted by the lever-like action of the pivot in the hull bracket into an oscillating movement. This design produced a substantial saving in material and working time as against the echelon-style running gear previously used. Ostensibly, this reduced the working time on the hull from 360 to 140 hours. Also, repair work on the tank could be performed more quickly by a simple exchange of the whole unit without disturbing the inner areas of the tank. Ten vehicles were fitted out with this running gear for test purposes. These trials went off satisfactorily yet after their completion there could be no thought of mass production because of the war situation.

The outcome of the researches undertaken by Krupps towards the end of 1944 as to the armament of all German tanks was the recommendation that the Tiger II be equipped with the 10.5cm L/68. As had happened previously in the case of the completed tests with the Panther into a stabilised suspension for the binocular sight, the installation, for this main armament, was to be a 'binocular with a gyro stabilised field of view'. This was an invention of Ernest Haas of the firm of Kreiselgeräte in Berlin. It had to be adopted to satisfy the desire for stabilised arrangements because the Americans had had one in their M3 tanks since 1941. While the Krupp design Hln-E151 applied to the installation of the 10.5cm KwK in the Tiger II, design Hln-E150 applied to the installation of a 12.8cm L/66 in the Tiger Panzerjäger. The traverse was 20 degrees, 10 left and 10 right. Neither re-arming was carried out.

The vehicle from the front.

The Jagdtiger seen from the right rear. The towing shackles are attached at the rear.

Both sides of a Jagdtiger with a shortened gun and spare track mounted on the superstructure.

A Jagdtiger fitted with Porsche running gear broke off a bogie wheel suspension frame during the experimental testing of the protective ventilating system. The photographs show the suspension frame and the point at which the bracket broke.

Both of these shots show details of the broken bracket and the fixing point.

The Jagdtiger with Porsche running gear.

Below *Krupp* made a proposal to re-arm all existing Tiger II vehicles with a 10.5 cm KwK L/68.

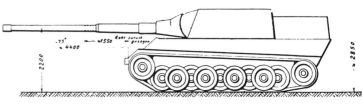

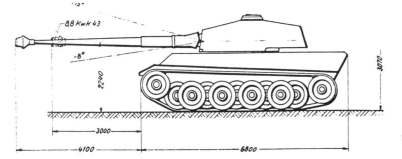

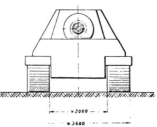

Likewise, the Jagdtiger was to be re-equipped with the longer 12.8 cm L/66.

The first prototype of the 38 cm Mortar Tank still had the Tiger E's rubber-tyred running gear.

Assault Tiger (Sturmtiger)

On 5th August 1943, Hitler proposed the manufacture of a Mortar Tiger (Tiger-Mörser) using a 38cm naval rocket projector. It was designated Gerät 562-Sturmmörserwagen 606/4 (Mortar Assault tank). Hitler said he agreed with Guderian's proposal that only one experimental vehicle be built to begin with. The planning objective was ten per month. On 20th October 1943, the iron model of the Panzermörser's 38cm on a Tiger I chassis was demonstrated at the troop training area at Arys. On 19th April 1944, Hitler ordered that, within the bounds of technical manufacturing practicability, up to a total of twelve superstructures and gun barrels for the Sturmmörser be prepared and erected on repaired Tiger I chassis. An output of a further seven Panzermörser 38cm was planned. The first vehicle was in fact to be completed on 15th September, and thereafter one a day so that seven could be delivered on 21st September.

The vehicle itself arose from the demand for self-propelled heavy artillery which could give infantry support and cover beneath tank gunfire. Hitler esteemed these vehicles as of great importance for special missions and took the preliminary view that a minimum of three hundred rounds of ammunition per month was necessary. The first vehicle with iron superstructure to be demonstrated was to be fitted by Alkett with a steel superstructure en route to its sphere of activity in the West after fulfilling its function in the East. The facilities needed for the job had been so heavily bombed that this reconstruction took three days to

The presentation before Hitler of the Tiger Assault Mortar Tank (Sturmmörserwagen) with a 38cm weapon.

38 cm Assault Mortar Tank, Sturmtiger

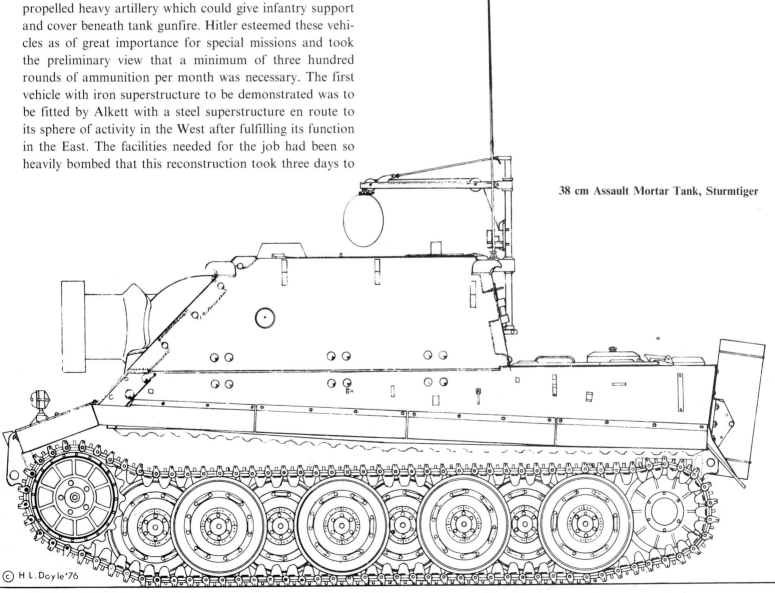

© H.L.Doyle '76

Four sides of the 38cm Mortar Tank of which only a few were built.

The photograph shows a 38cm Mortar Tank with a counterweight mounted on the barrel.

The inside of the 38cm Mortar Tank shows the ammunition loading tray and, to the right, the ammunition storage. The breech could be of lightweight construction since the gases were diverted to the front. The driver's position is at below left.

Stowed ammunition and sideways-folding ammunition loading tray.

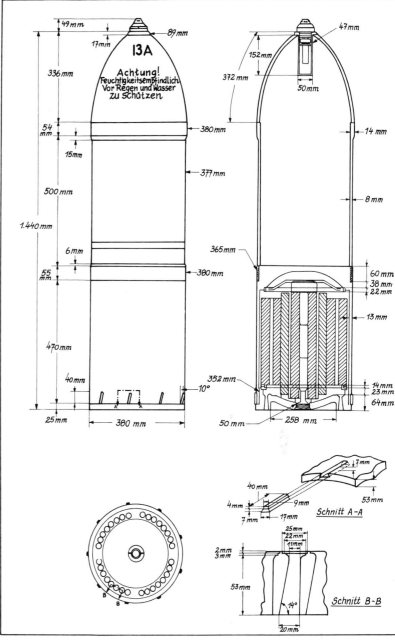

Construction of the 38cm Rocket-Shell 4581.

The chassis with the superstructure removed shows the shell stowage and roller-bearing loading tray. The driver's position is at the left front.

171

carry out. On 23rd September 1944, it was possible to tell Hitler that the special action taken by Alkett under the direction of Obermeister Hahne to produce ten Sturmmörsers had been a complete success. Hitler expressed his appreciation to those who had participated and ordered that five Tiger I chassis emerging from the repair shop each month should be converted in Tiger-Mörsers with a view to proving their fitness. In 1944, Alkett built eighteen of these vehicles in all.

Again on 5th January 1945, Hitler laid down that further building of Tiger Mörser should only take place using the repaired chassis of Tiger Is until the application of the projector on a lighter self-propelled gun carriage materialised. All repaired chassis were fitted with spring-rubber-rimmed steel bogie wheels. The all up weight was 65 tonnes. The sturdy tank superstructure with 150mm frontal armour was fabricated by the Branderburgisschen Eisenwerk, Kirchmoörser. There was a crew of five. Fourteen rounds of ammunition could be carried. The rocket launcher 61, 38cm L/5.4 shot the 350kp Rocket Assisted High Explosive Shell 4581 (R-Sprgs 4581) up to six kilometres. A crane mounted on the vehicle facilitated the loading of the vehicle. The breech could be kept light in weight since the explosive gases were discharged frontwards through a bypass in the rim of the muzzle. An MG34 was installed on a ball mounting in front of the driver.

In February 1945, sixteen of these vehicles in all were available. The first Sturmtiger saw action in Warsaw late in the summer of 1944.

Self-Propelled Guns (Selbstfahrlafetten)

In the New Year of 1942, the Army Weapons Department gave an order for a 17cm gun in armoured self-propelled mode. This Gerät 15-1702 (17cm K43) (Sfl) was to use the barrel, cradle, recoil mechanism, compressed air recuperator, compensator and mounting of the 17cm gun in a heavy howitzer carriage. The weight in running order was 53 tonnes; 13 tonnes of stores were carried. A vehicle using components of the Tiger chassis was put in hand with an expected target date for delivery of the spring of 1943.

Krupps had only dealt with the development of the 17cm and 21cm self- propelled gun; the requirement for an all-round firing capability, and the capability of dismounting the gun from the chassis, to act as an independent artillery piece, had to be solved taking account of the size

172

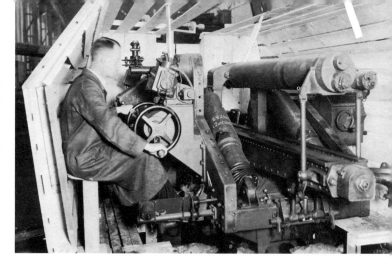

Parts of the Tiger chassis were to be used to provide heavier self-propelled guns. A wooden mock-up in the shape of the subsequent steel structure was made first of all to help establish the relevant measurements. In this way the seating requirements were established. The picture shows the first attempt at Krupp's Cricket 17 vehicle.

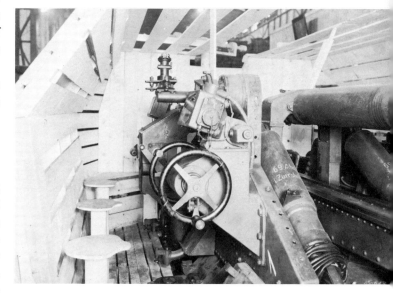

The full-scale wooden mock-up of the Mark VI self-propelled gun carriage (Geschützwagen).

The half-finished vehicle was captured in 1945 at Sennelager by the Allies. The upper sidewalls could be folded inwards for transportation by rail.

and weight involved. Krupps caused the vehicle to move, on its tracks, on a turntable until the centres of gravity and rotation were established and, in this way, achieved the all-round firing capability. The gun was dismounted by winching it backwards out of the chassis and setting it down on the turntable and its trail. For transportation, a well-wagon specially constructed for the Tiger was provided. So as to meet the loading gauge, the side walls of the tank's fighting room were hinged inwards.

An order to discontinue the weapon was given in 1944

Four views of the Mark VI self-propelled gun carriage for which an elongated Tiger B chassis was used.

Mark VI 17 cm K44 self-propelled gun carriage

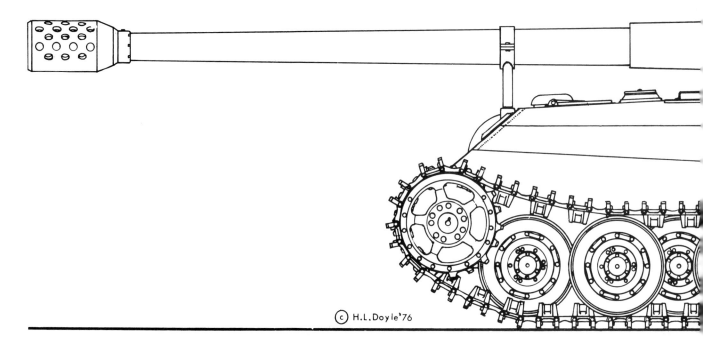

© H.L.Doyle'76

and new design requirements laid down a self-propelled gun of conventional construction. Construction of this 17cm K44 (Sf) GW VI was under way at Sennelager (an outworking of Henschel) in 1945, but it was not taken further. With a crew of eight, an ammunition supply of five rounds and frontal armour of 30mm, the fighting weight was 58 tonnes. The side armour was of 16-mm plate. Powerplant and running gear corresponded to that of the Tiger II although eleven bogie wheels were planned each side.

A similar layout also emerged for the Gerät 5-2107 (21cm Mrs 18/43) (Sfl). This armoured self-propelled gun with the 21cm 18 L/31 howitzer was to be ready by the spring of 1943. The weight in running order was established at 52.7 tonnes and for the gun itself 12.7 tonnes. The 21cm Mrs 18 (Sf)/GW VI required later was similar to the 17cm vehicle in appearance and weight. It could however only carry three rounds. Neither of these vehicles was completed.

The mobile arrangements ordered in January 1941 for the 24cm gun 4 was solved by Krupp by mounting it on a carriage supported between two unarmoured Tiger I chassis. Henschel were given written orders under OKH Wa J

Mark VI 21 cm heavy howitzer Mrs 18/43 self-propelled gun carria

© H.I.Doyle'76

174

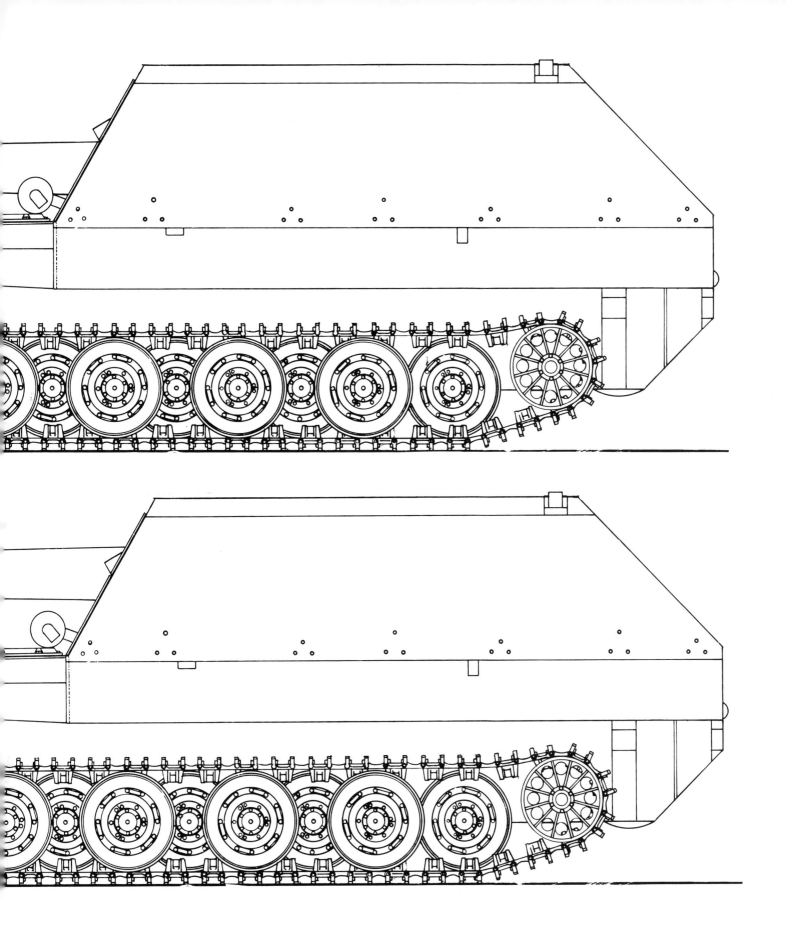

Rü (WuG 6) VIIIa2 Nr 9846/42 of 17th February 1942 to supply all of the necessary components for the chassis of the vehicles. Krupps were to perform the assembly. The order was designated 'Tiger H as transport vehicle for heaviest guns'.

The original method devised for loading Gerätes 040/041 on carriages left much to be desired in terms of mobility and cruising speed. At this stage, barrel and carriage together with the base plate and the four cantilever supports were to be suspended between two Tiger chassis. The unarmoured chassis weighed about 25 tonnes. Hydraulic jacks built into the chassis enabled the whole gun to be set down quickly so that both vehicles could be moved away without difficulty. When ready to move off, the weight of each vehicle came to almost 60 tonnes — no greater than the normal fighting weight of the Tiger tank.

To ensure uniformity of driving speed, the engines of the two carriages were linked up to a synchronising unit. On the road, the gun was to achieve a speed of 30 to 35 kilometres per hour. To make sure that road bridges would invariably have the weight of only one vehicle on them and that the second was on solid ground before and after cross-ing, the distance between vehicles was set at 20 to 22 metres.

On 23rd December 1942, Henschel stated that delivery of the additional chassis parts alongside mass production and the delivery of spare parts was unfortunately no longer possible since their production capacity was fully taken up with other commitments.

A similar type of transportation arrangement was planned by Friedrich Krupp of Essen for the movement of the 28cm K5 railway gun. Under these proposals, two tractors with Tiger B chassis — Gerät 566 Lastenträger (Load Bearer) für K5/3 (Tiger) — were to carry either gun, carriage or base plate between them. A further Tiger transporter was to carry the breech ring and the breech block.

Gerät 817 was to be manufactured for the 30.5cm mortar due for production in 1945, namely the gun carriage for 30.5cm GrW Sfl (606/9) on a Tiger chassis. However, like the self-propelled mounting for a 42cm mortar which it was proposed to assemble from parts of the Tiger, it was taken no further. Here again, the extended Tiger B running gear was to be used. The weight of the mortar was 18 tonnes and the completed vehicle weighed 65 tonnes. Both models were to be capable of all-round firing.

24 cm Gun 4 with Tiger I 'Loadbearers' (Lastenträger)

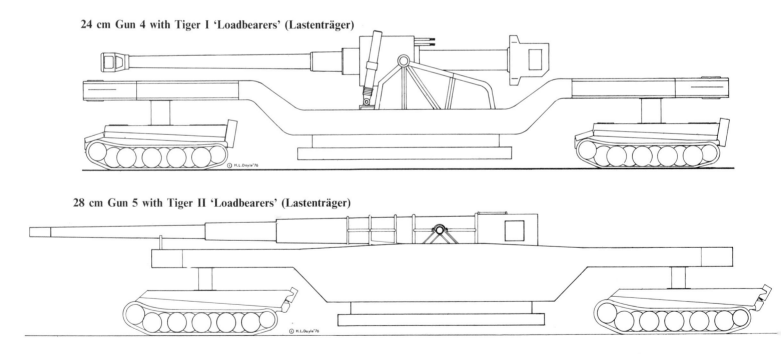

28 cm Gun 5 with Tiger II 'Loadbearers' (Lastenträger)

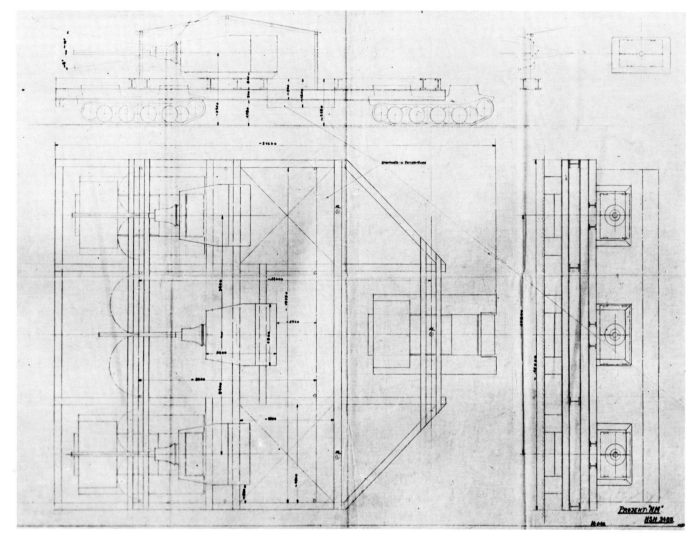

The Project NM dating from 1943 is still a mystery today. Here are obviously three turrets with guns of the magnitude of 12.8 cm and above set upon three Tiger E chassis acting as tractors.

Tank Command Vehicles (Panzerbefehlswagen)

It was planned to produce every tenth Tiger tank as a Command tank with special wireless equipment. Externally, the additional wireless equipment took the form of a multi-prong aerial whose case was mounted, in the first model, at the rear. On the second vehicle it became apparent that in this position the aerial crumpled with the shaking about it got from the heaving of the vehicle. It was therefore put back in its originally-planned position on the roof of the turret.

On 11th October 1943, it was ordered that from then on only every twentieth Tiger E turret was to be prepared as a Command turret. Those Tiger Command tanks fitted out with wireless equipment Fu 5 and 8 were given the SdKfz Number 267, and those with the Fu 5 and 7 equipment were furnished with the SdKfz Number 268.

On 9th June 1944, after the introduction of the model B, it was questioned how many Command vehicles of the new model should be built. Naturally, Command tanks were

A Tiger B Command tank. Externally, these vehicles were only identifiable by their additional antennae.

the first ordered after the introduction of the new production turrets (from vehicle 51).

Weapons Testing Department 7 had, in cooperation with a varnish manufacturer, developed a coloured contact varnish which was successfully used as a substitute for the tinning on bright contact points to eliminate radio interference caused by motor vehicles. It was prescribed in July 1944 as essential in both tanks and Command vehicles.

From August 1944, the 30-watt installation in the tank Command vehicle was transferred to the turret. The aerial inlet in the turret roof was simplified and was transferred to the hull by carrying out a simple procedure.

A conference on 17th July 1944 decided that in future all fighting vehicles should be so equipped and that they — whether in the field or in the ordnance depot — should be converted by means of an additional standard installation to the Command tank. The construction of special Command tanks in the factory could be reduced in this way. Vehicle number 284 was appointed by Weapons Testing Department C for these experiments. The firm of Wegmann had informally promised the completed turret for 12th September 1944. The design of the wireless installation differed

only slightly from that of a tank's.

As to the Command tank, only the Pz 20 box was discarded. It was replaced by the HSK 4218 assembly. Field generator GG 400, an accessories box for wireless parts and six extension rods were accommodated in the fighting compartment. The accessories box was smaller and floor space was found for it and the generator in the wireless area. The existing ammunition store in the command tank was changed. Instead, the new Command tank carried more ammunition than before. The exhaust outlet for the generator had to be changed to lead it outside the vehicle. The hollow dismountable antenna could be replaced by the extension rods up to a length of 0.7 metres. Six extension rods could — like a tent pole — be directly substituted on the base of the antenna.

Early in February 1945 the Inspector General of the Tank Corps ordered that the wireless installation previously provided for the Tiger Command tank should be further simplified. Fundamentally, wireless and intercommunication systems in tanks and also as modified in Command tanks were to be retained. In addition, cases 4, 6, 9 and 10 in the chassis and 3, 7 and 8 in the turret as well as the case for the wireless accessories were redundant. The following alterations already planned vis a vis the production series were to stand: replacement in tanks of antenna base number 1 with base number 2; replacement in the chassis of distribution box B 23 with cable distribution frame number 1; and installation of Pz connection boxes in Command tanks. For each tank, the tank commander's connection box was to be box Pz 30 Ausf A instead of box Pz 21. Box Pz 27 Ausf B (instead of 22 of the production series) beside the gunner had to be interchangeable with box Pz 30 as in the Command vehicle. The boxes 3, 7 and 8 being withdrawn from the turret were to be replaced by the box Pz 21 (Ausf C). The new turret was due to be delivered by Wegmann's to Henschel on 3rd February 1945.

After an inspection of the experimental vehicle, it was laid down inter alia that provision was to be made for a protective casing for the antenna inlet in each vehicle. Up to the beginning of production of the new series, antenna base number 2 instead of 1 was installed. To sum up, the necessary equipment for installation in a Command tank went under the description of 'set of wireless installation parts Fu 8 for the Tiger tank'. Once more, the experimental vehicle used was equipped and delivered as a standard tank.

Rescue and Recovery Tank (Bergepanzer)

The first edition of a Tiger Rescue and Recovery tank had probably been adapted from a Tiger I chassis by the troops themselves with the need for rescue and recovery clear in their minds. The turret was kept but the gun was removed and a cover plate was screwed over the opening left in the mantlet. A support for a crane boom was attached to the turret roof which was obviously linked to the elevating gear through a welded bracket. By this means, the makeshift crane could be raised and lowered. In odd cases, Tiger chassis minus turret were also used as a so-called salvage vehicle for recovery during action. Besides removing the heavy turret, the firm of J.S. Fries & Sohn of Frankfurt am Main produced a travelling portal crane with a 15-tonne lifting power. This piece of equipment was loaded on to two twin-wheeled chassis (tyre size 800-20) which was, despite its size, comparatively mobile. Four road wheels measuring 150 x 140mm allowed the equipment to be moved with its load. Eight men were able to get the equipment into action within twenty minutes. It was of great assistance in repair work in this field.

Two views of a Tiger Ausf E converted by the troops into a Recovery tank. The gun was removed, the opening was closed up with a sheet of armour. On the top of the turret there was a mounting support for a crane.

Late in 1943, a bulldozer attachment taking the form of a substantially strengthened V-shaped plough was ordered by the Regional Operations Office at Madgeburg in association with the firm of Krupp-Gruson for rubble clearing after air raids. It was possible to attach this plough in quick time to any tank available in the area. The arrangement weighed 1,580kp and cost between 1,200 and 1,500 Reichsmarks. Piles of rubble up to 80cm high could be moved without difficulty. The bulldozer arrangement extended about 25cm each side of the tank tracks. This Madgeburg street-clearing equipment had a blade width of 3.4 metres. The police chief of Kassel ordered a similar device in August 1944 which was built on to the front of a Tiger B. The work was carried out by the locomotive works — that is, in Henschel's main blacksmith's and boilermaking shop.

In view of the overstretched fuel situation, Henschel looked further into the development of a steam-driven caterpillar tractor. Originally this project was planned for use in tanks but the size of the boiler and condenser left insufficient space for the fighting compartment. The development was abandoned towards the end of the war. The Ordnance Department was no longer interested in a steam-powered tracked vehicle at that point.

From 1942 onwards, the fuel shortages in Germany called for drastic solutions. Those principally affected by the extremely meagre allocation of fuel were the reserve units and training battalions which were forced to use homemade fuel. Trials and modifications were carried out in experiments with liquid gas on all suitable vehicles, including the Tiger. The tank itself was not spared the installation of a generator for the production of gas from wood. Although the heavy vehicle could hardly be changed beyond second gear, a wood gas generator was even installed in a Tiger II at Fallingbostel in 1944. A truly sad spectacle.

179

6. EXPERIMENTAL ENGINES AND PROJECTS

During the war, some interesting engine developments sprang up because of the need to cope with the weight per horse-power of the heavy tank. The more acceptable are discussed in detail in this chapter.

The Motorenbau GmbH HL 230 type engine had a low power output and had to be improved. The engine which was designated the HL 234 was the outcome of a further two stages of development of the HL 230. First, the output was raised from 700 to 800hp by direct petrol injection. At the same time, the compression ratio was increased and a second cooling water pump was installed. Better distribution of coolant was insisted on. The normal valve springs were replaced by cup springs and the connecting rod bearings and cylinder head gasket were improved. Prototypes were built and subjected to test bed running. Mass production was planned from the middle of 1945. It was planned to develop the engine further by using a supercharger to bring its output up to almost 1,000hp with maximum revolutions per minute of 3,000. The supercharger was driven by a 1-litre 2-cylinder four-stroke engine rated to develop some 50hp. This unit was to be accommodated in the 'V' of the main engine. One of these engines was installed in the Tiger, but before the operating controls had been decided. The fuel consumption was about 235 grams per horse power per hour (g/PS/h) at 1,000rpm, 225 at 2,000rpm and 235 at 3,000rpm.

A 12-litre tandem engine was also under development by Maybach. The engine weighed 600kp and produced 500hp normally and 700hp with a supercharger. At the same time, experiments were taking place with a diesel version of the HL 234 but there were no indications of a reliable outcome. The injection unit for it was furnished by Bosch. There was no question of anything other than water cooling for all engines since Dr-Ing. h.c. Maybach insisted on this type of cooling as a matter of principle. His observation that he was water cooled when he came into the world ruled out any further discussion on the subject.

It was necessary for the fitting sequence of the HL 234, as it had been in the case of the HL 230, for the connecting piece between the air filter box and the flexible connector on the fan to be supplied at the same time as the engine. Again, the exhaust manifold had to be altered and it was necessary to incorporate the exhaust pipe, up till then supplied by Henschel ready-fitted to the rear of the hull, in the engine supply schedule. Because of the different housing of certain items in the Panther and Tiger engine rooms, it was necessary once again to produce slightly altered versions of the HL 234. The further development of the HL 234 engine was continued after the end of the war by Maybach Engineering in France. This was the engine type HL 295 of 1,000hp at 2,800rpm. It was later installed in the prototype of the French AMX 50 tank.

The German Army Command wanted nothing but petrol engines for tanks since German industry found it could not in practice manufacture synthetic diesel fuel. These considerations first became meaningless in 1942 since from then on synthetic diesel fuel could be produced in sufficient quantity. From that point, the development of a diesel engine for a tank was pushed. In this connection an order was also given by the Army Ordnance Department (Ordnance Inspection Department 6) to the firm Ruhrbenzin AG and I.G. Farbenindustrie AG for the development of a diesel fuel which was guaranteed to fire — exclusively for armoured vehicles. Its introduction depended upon the use of diesel engines in these vehicles. Lubricating oil, fuel for tropical use and Wehrmacht standard oil based on German raw materials were ordered at the same time.

Daimler-Benz's efforts to have the diesel MB 507 installed instead of the Maybach HL 230 finally failed towards the end of 1943. On 23rd December 1943, Lt Colonel Schaede who superintended the Departmental Production Group of the Ministry of Armaments and War Production made it clear that because there was insufficient manufacturing capacity it was under no circumstances to be considered as an engine for the Panther. Although the diesel engine had been passed over, it became one of the air-cooled motors which the Führer ordered to be developed. Nevertheless Daimler-Benz completed the experiments in hand on the MB 507 so as to be prepared, should the need arise, with suitable proposals.

Since 1942, Porsche had been carrying out experiments with an air-cooled 650hp diesel engine which was to be interchangeable with the Maybach HL 230 in existing tanks. Two experimental engines were built by Simmering-Graz Pauker AG of Vienna. This firm had also produced test-beds for this large engine and had undertaken similar experimental developments. Amongst others, Porsche had tested the single-cylinder experimental engines for use in tanks whose basic data are given in the adjacent table.

From the 2.3 litre unit (Porsche type 192), a sixteen-cylinder X- configuration engine was developed which was fitted with two BBC-Mannheim exhaust driven superchargers. The Simmering-Graz Pauker AG's pre-combustion chamber system was employed. This was especially suitable for the supercharger and for the combined scavenging and cooling of the combustion chamber. The cooling blower and oil cooler were assembled with the engine. Porsche's earlier experience with the arrangement of cylinder and cooling vanes was drawn upon extensively. Professor Kamm of Stuttgart designed the supercharger. The supercharger pressure was held at the least possible excess atmospheric pressure of 0.5 so as to maintain the Ordnance Departments requirements for a long engine serviceability interval. The engine had a dry weight of about 2,000Kp and it measured 1,680 by 2,500 x 1,150mm. It was planned to increase the output by an increase in crankshaft rotational speed from 2,000 to 3,000rpm. The single cylinder set-up of this engine had completed a 100-hour run on the test bed in Vienna and had produced an output of 47hp at 2,100rpm. The compression ratio lay between 13.8 and 14:1. In order to deduce the output of the complete engine, it had to be remembered that no allowance was made during the trials for the power required to run the cooling fan.

On 5th January 1945, Hitler was given a progress report by Colonel Holzhauer on the development of the Porsche-Simmering sixteen-cylinder air-cooled diesel engine. Hitler emphasised the importance of this project at that point in time. He expected to receive further continuous reports about the results of the tests on the experimental engine as well as on the experimental vehicle.

One of these engines was installed in a Tiger B at the Nibelungenwerk which meant that it had to have a completely re-designed engine room. Both the hull and the track adjustment equipment also required to be altered considerably. In pursuit of an increase in the output of this engine, the use of the Porsche type 213 3-litre single-cylinder unit

Porsche Single-Cylinder Engines

Type	Engine	Bore x Stroke	Swept Volume	Fuel	System	Remarks
117	101	115x145mm	1.5 litres	Petrol	Carburettor	Cylinder head A
119	101	115x145mm	1.5 litres	Petrol	Carburettor	Cylinder head B
158	101	115x145mm	1.5 litres	Diesel	Diesel injection	
159	101	115x145mm	1.5 litres	Diesel	Simmering	
191	190	120x145mm	1.64 litres	Diesel	Pre-combustion chamber	
192	203	135x160mm	2.3 litres	Diesel		Eighteen cylinder composite project
193	101/93	120x145mm	1.64 litres	Petrol	(Injection)	
213	212	150x170mm	3 litres	Diesel		

was tried. With a total piston displacement of 48 litres, an output of 1,500hp at 2,500rpm was expected. The Simmering-Graz-Pauker AG designation for this engine was type Sla 16 and the Porsche designation was type 212.

The V6 11.5/16 twelve-cylinder blown engine developed by MAN was to be ready for manufacture in 1941. However, this 400hp engine was not even ready in 1943 and was thereupon cancelled since its output was too small.

An air-cooled twelve or sixteen-cylinder diesel engine with an output of 800hp in which Argus cooperated did not get beyond the project stage. In addition, it would have required fundamental alterations to the hull of the tank.

A 30-litre twelve-cylinder carburettor engine with rotary valves was planned by Auto-Union. It was to have an output of 900hp.

The three photographs below show the sixteen-cylinder 'X' configuration engine developed by Porsche. At the left is the open camdrive with two of the injection pumps visible. In the middle is the open flywheel. At the right, the cylinder head has been removed to expose the rocker arms on the valve gear.

Above and below *The completed assembly with the blowers; it could be accommodated in the engine room of the Tiger B with the minimum of alterations.*

Above and below *The Type Sla 16 engine in assembled form but still without the blowers.*

A single-cylinder experimental engine formed the Adler-Werke's experimental basis for a tank engine. This 2.5-litre unit produced an output of 87.5hp at 3,000rpm. This promised an output of 1,050hp from a twelve-cylinder engine. A trial engine was to be completed by July 1945.

Towards the end of 1943, Klöckner-Humboldt-Deutz AG were given an order for the development of a diesel engine yielding a peak output of 700hp at 2,000rpm. It was laid down that a primary condition of any newly-developed engine was that it could be installed in the existing engine room of a tank without the vehicle needing to be altered fundamentally. The construction experiment showed that requirements could only be met by a V-8 two-stroke diesel motor with a cylinder bore of 170mm and a stroke of 180mm.

To clarify questions of scavenging, combustion, bearings, lubrication and piston, two single-cylinder experimental engines were first of all built and set running. The peak load of the cylinder of 86.5hp at 2,000rpm corresponded to an average real piston pressure of 4.8Kp/cm². The compression ratio was 15:1. Already, the first experiments showed that the desired output was attainable without great difficulty.

After the first satisfactory single-cylinder trials, three eight-cylinder engines of the TM type 118 in 90 degrees V-

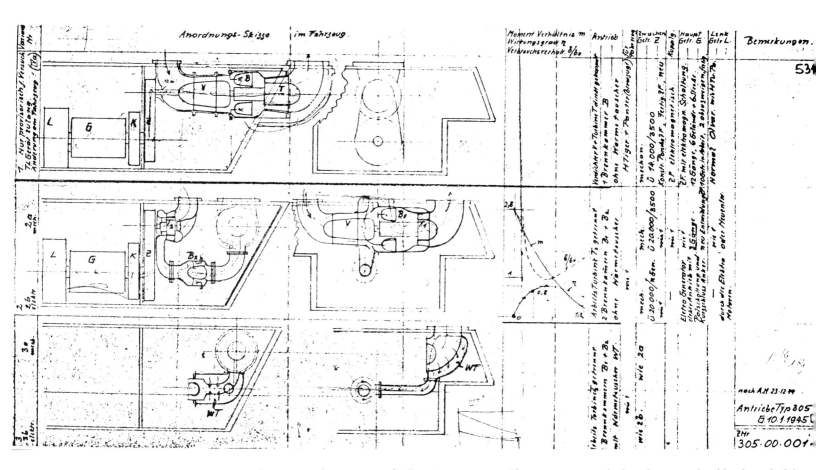

These drawings depict Porsche's investigations into housing a turbine engine in the Tiger's engine room. These investigations had not been completed by the end of the w

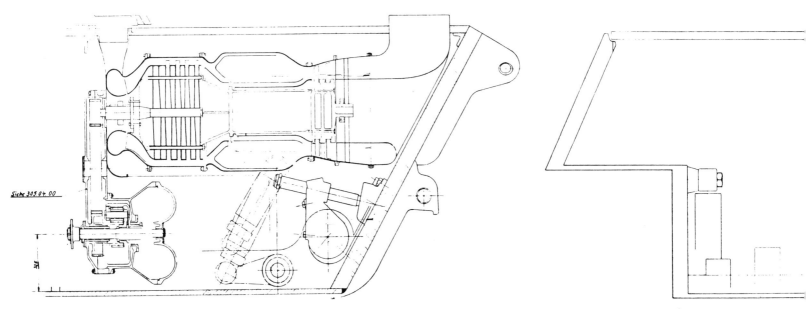

184

form were put in hand. The preference was to manufacture only one of these engines in the first instance. With the evacuation of the experimental establishment at Altmorschen in February 1945 and the further removal from there to Ulm at the end of March 1945, a large part of the components already manufactured for the engine was lost.

Even a modified BMW radial aircraft engine was to be installed in the Tiger B. The necessary alterations to the hull turned out to be too extensive. This development was not pursued any further.

Porsche was given the task of developing a turbine engine with an output of 1,000hp. Its installation in a tank was to be looked at and it was to be ascertained whether the *Luftwaffe*'s newly-launched jet powerplant could find an application for this design. An exact calculation of the fuel requirement and torque flow showed the impossibility of using existing turbines or their components. The torque flow was unsuitable for use in the tank and the fuel consumption at full load varied between 600 and 700 grams per horsepower per hour. At part load it rose still higher.

After that, a new unit was planned (Porsche type 305) which had the following notable features in its construction. It had an axial flow compressor with a combustion chamber and a turbine which served as the exclusive power source for the compressor. Between the compressor and the combustion chamber, a part of the compressed air was diverted into a second combustion chamber. The exhaust gases from the second combustion chamber supplied a special driving turbine which was to drive the vehicle via a transmission. This arrangement promised to yield a torque flow five times greater than the torque at highest rotational speed. The fuel requirement was less than that of the project without a special driving turbine but it still did not come up to a satisfactory standard. To improve the efficiency, a heat exchanger was taken into consideration. It might have been permissible under the project with the separate driving turbine to have got by with a two-stage gear transmission. Porsche was in the position to confirm this from the results of its various trials. The project was not taken to the experimental stage because of the way the war was going. The work itself was largely undertaken by the experimental station of the Waffen-SS at Vienna.

In all the new engine experiments the firm of Maybach was by far the most progressive. The desire for increased engine output and a resulting improvement in the weight per horse power of heavy tanks overshadowed all other considerations. Saving space in the confined engine room was of lesser value than the importance attached to accessibility for maintenance. In spite of all the endeavours in the field of engine development, it was still the Maybach HL 230 engine that was installed up to the end of the war in the Panther and Tiger tanks.

Transmission, Steering and Running Gear

Better efficiency from the transmission gears was also sought. Reducing the weight of operating apparatus and simpler design was required. The firm of J.M. Voith of Heidenheim therefore built a so-called PANTA hydraulic gearing unit which was to be installed in the Tiger B. The experiments were broken off on 15th November 1944. Likewise, the AEG Railway Division was busy in the year 1943/44 with the design of a Föttinger fluid torque converter (turbine pumps and turbines, three transmission steps). AEG had already developed a fluid torque converter in 1939 for Henschel but because of its size and weight, it could not at that time be installed in the tank. A transmission gear unit for the Tiger B was under consideration but it came nowhere near installation.

The firm of Pulsgetriebe GmbH of Leipzig had produced an eight-gear transmission, type PP 33, in 1944 which was able to transfer a maximum output of 1,000hp at 3,000rpm at a total reduction of 1:18.7 and an average gradient factor of 1.5. With an aluminium casing, it weighed 850Kp. The eight forward gears operated through three sets of planet pinions operating in series. The fourth set shifted all eight forward gears to reverse drive at half speed through a dog clutch. The transmission was tensionally connected and free running and indeed such that the full engine torque was transferred smoothly whether the gear shift was in forward or reverse. The engine clutch was only used for starting up. In the gearbox only unpolished case hardened gear wheels of remarkably small pitch were used. Although Henschel was not convinced of its mode of operation, one of these gearboxes was sent on to Sennelager to be installed in a Tiger tank.

As had already happened in the case of the Mark IV tank, the Army High Command ordered the Gear Wheel factory at Augsberg (formerly Joh. Renk AG) under Order number SS 4912.0006.4819.42, to develop a new type of hydrostatic fluid steering mechanism for tanks. They were earmarked for the 'Kätzchen' (Little Cat) tank — an armoured fully tracked multi-purpose vehicle ordered under reference SS 006-6032/42 from Auto-Union with a Maybach HL 50 Z engine and a ZFAK 8-45 gearbox. In priority order DE 504, dealing with the appropriation of Reichsmarks, a similar steering unit was ordered under BuM number 5872/43 of 25th February 1943 for the E10, Tiger I, Tiger II and Panther II tanks. The firm was also occupied with a newly-developed OLVAR gearbox. The installation of a hydrostatic steering mechanism (infinitely variable with uninterrupted changes in the radii of turn) was anticipated but it went no further than that.

The Gear Wheel factory at Freidrichshafen had at this point developed a so-called 'electric gearbox' but it was plagued with persistent difficulties with the clutches. An electric clutch was provided for each pair of spur wheels. In the event of a breakdown in Maybach's production, it was planned that if need be the dog clutch constant mesh gearbox type AK 7-400 used for the Panther would also be used for the Tiger B. A V-n graph provided by the author in Sennelager in 1944 showed a top speed of 46 kilometres per hour in seventh gear at 3,000rpm. The experiment was not too successful principally because the gear reduction was too small. The experiments were wound up in order, if need be, to have an alternative gearbox available for the Tiger. (ZF also built experimentally two Mekydro gear change mechanisms under order SS 0006-6423/43 for the Tiger.)

Assembly possibilities of various steering gears and gearboxes.

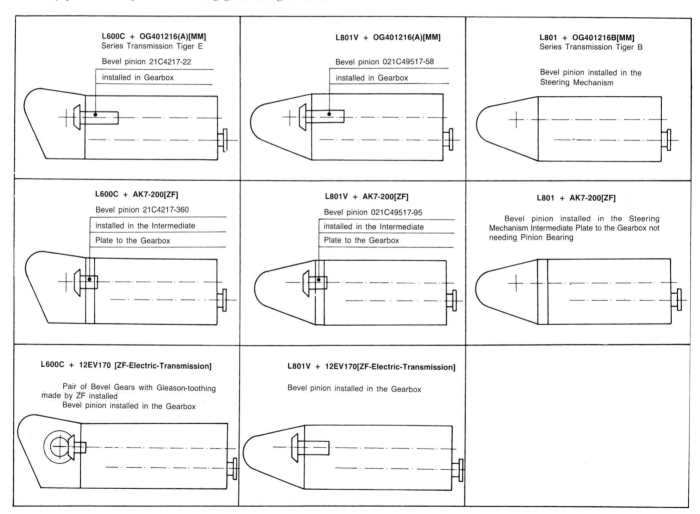

The author's V-n graph for a Tiger B with a ZF AK 7-400 dog clutch constant mesh gearbox which he produced in Sennelager in 1944. The vertical axis n is rpm; the horizontal axis V is speed (km/hr); and the graph shows speed in each of seven gears ('gang')

Henschel was working in the meantime on an improved steering mechanism for the Tiger. This type L 1201 was easier in its basic construction and could transfer more power. Approximately 80 per cent of the detailed designs had already been finished and the expectation was that the steering gear would return an increase of about 50 per cent in power and that smaller gear wheels and 25 per cent fewer ball bearings would be needed.

As to the design of the running gear and the choice of suspension, it has to be accepted that towards the end of the war the trend was clearly to do away with torsion bar suspension. The main reason was quite emphatically that torsion springing took up too much room inside the hull and that it was too expensive to manufacture. The firm of Adler provided plans for a self-contained suspension for the Panther and Tiger tanks which provided for externally mounted sets of plate springs. These suspension units were maintenance-free and could be easily replaced and installed in the Tiger.

The systematic destruction of the ball bearing factories was the reason for the order to replace as many roller-friction bearings as possible with plain bearings. In this connection the impracticability of such a conversion in real and functional terms was quickly emphasised. For all that, replaceable designs were drawn up and tested out for the Tiger E and B.

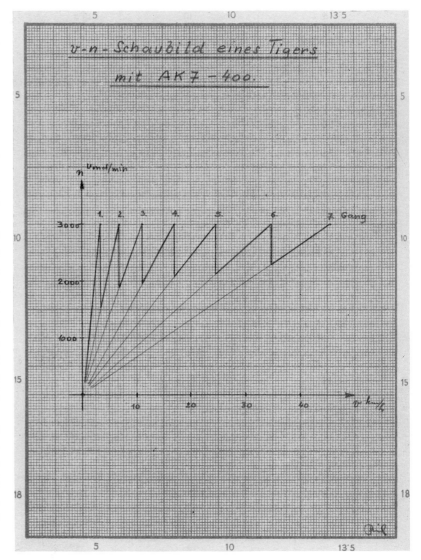

187

Conclusions

It is obvious that a great deal of trouble was taken to improve and provide the only two tanks still remaining in production — the Panther II and Tiger II — as soon as possible. They would have been, with the planned adjustments, the most advanced tanks of the Second World War. Yet grave doubts emerged towards the end of 1944 as to whether a tank of the Tiger class was not already too heavy and too lacking in mobility for tactical use. Even Henschel engineers were of the opinion that the Panther was better suited to mass production and had positive tactical advantages. In view of the economy measures of industry and their effect on the hours of work expended per tank and also the manufacturing difficulties stemming from air raids and shortages of raw materials, a smaller vehicle and one quicker to manufacture would have been preferable.

As late as January 1945, front-line officers urgently demanded a 35-tonne tank from Henschel's experimental station as speedily as it could be manufactured from tried and tested components. On the other hand, after the Allied landings in France, industry abandoned hope and all so-called Tank Building Programmes were no longer treated seriously.

There was little doubt that with vehicles of the Tiger class the limits of the useful size and weight of a tank, which it had been necessary to define, had been reached. It also remains without doubt that the stamina to see the Tiger through was sustained in two ways. First, by the very existence of the powerful tank and, secondly, by the greater fighting spirit it inspired in its crews. Moreover, the superiority of the tank's main armament in tank warfare was obvious. On the other hand there were the sensitivity and the weakness of powerplant and running gear — too great a specific ground pressure as well as too small a specific weight.

No matter how legendary the Tiger tank became, the troops themselves might have been better served by a greater number of lighter, more mobile and more reliable tanks.

This Tiger Ausf B stands outside the Combat Training School 2, Munster, the sole Tiger in Germany.

APPENDICES

APPENDIX A Technical Specifications of Tiger E (Old Turret)

GENERAL DATA

Combat weight (kg)	57,000
Transportation weight (with Transportation Tracks) (kg)	52,500

Speed

Cruising speed (km/hr)	
road (motorway)	40
roughish country	20/25
Range	
road (motorway) (km)	195
roughish country (km)	110

Performance

Trench crossing capability (m)	2.5
Step crossing capability (m)	0.0790
Climbing capability (°)	
forwards	35
backwards	35
Fording capability (m)	1.60
Submersion depth (m)	4.0
Crew	Five

Principal Measurements

Overall length (mm)	
gun at 12 o'clock	8,450
gun at 6 o'clock	8,434
without overhang of gun	6,316
Overhang of gun at 12 o'clock (mm)	2,116
Overall width with Combat Tracks (with track cover) (mm)	3,705

Overall height (mm)	3,000
Length at track level (mm)	5,850
Width track to track (mm)	
Combat Tracks	3,547
Transportation Tracks	3,142
Track surface contact per track (mm)	3,605
Track surface contact per track, settlement depth of 20cm (projected from level) (mm)	5,150
Track gauge (mm)	
Combat Tracks	2,822
Transportation Tracks	2,622
Outside height ground to superstructure roof (mm)	1,800
Height, ground to axis of gun barrel (mm)	2,195
Terrain clearance, both front and rear (mm)	470

Hull with Superstructure (mm)

Greatest external length	5,965
External width (mm)	
at running gear level	1,920
at side extension level (ave)	3,140
Inside width of hull (mm)	
at running gear level	1,800
at side extension level (ave)	2,980
Height of hull from floor to top	1,335

Hull armour

	Thickness (mm)	Degrees off Horizontal (°)
In front of driver	100	81
Nose	100	10
Side	60	90
Rear	80	81

Top 25
Floor 25
Weight of completely
machined hull with top (kg) 20,800

Running Gear

	Combat Track	Transportation Track
Number of Guide teeth per link	Two	Two
Length of track pin (mm)	716	658.5
Diameter of pin (mm)	28	28
Ground pressure per unit area (Weight ÷ 2 x track surface contact x width of track) (kg/cm²)	1.05	1.46
Ground pressure at settlement depth of 20cm (kg/cm²)	0.735	1.02
Track print/track surface contact	1:1.278	1:1.384

Bogie Wheels

Type of running gear   Stacked
Type of bogie wheels   steel with
                                  rubber-cushioned rim
Number of bogie wheels each side   Eight
Diameter of bogie wheels (mm)   800
Loading per bogie wheel (kg)   3,440
Distance between axis wheel to wheel (mm)   515
Play between bogie wheel and track teeth (mm)   2

Crank Axles and Suspension

Material for bearing bushes   Novotext
Type of suspension   Torsion bars
Number of torsion bars   Sixteen
Diameter of torsion bars (mm)
  front and rear   58
  middle   55
Diameter of head (m)   80, 85 respectively
Sprung length of torsion bar (mm)   1,730
Total length of torsion bar (mm)   1,890
Distance from floor of hull
  to centre of torsion bar (mm)   95

Sprocket, Idler Wheel, Shock Absorber

Pitch circle — diameter of sprocket (mm)   841.37
Pitch of driving sprocket (mm)   131
Diameter of idler wheel (mm)   600
Maximum travel of track adjuster (mm)   115
Number of shock absorbers   Four

Engine Installation

Engine   Maybach Motorenbau GmbH
Type   HL 230 P 45
Output at 3,000rpm, air temperature
  20 degrees C and atmospheric pressure
  760mm (Torricellean tube) (hp)   700
Weight of engine (kg)   1300
Number of cylinders   Twelve
Bore and Stroke (mm)   130 x 145
Swept volume (cm³)   23,000
Compression ratio   6.8:1
Ignition   Two magnetos with
                                  in-built impulse starters
Fuel consumption (litres/hp/hr)   1
Fuel consumption (litres/100km)
  road   270
  roughish country   280

Cooling System

Type of cooling   Water
Number of radiators   Two
Height of radiators (mm)   490
Width of radiators (core) (mm)   892
Thickness of radiators (mm)   200
Front surface of radiators (mm²)   437
Number of fans (double fans)   Two
Diameter of fan blades (mm)   437
Rpm of fans at max. engine rpm
  summer (tropical)   4,150
  winter   2,950
Type of fan drive   Bevel gears and drive-shafts
Maximum power requirement (hp)   50
Number of air filters   Two
Manufacturer and type
  of air filter   Fa. Mann and Henschel

Gearbox and Steering gear

Maximum solid angle of drive-shaft (°)   front 1; rear 2
Length of drive-shaft (mm)   front 885; rear 840

Transmission

Manufacturer   MM/Adler
Type   0G 40 12 16 A
Number of forward gears   Eight
Number of reverse gears   Four
Clearance of transmission shaft (mm)   181.5
Overall length of gearbox (mm)   1372
Overall width of gearbox (mm)   556
Overall height of gearbox (mm)   591
Reduction gearing of gearbox   1:11

Permissible speeds at engine revolutions of 3,000rpm (km/hr)

1st gear	2.84
2nd gear	4.34
3rd gear	6.18
4th gear	9.17
5th gear	14.1
6th gear	20.9
7th gear	30.5
8th gear	45.4
In Reverse	3.75
Total reduction of gearbox	1:16
Type and tooth construction of the bevel gearing	Klingelnberg-Palloid Spiral
Bevel gearing reduction ratio	1:1.06

Steering Gear

Design — Steering gear with two radii of turn	L 600c
Steering gear reduction ratio	1:1.3333
Number of epicyclic steering gears	Two
Number of steering clutches to epicyclic steering gears	Four
Material of clutch disc coating	Jurid alternatively Emero
Number of gear wheels	Twenty-nine
Minimum turning radius (m)	3.44
Maximum turning radius (m)	165
Operation of steering (oil pressure 6.5 x atmospheric pressure)	Argus Lenkapparat
Total length of gear and steering gear block (mm)	1,812
Total weight of gear and steering gear block (kg)	1,345

Final Drive and Brakes

Final drive gear reduction	1:10.7
Type of brakes	Argus Disc Brakes
Position of brakes	Between steering gear and track drive
Footbrake operates on two steering gear shafts	(Two brakes)
Diameter of brake drums – external (mm)	550
Material of disc coating	Emero
Brake cooling	Cooling vanes on brake housing
Type of brake operation	Mechanical by foot pedal and hand lever

Fuel and Water capacity

Fuel	
four tanks (litres)	540 without reserve tank
20-litre jerry cans (litres)	—
Water capacity	
radiator and engine (litres)	—
tanks (litres)	—

Turret

Weight (kg)	11,000
Height with commander's cupola (mm)	1,200
Inside diameter of operational area in turret (mm)	1,830

Armament

KwK 36 8.8cm L/56

Rounds of fixed ammunition	Ninety-two
MG42 (MG34 in interim)	(Two)
Thirty-nine bags of 150-round belts	5,850 rounds
Machine pistol	One
Six magazines of thirty-two rounds	192 rounds
HE shell	Three

With the installation of the new turret (with a commander's cupola/exit hatch which was hinged to swing sideways) the following measurements were altered.

Overall length	
gun barrel at 12 o'clock (mm)	8,455
gun barrel at 6 o'clock (mm)	8,411
without overhang of gun barrel (mm)	6,355
Overhang of gun barrel, gun at 12 o'clock (mm)	2,122 mm
Overall height (mm)	2,855 mm

State of modification 'a' after those of 10th May 1944

APPENDIX B Technical Specifications of Tiger B
(from Vehicle Number 51)

GENERAL DATA

Combat weight (kg)	69,800*
Transportation weight (kg)	66,300*

Speed

Cruising speed (km/hr)	
road (motorway)	38
roughish country	15/20
Range (km)	
road (motorway)	170
roughish country	120

Performance

Trench crossing capability (m)	2.50
Step crossing capability (m)	0.85
Climbing capability (°)	
forwards	35
backwards	35
Fording capability (m)	1.60
Crew	Five

Principal Measurements

Overall length (mm)	
gun at 12 o'clock	10,286*
gun at 6 o'clock	9,966*
without overhang of gun	7,380*
Overhang of gun at 12 o'clock (mm)	2,906*
Overall width with Combat Tracks	
including track cover (mm)	3,755
Overall height (mm)	3,090
Length at track level (mm)	6,400
Width track to track (mm)	
Combat Track including projection of track pin	3,625
Transportation Tracks	3,270
Track surface contact per track (mm)	4,120

Track surface contact per track	
at settlement depth of 20cm	
(projected from ground level) (mm)	5,400
Track gauge (mm)	
Combat Tracks	2,790
Transportation Tracks	2,610
Outside height ground to superstructure roof (mm)	1,860
Height, ground to axis of gun barrel (mm)	2,260
Terrain clearance (mm)	
front	495
rear	510

Weight and Cubic capacity

Weight of ready to run chassis without turret, weapons and ammunition, fitments and installations (kg)	about 52,000
Total cubic capacity (m³)	17.4
fighting compartment (m³)	about 11
engine room (m³)	about 2.2
turret above the underside of the top of the hull (m³)	about 4.2
the rest excluding engine room and fighting compartment (m³)	about 2

Hull

Gross weight (kg)	28,000
Deadweight after machining (kg)	27,700
Greatest external length of hull (mm)	7,134
External width	
at running gear level (mm)	1,928
at side extension level (mm) (average)	2,938
Inside width of hull	
at running gear level (mm)	1,768
at side extension level (mm) (average)	2,778
Height of hull from floor to top	
forward (mm)	1,365
rear (mm)	1,350

193

Hull armour

	Thickness (mm)	Degrees off Horizontal (°)
In front of driver	150	40
Nose	100	40
Side	80	lower 90
		upper 65
Rear	80	60
Top	40	
Floor		
front	40	
rear	25	

Running Gear

	Combat track	Transportation track
Number of guide teeth per link	Two	Two
Length of track pin (mm)	818	658.5
Diameter of track pin (mm)	24	24
Ground pressure per unit area on firm ground (Weight ÷ 2 x track surface contact x width of track) (kg/cm²)	1.02	1.23
Ground pressure at settlement depth of 20cm (kg/cm²)	0.777	0.943
Track print/Track surface contact	1:1.475	1:1.1578

Bogie Wheels

Type of running gear	echelon
Type of bogie wheel	Steel with rubber-cushioned rim
Number of bogie wheels each side	Nine
Diameter of bogie wheel (mm)	800
Loading per bogie wheel (kg)	3,610
Distance between axles, wheel to wheel (mm)	515
Play between bogie wheel and track teeth (mm)	2 or 4

Crank Axles and Suspension

Material for bearing bushes	Novotext
Type of suspension	Torsion bar
Number of torsion bars	Eighteen
Diameter of torsion bars (mm)	60 or 63
Diameter of torsion bar head (mm)	90
Sprung length of torsion bar (mm)	1,800
Total length of torsion bar (mm)	1,960
Distance from floor of hull to centre of torsion bar (mm)	95

Sprocket, Idler Wheel, Shock Absorbers

Pitch circle — diameter of sprocket (mm)	870
Pitch of driving sprocket (mm)	151
Diameter of idler wheel (mm)	650
Maximum travel of track adjuster (mm)	210
Number of shock absorbers	Four

Engine Installation

Engine	Maybach Motorenbau GmbH
Type	HL 230 P 30
Output at 3,000rpm, air temperature 20 degrees C, and atmospheric pressure 760mm (Torricellean tube) (hp)	700
Weight of engine (kg)	1,300
Number of cylinders	Twelve
Bore and Stroke	130 x 145mm
Swept volume (cm²)	23,000
Compression ratio	6.8:1
Ignition	Two magnetos with in-built impulse starters
Fuel consumption (litres/hp)	1/PS/h
Fuel consumption	
road (litres/100km)	500
roughish country (litres/100km)	700

Cooling System

Type of cooling	Water
Number of radiators	Four
Height of radiator core (mm)	324
Width of radiator core (mm)	522
Thickness of radiators (mm)	200
Front surface of radiators (mm²)	0.169
Number of fans	Two double fans
Diameter of fan blades (mm)	520
Rpm of fans at maximum engine rpm	
summer (tropical)	3,765
winter	2,680
Maximum power requirement (hp)	40
Number of air filters	Two
Manufacturer and type of air filter	Fa, Mann and Hummel

Gearbox and Steering Gear

Maximum solid angle of drive-shaft	front 2:25 degrees; rear 2 degrees
Length of drive-shaft	
front (mm)	993
rear (mm)	1,187

Gearbox

Manufacturer	MM/ZF

Type	OG 40 12 16 B
Number of gears	
forward	Eight
reverse	Four
Clearance of transmission shaft (mm)	181.5
Overall length of gearbox (mm)	1,266
Overall width of gearbox (mm)	600
Overall height of gearbox (mm)	620
Reduction gearing of gearbox	1:11
Permissible speed at 3,000rpm (km/hr)	
1st gear	2.57
2nd gear	3.83
3rd gear	5.62
4th gear	8.33
5th gear	12.75
6th gear	18.95
7th gear	27.32
8th gear	41.5
Reverse gear	3.39
Total reduction of gearbox	1:16
Type and tooth construction	
of the bevel gearing	Klingelnberg-Palloid-spiral
Bevel gearing reduction ratio	1:1.05

Steering gear

Manufacturer	H & S
two radii of turn	L801
Steering gear reduction ratio	1:1.2955
Number of epicyclic steering gears	Two
Number of steering clutches	
to epicyclic steering gears	Four
Material of clutch disc coating	Jurid,
	alternatively Emero
Number of gear wheels	25
Minimum turning radius (m)	2.08
Maximum turning radius (m)	114
Operation of steering	Argus-Lenkapparat
Total length of gearbox and steering gear (mm)	1,690**
Total weight of gearbox and steering gear (kg)	1,200

Final drive and Brakes

Final drive gear reduction	1:12.56
Type of brakes	Argus Disc Brakes LB900.4
Position of brakes	Between steering gear and track shoe

Footbrake operates on	Steering gear shaft only
External diameter of brake drums (mm)	565
Material of disc coating	Emero
Brake cooling	Cooling vanes on brake housing
Type of brake operation	Mechanical by foot pedal
	and hand lever

Fuel and Water capacity

Fuel in tanks (without reserve tank) (litres)	860
Fuel in 20-litre jerry cans (litres)	–
Water capacity of radiators and engine, about (litres)	–

Turret

Weight (kg)	13,500
Deadweight after machining,	
turret without gun (kg)	about 8,000
Height of turret with commander's cupola (mm)	1,217
Inside diameter of operational area in turret (mm)	1,850

Armament

KWK43 8.8cm (L/71)	
Rounds of fixed ammunition	84*
= stowed	68
+ stacked on turret platform	16
Machine-gun MG42 (MG34 in interim)	Three
(one anti-aircraft weapon)	
Thirty-two bags of 150-round belts	4,800 rounds
Machine pistol	One
Six magazines of six rounds	192 rounds
HE shell	Three rounds

*The data with a single asterisk differ for vehicles 1 to 50 which were fitted with the older turret (Porsche) as follows:

Combat weight (kg)	68,500
Transportation weight (kg)	65,000
Overall length	
gun barrel forward (mm)	10,280
gun barrel rearwards (mm)	9,960
Forward overhang of gun barrel (mm)	2,900

**Total length of gearbox and steering gear. For LS01 experimental model (twelve in all) with OG 40 12 16, length = 1790mm

APPENDIX C 8.8cm Tank Gun 43 (L/71): Dimensions, Weight and Performance

Dimensions

Calibre (cm)	8.8
Length of barrel (mm)	6,300
Length of barrel in calibres	71
Length of barrel with muzzle brake (mm)	6,595
Distance of rear breech plate surface from rim at the front breech recess surface (mm)	290
Length of bore from rim at the front of the breech recess surface to the muzzle (mm)	6,010
Length of rifled section (mm)	5,150.5
Length of rifled section in calibres	58.5

Rifling

Number	Thirty-two
Depth (mm)	1.2
Width (mm)	5.04
Width of flats (mm)	3.6

Chamber

Diameter of rear tapered sections	
rear (mm)	132.4
front (mm)	123.9
Diameter of front tapered sections	
rear (mm)	92.5
front (mm)	88
Length of chamber (mm)	859.5
Rifling (27.57 calibre) (°)	6.30
Ground to axis of barrel (mm)	2,245mm
Depression/elevation (°)	-8 +15
Traverse (°)	360

Recoil Gear Hydraulic Buffer

Average braking force (Kp)	9,000
Fluid content (litres)	6
Length of recoil, least (mm)	380
Length of recoil, greatest (mm)	580

Hydro-Pneumatic Recuperator

Initial stress (Kp/cm²)	60-65
Fluid content (litres)	5.3

Hydro-Pneumatic Balance Compensator

Initial stress (Kp/cm²)	44
Fluid content (litres)	1.78

Weight (Kp)

Barrel complete with breech block and muzzle brake (Kp)	1,605
Barrel complete with breech (Kp)	1,570
Monoblock barrel (Kp)	1,155
Breech plate minus breech (Kp)	260
Breech ring securing collar (Kp)	26
Falling wedge breech block with inner parts (Kp)	55
Breech action (Kp)	13
Muzzle brake (Kp)	35
Recoil brake (Kp)	65
Counter-recoil mechanism (Kp)	60
Total weight of gun (Kp)	2,265

Ballistic Data

	8.8cm PzGr39/43	8.8cm PzGr40/43	8.8cm SprGr43	8.8cm H1Gr39
Weight of projectile (Kp)	10.16	7.5	9.4	7.65
Filler (Kp)	0.050	–	1.0	0.77
Muzzle velocity (m/sec)	1,000	1,130	750	600
Max. range at 15° elevation (m)			10,000	7,400
Kinetic energy at muzzle (mt)	516	480	269	140.4
Kinetic energy at muzzle (per Kp)				
Weight of barrel (mKp)	311	290	162	98
Design gas pressure (Kp/cm²)	3,700	3,700	3,700	3,700
Operating gas pressure at 10° (Kp/cm²)	2,900	2,900	1,450	850

Penetration of projectile (mm) at 90° angle of incidence shown (m)	Range	mm	mm	mm
	500m	185* (205**)	217 (270)	90
	1,000m	165 (186)	193 (233)	90
	1,500m	147 (170)	170 (205)	90
	2,000m	132 (154)	152 (175)	90
Weight of cartridge (Kp) (fixed ammunition)		22.8	19.9	18.6	15.35
Length of cartridge (mm)		1,125.3	1,103.1	1,167.2	1,157.4
Volume of combustion chamber (litres)		9.0	9.14	8.8	9.0
Propellant charge (Kp)		6.8	6.8	3.8	2.0
Weight of cartridge case (Kp)		5.8	5.8	5.8	5.8
Length of cartridge case (mm)		822	822	822	822
Diameter of cartridge base (mm)		132	132	132	132

Performance data of the 8.8cm Tank Gun 36 (L/56) for comparison

	8.8cm PzGr39	8.8cm PzGr40	8.8cm H1Gr
Weight of projectile (kp)	10.16	7.5	7.65
Muzzle velocity (m/sec)	810	930	600

Penetration of projectile (mm) at 90° angle of incidence at ranges shown (m)	Range	mm	mm	mm
	500	111	156	90
	1,000	100	140	90
	1,500	92	125	90
	2,000	84	110	90

*after senior cadet course training file 1944
**after Senger and Ettelin (*Tanks 1916-1966*)

The 8.8cm KwK 36 (L/56) installed in the Tiger I differed hardly at all in penetration from the Panther tank's 7.5cm KwK 43 L/70. However, further development resulting in the 8.8cm KwK 43 L/71 employed in the Tiger II showed a considerable increase in performance when compared with the Panther's gun.

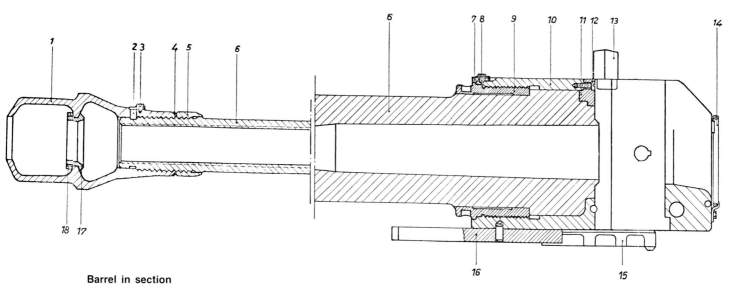

Barrel in section

1. Muzzle brake
2. Locating key
3. Screw securing locating key
4. Tab washer
5. Locking ring
6. Monoblock barrel
7. Stop
8. Hexagonal screw on stop
9. Breech ring securing collar
10. Breech plate
11. Safety lug
12. Cheese head screw
13. Recoil lug
14. Connecting tube on 'blow off' arrangement
15. Breech opening mechanism
16. Recoil guide shoe
17. Insert ring
18. Locking ring

APPENDIX D 12.8cm Tank Hunter Gun 80 (Panzerjägerkanone 80): Dimensions, Weight and Performance

Barrel

Calibre (cm)	12.8
Length of barrel (mm)	7,020
Length of barrel in calibres	55
Distance of rear breech plate from rim at the front breech recess surface (mm)	400
Length of bore (mm)	6,610
Length of rifled section (mm)	5,533
Length of rifled section in calibres	43

Rifling

Number	Forty
Depth (mm)	1.7
Width (mm)	6.05 + 0.6
Width of flats (mm)	4.0 − 0.6

Chamber

Diameter of rear tapered sections	
rear (mm)	176.4 + 0.2
front (mm)	162.8 + 0.2
Diameter of front tapered section (forcing cone)	
rear (mm)	162.8 + 0.2
front (mm)	133.5 + 0.2
Length of chamber (mm)	1,077
Capacity of chamber (litres)	22.88
Rifling, constant (27 calibre)	6° 38′ 13″
Centre to centre spacing of rear of barrel	
with breech (mm)	1,830
without breech (mm)	1,920

Gun Carriage Dimensions

Elevation/Depression (°)	+15° -7°
Traverse both left and right (%)	10
Ground to axis of barrel (mm)	2,150

Recoil Gear Hydraulic Buffer

Average braking force (Kp)	about 33,000
Fluid content (litres)	12.25
Length of recoil, normal (mm)	870
Length of recoil (max.) interval (mm)	900

Hydro-Pneumatic Recuperator

Initial air pressure (Kp/cm²)	50
Fluid content (litres)	11.61

Dial Sight 2/1

Range of setting for 12.8cm PzGr43 (m)	0 to 4,000
Range of setting for 12.8cm SprGr L/50 (m)	0 to 8,000
Graduation	0 to 176

1. Monoblock barrel
2. Safety lug
3. Cheese head screw
4. Breech ring securing collar
5. Breech plate
6. Recoil lug
7. Recuperator lug
8. Rifling cam
9. Straight cylindrical pin

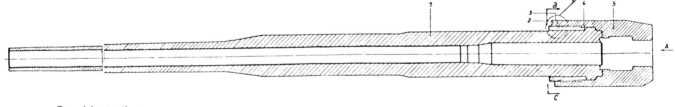

Barrel in section

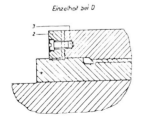

Einzelheit bei D

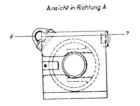

Ansicht in Richtung A

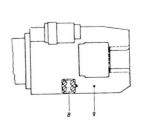

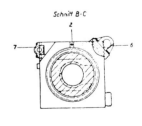

Schnitt B-C

Weight (Kp)

Barrel, complete with breech (Kp)	3,300
Monoblock barrel (Kp)	2,200
Breech plate minus breech (Kp)	810
Breech Ring Securing collar (Kp)	84
Falling wedge breech block with inner parts (Kp)	192
Recoil brake (Kp)	121
Counter recoil mechanism (Kp)	121
Total weight of gun (Kp)	7,000

Loading Dimensions

Gun without vehicle

length (mm)	8,000
width (mm)	1,600
height (mm)	1,390
Barrel overhangs the front of the chassis by	3,050mm

Weight of Ammunition (Packed)

12.8cm PzGr43:

Shell with packing (Kp)	31.8
Cartridge case with packing (Kp)	36.6

12.8cm SprGrL/50:

Shell with packing (Kp)	31.5
Cartridge case with packing (Kp)	33.8

Performance Details

	12.8cm PzGr43	12.8cm SprGr
Length of shell (mm)	496.5	623
Weight of shell (Kp)	28.3	28.0
Bursting charge (Kp)	0.55	3.60
Muzzle velocity (m/sec)	920	750
Max. range at 15° elevation (m)	–	12,200
Kinetic energy at muzzle (mt)	1,270	800
Design gas pressure (Kp/cm²)	3,700	3,700
Usual gas pressure (Kp/cm²)	3,000	2,500
Length of combustion chamber (mm)	967.5	967.5
Volume of combustion chamber (litres)	20.4	20.4
Propellant charge, weight (Kp)	15.0	12.2
Weight of cartridge case (Kp)	11.6	11.6
Length of cartridge case (mm)	870	870
Diameter of cartridge case rim (mm)	192	192
Volume of cartridge (litres)	18.24	18.24

APPENDIX E
Technical Data

Vehicle	VK 3001(P) Tank	12.8 cm Self-Propelled Gun L/61 (PzSfl V)
Designation		
Model	—	—
Type	100	VK 3001(H)
Manufacturer	Nibelungenwerke	Henschel/Rheinmetall
Year of manufacture	1939–41	1939–42
Source of information	Porsche design of 26/04/40	Various

Engine

Manufacturer, type	Two Porsche 100	Maybach HL 116S
Cylinders: configuration/N°	72° V-10	in-line 6
Firing order	1–8–3–10–5–9–4–7–2–6	1–5–3–6–2–4
Bore/stroke (mm)	105 x 115	125 x 150
Swept volume (cm³)	10,000	11,048
Compression ratio	5.9:1	6.5:1
rpm, normal/maximum	2,500	2,600/3,300
Maximum output (hp)	One engine 210, together 410	265/300
Valve arrangement	Overhead	Overhead
Crankshaft bearings	Six plain	Eight plain
Carburetter	Solex 40 JFF II	Two Solex 40 JFF II
Starting motor	Bosch AL 24 V	Bosch BNG 4/24
Lighting dynamo	Bosch GQL 300/12–900	Bosch GQL 300/12–900
Battery: N°/volts/amps	Two/12/120	Two/12/105
Fuel consumption (grams/hp/hr)	230–250	—
Fuel capacity (litres)	—	450
Fuel feed	Pumps	Pumps
Cooling	Air, ventilaor fan	Water

Drive and Steering

Clutch	None: petrol electric direct drive	Triple dry
Gearbox	Porsche/Siemens	ZF SSG 77 synchromesh
N° of gears: forward/reverse	Two/two	Six/one
Track driving sprockets	At front	At front
Final drive gear reduction	1:	1:
Maximum speed (km/hr)	60	19.6
Radius of action: road/country (km)		
Type of steering	Porsche/Siemens	DB/Wilson clutch
Diameter of turning circle (m)	—	

Track, Suspension and Running Gear

Suspension	Torsion bar mounted lengthwise	Torsion bar mounted crosswise
Chassis lubrication system	Central and high pressure	High pressure
Brake installation		
Manufacturer	Porsche/Siemens	DB/Henschel
Mode of operation	Electric	Mechanical
Type of brake	Disc	Internal expanding
Brake system operates on	Drive	Drive
Type of running gear	Tread and track supporting rollers	Tread and track supporting rollers
Size of bogie wheels (mm)	600	700/98–550
Track gauge (mm)	2,600	2,100
Track surface contact (mm)	3,225	4,750
Width of track (mm)	600	520
N° of links per track	88	85
Track type	—	—
Terrain clearance (mm)	490	280
Ground pressure (kp/cm²)	0.9	0.8

Measurements

Tank dimensions		
Overall length (mm)	6,600 without gun	9,800/7,200 without gun
Overall width (mm)	3,200	3,170
Overall height (mm)	3,030	2,670
Armour		
Hull		
front (mm)	50	40
side (mm)	40	30
rear (mm)	30	20
Turret		
front (mm)	—	30
side (mm)	—	15
rear (mm)	—	15
Combat weight (kp)	30,000	35,000

Performance

Climbing (°)	—	24
Step Crossing (mm)	—	—
Fording (mm)	—	—
Trench crossing (mm)	—	—

Armament and Crew

Armament		
Main	One 7.5 cm L/24 or 10.5 cm	One 12.8 cm K 40 (18)
Secondary	—	—
Crew	Four	Five

Comments

	—	—

200

Vehicle	Mark VII Tank (VK 6501)	Tank Mark VI (VK 3601*)
Designation		
Model	—	—
Type	SW	VK 3601
Manufacturer	Henschel	Henschel
Year of manufacture	1940–41	1942
Source of information	Ordance Department Manual Page 42	Ordnance Department Manual Page D36
Engine		
Manufacturer, type	Maybach HL 224	Maybach HL 174**
Cylinders: configuration/N°	60° V–12	60° V–12
Firing order	1–12–5–8–3–10–6–7–2–11–4–9	1–12–5–8–3–10–6–7–2–11–4–9
Bore/stroke (mm)	125 x 145	125 x 130
Swept volume (cm³)	21,353	9,144
Compression ratio	6.5:1	6.5:1
rpm, normal/maximum	3,000	3,000
Maximum output (hp)	600	550
Valve arrangement	Overhead	Overhead
Crankshaft bearings	Seven Roller	Seven rollers
Carburetter	Two Solex Fallstrom	Two Solex 40 JFF II
Starting motor	Bosch 24 V	Bosch BNG 4/24
Lighting dynamo	Bosch GULN 700/12	Bosch GQL 300/12–900
Battery: N°/volts/amps	Four/6/105	Two/12/105
Fuel consumption (grams/hp/hr)		
Fuel capacity (litres)	—	—
Fuel feed	Pumps	Pumps
Cooling	Water	Water
Drive and Steering		
Clutch	Multiple Disc	Wet multiple disc
Gearbox	Maybach	Maybach OLVAR 401216
N° of gears: forward/reverse	Five/one	Eight/one
Track driving sprockets	At front	At front
Final drive gear reduction	1:1	1:10.75
Maximum speed (km/hr)	26	40
Radius of action: road/country (km)		—
Type of steering	Three radii of turn	Henschel two radii of turn
Diameter of turning circle (m)	—	7
Track, Suspension and Running Gear		
Suspension	Torsion bar mounted crosswise	Torsion bar mounted crosswise
Chassis lubrication system	High pressure	Central high pressure
Brake installation		
Manufacturer	Perrot	Südd Arguswerke
Mode of operation	Mechanical	Mechanical
Type of brake	Internal expanding	Disc
Brake system operates on	Drive	Drive
Type of running gear	Tread and track supporting rollers	Stepped
Size of bogie wheels (mm)	—	—
Track gauge (mm)	—	2,620
Track surface contact (mm)	—	3,640
Width of track (mm)	800	520
N° of links per track	—	—
Track type	—	—
Terrain clearance (mm)	—	450
Ground pressure (kp/cm²)	—	—
Measurements		
Tank dimensions		
Overall length (mm)	—	6,050
Overall width (mm)	—	3,140
Overall height (mm)	—	2,700
Armour		
Hull		
front (mm)	100	100
side (mm)	—	60
rear (mm)	—	60
Turret		
front (mm)	—	80
side (mm)	—	60
rear (mm)	—	60
Combat weight (kp)	65,000	36,000–40,000
Performance		
Climbing (°)	—	
Step Crossing (mm)	—	35
Fording (mm)	—	790
Trench crossing (mm)	—	2,300
Armament and Crew		
Armament		
Main	One 7.5 cm KwK L/24	One 0725 weapon
Secondary	Two MG34	Two MG34
Crew	Five	Five
Comments	—	*intermediate development **later HL 210 P45

201

	Tiger I Tank	38 cm Assault Mortar Tiger Tank
Vehicle		
Designation	(SdKfz 181)	(38 cm Sturmmörser Tiger)
Model	E	—
Type	VK 4501(H)	VK 4501(H)
Manufacturer	Henschl	Alkett (Modification)
Year of manufacture	1942–44	1944–45
Source of information	D 656/23 of 10/05/44	Ordnance Department Manual Page G369
Engine		
Manufacturer, type	Maybach HL 210 P45*	Maybach HL 210 P45
Cylinders: configuration/N°	60° V–12	60° V–12
Firing order	12–1–8–5–10–3–7–6–11–2–9–4	12–1–8–5–10–3–7–6–11–2–9–4
Bore/stroke (mm)	125 x 145	125 x 145
Swept volume (cm^3)	21,353	21,353
Compression ratio	7:1	7:1
rpm, normal/maximum	2,500/3,000	2,500/3,000
Maximum output (hp)	650	650
Valve arrangement	Overhead	Overhead
Crankshaft bearings	Seven roller	Seven roller
Carburetter	Four Solex 52 JFF IID	Four Solex 52 JFF II D
Starting motor	Bosch BPD 6/24	Bosch BPD 6/24
Lighting dynamo	Bosch GULN 1000/12–1000**	Bosch GULN 1000/12–1000*
Battery: N°/volts/amps	Two/12/120 or 150	Two/12/120 or 150
Fuel consumption (litres/100km)	535/935	535/935
Fuel capacity (litres)	534 (four tanks)	534 (four tanks)
Fuel feed	Two Solex pumps	Two Solex pumps
Cooling	Water	Water
Drive and Steering		
Clutch	Wet multiple disc	Wet multiple disc
Gearbox	Maybach OLVAR OG 401216A	Maybach OLVAR OG 401216A
N° of gears: forward/reverse	Eight/four	Eight/four
Track driving sprockets	At front	At front
Final drive gear reduction	1:10.75	1:10.75
Maximum speed (km/hr)	45.4	45.4
Radius of action: road/country (km)	100/60	100/60
Type of steering	HS L600C two radii of turn	HS L600C two radii of turn
Diameter of turning circle (m)	7	7
Track, Suspension and Running Gear		
Suspension	Torsion bar mounted crosswise	Torsion bar mounted crosswise
Chassis lubrication system	Direct high pressure group	Direct high pressure group
Brake installation		
Manufacturer	Südd Arguswerke	Südd Arguswerke
Mode of operation	Mechanical	Mechanical
Type of brake	Disc	Disc
Brake system operates on	Steering gear shaft	Steering gear shaft
Type of running gear	Box formation	Box formation
Size of bogie wheels (mm)	800 x 95E	800 x 95E
Track gauge (mm)	2,822/Transportation 2,622	2,822/Transportation 2,622
Track surface contact (mm)	3,605	3,605
Width of track (mm)	725/Transportation 520	725/Transportation 520
N° of links per track	96	96
Track type	Kgs 63/520/30 (Transportation)	Kgs 63/520/30 (Transportation)
	Kgs 63/725/130 (Combat)	Kgs 63/725/130 (Combat)
Terrain clearance (mm)	470	470
Ground pressure (kp/cm^2)	1.04	1.5
Measurements		
Tank dimensions		
Overall length (mm)	–8,450/8,434–/6,316	6,280
Overall width (mm)	3,705	3,570
Overall height (mm)	3,000	2,850
Armour		
Hull		
front (mm)	100	150
side (mm)	80 above; 60 below	80 above; 60 below
rear (mm)	80	80
Turret		
front (mm)	100	150
side (mm)	80	80
rear (mm)	80	80
Combat weight (kp)	56,900	65,000
Performance		
Climbing (°)	35	35
Step Crossing (mm)	790	790
Fording (mm)	1,200	1,200
Trench crossing (mm)	2,300	2,300
Armament and Crew		
Armament		
Main (rounds)	One 8.8 cm KwK 36 L/56 (92)	One 38 cm StuM 61 L/5.4 (14)**
Secondary (rounds)	Two MG (3,920)	One MG 34 (3,920)
Crew	Five	Five
Comments	*From N° 251 HL 230 P45	*In some also 700W
	**in some cases also 700W	**Assault mortar, rocket Projector

Vehicle	Mark VI Tank Tiger (P)	Tiger (P) with Ram
Designation	VK 4501(P)	(design)
Model	—	—
Type	101	101
Manufacturer	Nibelungenwerke	Not built
Year of manufacture	1941–42	Proposed for 1942
Source of information	Ordnance Department Manual Page D41	Porsche SK 8252
Engine		
Manufacturer, type	Two Porsche 101/1	Two Porsche 101/1
Cylinders: configuration/N°	72° V-10	72° V-10
Firing order	1-8-3-10-5-9-4-7-2-6	1-8-3-10-5-9-4-7-2-6
Bore/stroke (mm)	115 x 145	115 x 145
Swept volume (cm^3)	15,060	15,060
Compression ratio	5.9:1.	5.9:1
rpm, normal/maximum	2,000/2,500	2,000/2,500
Maximum output (hp)	One engine 320; together 640	One engine 320; together 640
Valve arrangement	Overhead	Overhead
Crankshaft bearings	Six plain	Six plain
Carburetter	One Solex 50 JFF II	One Solex 50 JFF II
Starting motor	Bosch AL/SED	Bosch AL/SED
Lighting dynamo	Bosch LQ 3000/24	Bosch LQ 3000/24
Battery: N°/volts/amps	Two/12/150	Two/12/150
Fuel consumption (grams/hp/hr)	250–270	250–270
Fuel capacity (litres)	520	520
Fuel feed	Pumps	Pumps
Cooling	Air, ventilation fans	Air, ventilation fans
Drive and Steering		
Clutch	None: petrol-electric direct drive	None: petrol-electric direct drive
Gearbox	Porsche/Siemens Speed Switch	Porsche/Siemens Speed Switch
N° of gears: forward/reverse	Three/three	Three/three
Track driving sprockets	At rear	At rear
Final drive gear reduction	1:15	1:15
Maximum speed (km/hr)	35	35
Radius of action: road/country (km)	80	80
Type of steering	Porsche/Siemens	Porsche/Siemens
Diameter of turning circle (m)	2.15	2.15
Track, Suspension and Running Gear		
Suspension	Torsion bar mounted lengthwise	Torsion bar mounted lengthwise
Chassis lubrication system	Direct high pressure group	Direct high pressure group
Brake installation		
Manufacturer	Porsche/Siemens	Porsche/Siemens
Mode of operation	Hydraulic/mechanical	Hydraulic/mechanical
Type of brake	Disc	Disc
Brake system operates on	Drive	Drive
Type of running gear	Steel bogie wheels	Steel bogie wheels
Size of bogie wheels (mm)	794	794
Track gauge (mm)	2,640	2,640
Track surface contact (mm)	4,175	4,175
Width of track (mm)	640	640
N° of links per track	109	109
Track type	Kgs 62/640/130	Kgs 62/640/130
Terrain clearance (mm)	480	480
Ground pressure (kp/cm^2)	1.06	1.14
Measurements		
Tank dimensions		
Overall length (mm)	–9,340/6,700	8,430
Overall width (mm)	3,140	3,600
Overall height (mm)	2,800	2,550
Armour		
Hull		
front (mm)	100	100
side (mm)	80	80
rear (mm)	80	80
Turret		
front (mm)	100	30
side (mm)	80	30–50
rear (mm)	80	30
Combat weight (kp)	57,000–59,000	60,170
Performance		
Climbing (°)	30	30
Step Crossing (mm)	780	780
Fording (mm)	1,000	1,000
Trench crossing (mm)	2,640	2,640
Armament and Crew		
Armament		
Main (rounds)	One 8.8 cm KwK 36 L/56 (70)	None
Secondary	Two MG 34	None
Crew	Five	One
Comments	—	—

Vehicle	Tank Hunter Tiger (P) Elephant (SdKfz 184) previously Ferdinand	Tiger (P) Recovery Tank VK 4501(P)
Designation		
Model	—	—
Type	101	101
Manufacturer	Nibelungenwerke	Nibelungenwerke
Year of manufacture	1942–43	1943
Source of information	D 656/1 of 01/05/43	D 656/1 of 01/05/43

Engine

Manufacturer, type	Two Maybach HL 120 TRM	Two Maybach HL 120 TRM
Cylinders: configuration/N°	60° V–12	60° V–12
Firing order	1–12–5–8–3–10–6–7–2–11–4–9	1–12–5–8–3–10–6–7–2–11–4–9
Bore/stroke (mm)	105 x 115	105 x 115
Swept volume (cm^3)	11,867	11,867
Compression ratio	6.2–6.5:1	6.2–6.5:1
rpm, normal/maximum	2,600	2,600
Maximum output (hp)	One engine 265, together 530	One engine 265, together 530
Valve arrangement	Overhead	Overhead
Crankshaft bearings	Seven roller	Seven roller
Carburetter	Two Solex 40 JFF II	Two Solex 40 JFF II
Starting motor	Bosch BNG 4/24	Bosch BNG 4/24
Lighting dynamo	Bosch GQL 300/12–900	Bosch GQL 300/12–900
Battery: N°/volts/amps	Four/12/120	Four/12/120
Fuel consumption (litres/100km)	1,200	1,200
Fuel capacity (litres)	1,080 (= 540 + 540)	1,080 (= 540 + 540)
Fuel feed	Pumps	Pumps
Cooling	Water	Water

Drive and Steering

Clutch	None: petrol-electric direct drive	None: petrol-electric direct drive
Gearbox	Porsche/Siemens	Porsche/Siemens
N° of gears: forward/reverse	Three/three	Three/three
Track driving sprockets	At rear	At rear
Final drive gear reduction	1:16.75	1:16.75
Maximum speed (km/hr)	20	25
Radius of action: road/country (km)	150/90	160/100
Type of steering	Porsche/Siemens	Porsche/Siemens
Diameter of turning circle (m)	2.15	2.15

Track, Suspension and Running Gear

Suspension	Torsion bar mounted lengthwise	Torsion bar mounted lengthwise
Chassis lubrication system	Direct high pressure group	Direct high pressure group
Brake installation		
Manufacturer	Porsche/Siemens	Porsche/Siemens
Mode of operation	Compressed air/electric	Compressed air/electric
Type of brake	Internal expanding	Internal expanding
Brake system operates on	Drive	Drive
Type of running gear	Steel bogie wheels	Steel bogie wheels
Size of bogie wheels (mm)	794	794
Track gauge (mm)	2,680	2,860
Track surface contact (mm)	4,175	4,175
Width of track (mm)	640	640
N° of links per track	109	109
Track type	Kgs 62/640/130	Kgs 62/640/130
Terrain clearance (mm)	480	480
Ground pressure (kp/cm^2)	1.23	0.9

Measurements

Tank dimensions		
Overall length (mm)	8,140	6,700
Overall width (mm)	3,380	3,380
Overall height (mm)	2,970	—
Armour		
Hull		
front (mm)	100 + 100	100
side (mm)	80	80
rear (mm)	80	80
Turret		
front (mm)	200	—
side (mm)	80	—
rear (mm)	80	—
Combat weight (kp)	65,000	47,200

Performance

Climbing (°)	22	22
Step Crossing (mm)	780	780
Fording (mm)	1,000	1,000
Trench crossing (mm)	2,640	2,640

Armament and Crew

Armament		
Main (rounds)	One 8.8 cm StuK 43/1 L/71 (55)	None
Secondary	One unmounted MG34 (600)	One MG34
Crew	Six	Four

Comments

	—	—

	Tank VK 4501(P)HA	Tank VK4502(P)
Vehicle		(Design)
Designation		
Model	—	—
Type	102	180/181*
Manufacturer	Nibelungenwerke	Not built
Year of manufacture	1942	Proposed for 1943–44
Source of information	Porsche KG archives	Porsche design K 3501
Engine		
Manufacturer, type	Two Porsche 101/1	Two Porsche 101/4
Cylinders: configuration/N°	72° V–10	72° V–10
Firing order	1–8–3–10–5–9–4–7–2–6	1–8–3–10–5–9–4–7–2–6
Bore/stroke (mm)	115 x 145	115 x 145
Swept volume (cm³)	15,060	15,060
Compression ratio	5.9:1	6.4:1
rpm, normal/maximum	2,000/2,500	3,200
Maximum output (hp)	One engine 320, together 640	One engine 350, together 670
Valve arrangement	Overhead	Overhead
Crankshaft bearings	Six plain	Six plain
Carburetter	Solex 50 JFF II	Solex 50 JFF II
Starting motor	Servo-Motor T141, 9hp	Bosch AL/SED
Lighting dynamo	Bosch LW 3000/24	Bosch LW 3000/24
Battery: N°/volts/amps	Two/12/120	Four/12/120
Fuel consumption (grams/hp/hr)	250/270	270
Fuel capacity (litres)	520	—
Fuel feed	Pumps	Pumps
Cooling	Air, ventilation fans	Air, ventilated fans
Drive and Steering		
Clutch	Hydraulic	None: petrol-electric drive
Gearbox	Voith NITA torque converter	Porsche/Siemens
N° of gears: forward/reverse	Two/one	Two/one
Track driving sprockets	At rear	At rear
Final drive gear reduction	1:15	1:
Maximum speed (km/hr)	35	35
Radius of action: road/country (km)	80	—
Type of steering	Porsche/Siemens	Porsche/Siemens
Diameter of turning circle (m)	2.15	2.15
Track, Suspension and Running Gear		
Suspension	Torsion bar mounted lengthwise	Torsion bar mounted lengthwise
Chassis lubrication system	Direct high pressure group	Direct high pressure group
Brake installation		
Manufacturer	Südd Arguswerke	Porsche/Siemens
Mode of operation	Hydraulic	Hydraulic/mechanical
Type of brake	Disc	Disc
Brake system operates on	Drive	Drive
Type of running gear	Steel bogie wheels	Steel bogie wheels
Size of bogie wheels (mm)	794	794
Track gauge (mm)	2,640	2,700
Track surface contact (mm)	4,115	4,115
Width of track (mm)	640	700/Transportation 500
N° of links per track	109	109
Track type	Kgs 62/640/130	Kgs 62/640/130
Terrain clearance (mm)	480	480
Ground pressure (kp/cm²)	1.06	1.15
Measurements		
Tank dimensions		
Overall length (mm)	6,700	8,345
Overall width (mm)	3,140	3,400/Transportation 3,140
Overall height (mm)	2,800	2,740
Armour		
Hull		
front (mm)	100	150
side (mm)	80	80
rear (mm)	80	80
Turret		
front (mm)	—	100
side (mm)	—	80
rear (mm)	—	80
Combat weight (kp)	59,000	64,000
Performance		
Climbing (°)	30	30
Step Crossing (mm)	780	—
Fording (mm)	1,000	—
Trench crossing (mm)	2,640	—
Armament and Crew		
Armament		
Main	—	One 8.8 cm Kwk 43 L/71 (68)
Secondary	—	Two MG 34
Crew	Five	Five
Comments	Vehicle with hydraulic drive	*Type 181 planned with hydraulic drive as for Type 102

	Tiger II Tank (SdKfz 182)	Tiger II Tank (SdKfz 182)
Vehicle		
Designation		
Model	B	B
Type	VK 4503	VK 4503
Manufacturer	Henschel	Henschel
Year of manufacture	1943–44	1944–45
Source of information	D 656/43 of 01/09/44	D 656/43 of 01/09/44
Engine		
Manufacturer, type	Maybach HL 230 P30	Maybach HL 230 P30
Cylinders: configuration/N°	60° V–12	60° V–12
Firing order	1–8–5–10–3–7–6–11–2–9–4–12	1–8–5–10–3–7–6–11–2–9–4–12
Bore/stroke (mm)	130 x 145	130 x 145
Swept volume (cm³)	23,095	23,095
Compression ratio	6.8:1	6.8:1
rpm, normal/maximum	2,600/3,000	2,600/3,000
Maximum output (hp)	600/700	600/700
Valve arrangement	Overhead	Overhead
Crankshaft bearings	Seven + one roller	Seven + one roller
Carburetter	Four Solex 52 JFF IID	Four Solex 52 JFF IID
Starting motor	Bosch BPD 6/24 ARS 146 + AL/ZMJ/R 12	Bosch BPD 6/24 ARS 146 + AL/ZMJ/R 12
Lighting dynamo	Bosch GTLN 700/12–1500 L1	Bosch GTLN 700/12–1500 L1
Battery: N°/volts/amps	Two/12/150	Two/12/150
Fuel consumption (litres/100km)	750/1,000	750/1,000
Fuel capacity (litres)	860 (= 85 + 145 + 145 + 80 + 65 + 170)	860 (= 85 + 145 + 145 + 80 + 65 + 170)
Fuel feed	Two Solex twin pumps	Two Solex twin pumps
Cooling	Water	Water
Drive and Steering		
Clutch	Wet multiple disc	Wet multiple disc
Gearbox	Maybach OLVAR B 401216	Maybach OLVAR B 401216
N° of gears: forward/reverse	Eight/four	Eight/four
Track driving sprockets	At front	At front
Final drive gear reduction	1:12.56	1:12.56
Maximum speed (km/hr)	41.5	41.5
Radius of action: road/country (km)	170/120	170/120
Type of steering	HS L 801 two radii of turn	HS L 801 two radii of turn
Diameter of turning circle (m)	4.16	4.16
Track, Suspension and Running Gear		
Suspension	Torsion bar mounted crosswise	Torsion bar mounted crosswise
Chassis lubrication system	Four central direct high pressure group	Four central direct high pressure group
Brake installation		
Manufacturer	Südd Arguswerke, Type LB 900–4	Südd Arguswerke, Type LB 900–4
Mode of operation	Mechanical	Mechanical
Type of brake	Disc, diameter 565 mm	Disc, diameter 565 mm
Brake system operates on	Drive	Drive
Type of running gear	Echelon	Echelon
Size of bogie wheels (mm)	800	800
Track gauge (mm)	2,790/Transportation 2,610	2,790/Transportation 2,610
Track surface contact (mm)	4,120	4,120
Width of track (mm)	800/Transportation 660	800/Transportation 660
N° of links per track	92	92
Track type	Kgs 73/800/52	Kgs 73/800/52
Terrain clearance (mm)	485	485
Ground pressure (kp/cm²)	1.02	1.02/Transportation 1.23
Measurements		
Tank dimensions		
Overall length (mm)	10,280	10,286
Overall width (mm)	3,625/with skirts 3,755	3,625/with skirts 3,755
Overall height (mm)	3,075	3,090
Armour		
Hull		
front (mm)	150	150
side (mm)	80	80
rear (mm)	80	80
Turret		
front (mm)	100	180
side (mm)	80	80
rear (mm)	80	80
Combat weight (kp)	68,500	69,800
Performance		
Climbing (°)	35	35
Step Crossing (mm)	850	850
Fording (mm)	1,750	1,600
Trench crossing (mm)	2,500	2,500
Armament and Crew		
Armament		
Main (rounds)	One 8.8 cm KwK 43 L/71 (72)	One 8.8 cm KwK 43 L/71 (84)
Secondary (rounds)	Two MG34 (5,850)	Two MG34 (5,850)
Crew	Five	Five
Comments	Model with Porsche turret	Model with production turret

Vehicle		
Designation	Tiger Tank Hunter	Tiger Tank Hunter
	Hunting Tiger (Jagdtiger SdKfz 186)	(Experimental)
Model	B	B
Type	VK 4503	212/258
Manufacturer	Nibelungenwerke	Nibelungenwerke
Year of manufacture	1944–45	1944–45
Source of information	Ordnance Department Manual Page G360	FIAT Final Report 1945

Engine		
Manufacturer, type	Maybach HL 230 P30	SGP SLa 16
Cylinders: configuration/N°	60° V–12	X–16
Firing order	1–8–5–10–3–7–6–11–2–9–4–12	1–13–12–15–9–14–11–16–10–6–3–8–2–5–4–7
Bore/stroke (mm)	130 x 145	135 x 160
Swept volume (cm^3)	23,095	36,800
Compression ratio	6.8:1	14.5:1
rpm, normal/maximum	2,600/3,000	2,000
Maximum output (hp)	600/700	750
Valve arrangement	Overhead	Overhead
Crankshaft bearings	Seven + one roller	Five friction
Carburetter	Four Solex 52 JFF IID	Four Bosch PE 4 Diesel injectors
Starting motor	Bosch BPD 6/24 ARS 146 + AL/ZMJ/R 12	Bosch 10/24
Lighting dynamo	Bosch GTLN 700/12–1500 L1	Bosch GULN 1000/24
Battery: N°/volts/amps	Two/12/150	Two/12/150
Fuel consumption (litres/100km)	800/1,100	800/1,100
Fuel capacity (litres)	860 (= 85 + 145 + 145 + 80 + 65 + 170)	860 (seven tanks)
Fuel feed	Two Solex twin pumps	Pumps
Cooling	Water	Air, ventilator fans

Drive and Steering		
Clutch	Wet multiple disc	Wet multiple disc
Gearbox	Maybach OLVAR B 401216	Maybach OLVAR B 401216
N° of gears: forward/reverse	Eight/four	Eight/four
Track driving sprockets	At front	At front
Final drive gear reduction	1:12.56	1:1
Maximum speed (km/hr)	41.5	35
Radius of action: road/country (km)	170/120	170/120
Type of steering	HS L 801 two radii of turn	HS L 801 two radii of turn
Diameter of turning circle (m)	4.16	4.8

Track, Suspension and Running Gear		
Suspension	Torsion bar mounted crosswise	Torsion bar mounted lengthwise (Porsche Type 258)
Chassis lubrication system	Four central direct high pressure group	Four central direct high pressure group
Brake installation		
Manufacturer	Südd Arguswerke Type LB 900–4	Südd Arguswerke
Mode of operation	Mechanical	Mechanical
Type of brake	Disc, diameter 565 mm	Disc
Brake system operates on	Drive	Drive
Type of running gear	Echelon formation bogie wheels	Steel bogie wheels
Size of bogie wheels (mm)	800	800
Track gauge (mm)	2,790/Transportation 2,610	2,790
Track surface contact (mm)	4,240	4,415
Width of track (mm)	800/Transportation 660	800/Transportation 660
N° of links per track	92	92
Track type	Kgs 73/800/52	Kgs 73/800/52
Terrain clearance (mm)	490	565
Ground pressure (kp/cm^2)	1.06	1.05

Measurements		
Tank dimensions		
Overall length (mm)	10,654	10,370
Overall width (mm)	3,625	3,590
Overall height (mm)	2,945	3,050
Armour		
Hull		
front (mm)	150	150
side (mm)	80	80
rear (mm)	80	80
Turret		
front (mm)	250	250
side (mm)	80	80
rear (mm)	80	80
Combat weight (kp)	75,200	74,000

Performance		
Climbing (°)	35	35
Step Crossing (mm)	880	880
Fording (mm)	1,750	1,750
Trench crossing (mm)	2,500	2,500

Armament and Crew		
Armament		
Main (rounds)	One 12.8 cm Pak 44 L/55 (40)	One 12.8 cm Pak 44
Secondary (rounds)	Two MG34 (1,500)	One MG42
Crew	Six	Six

Comments		
	—	—

Vehicle

Designation	Tiger II Tank
	(Experimental)
Model	B
Type	VK 4503
Manufacturer	Henschel
Year of manufacture	1945
Source of information	Maybach data

Engine

Manufacturer, type	Maybach HL 234
Cylinders: configuration/N°	60° V–12
Firing order	12–1–8–5–10–3–7–6–11–2–9–4
Bore/stroke (mm)	130 x 145
Swept volume (cm³)	23,095
Compression ratio	7:1
rpm, normal/maximum	3,000
Maximum output (hp)	800
Valve arrangement	Overhead
Crankshaft bearings	Seven plain
C a r b u r e t t e r	Bosch Petrol Injector PZ 12
Starting motor	Bosch BPD 6/24
Lighting dynamo	Bosch GULN 1000/24–1000
Battery: N°/volts/amps	Two/12/150
Fuel consumption (grams/hp/hr)	235
Fuel capacity (litres)	860 (seven tanks)
Fuel feed	Pumps
Cooling	Water

Drive and Steering

Clutch	Wet multiple disc
Gearbox	Maybach OLVAR B 401216
N° of gears: forward/reverse	Eight/four
Track driving sprockets	At front
Final drive gear reduction	1:
Maximum speed (km/hr)	41.5
Radius of action: road/country (km)	170/120
Type of steering	HS L 801 two radii of turn
Diameter of turning circle (m)	4.8

Track, Suspension and Running Gear

Suspension	Torsion bar mounted crosswise
Chassis lubrication system	Four central direct high pressure group
Brake installation	
Manufacturer	Südd Arguswerke
Mode of operation	Mechanical
Type of brake	Disc
Brake system operates on	Drive
Type of running gear	Echelon formation bogie wheels
Size of bogie wheels (mm)	800
Track gauge (mm)	2,790
Track surface contact (mm)	4,100
Width of track (mm)	800
N° of links per track	92
Track type	Kgs 73/800/52
Terrain clearance (mm)	485
Ground pressure (kp/cm²)	1.03

Measurements

Tank dimensions	
Overall length (mm)	7,260
Overall width (mm)	3,625
Overall height (mm)	—
Armour	
Hull	
front (mm)	150
side (mm)	80
rear (mm)	80
Turret	
front (mm)	—
side (mm)	—
rear (mm)	—
Combat weight (kp)	68,000

Performance

Climbing (°)	35
Step Crossing (mm)	850
Fording (mm)	1,750
Trench crossing (mm)	2,000

Armament and Crew

Armament	
Main	One 8.8 or 10.5 cm KwK
Secondary	Two MG42
Crew	Five

Comments

—

APPENDIX F   Maybach Engine Data

Prototype HL	N° of Cylinders	Bore x Stroke (mm)	Volume (litres) Single Cylinder	Volume (litres) Total Capacity	rpm	hp	kp/hp
10	Two	100x 70	0.5498	1.0996	5,000	70	—
30	Four	95x110	0.780	3.1188	3,500	113	2.18
33	Four	100x106	0.832	3.3301	4,000	120	—
42	Six	90x110	0.700	4.1987	3,000	100	3.8
45	Six	95x110	0.780	4.6782	3,800	147	2.32
50	Six	100x106	0.832	4.9951	4,000	180	—
54	Six	100x115	0.903	5.4193	2,600	110	4.13
62	Six	105x120	1.039	6.2345	2,600	135	3.96
66	Six	105x130	1.126	6.7540	3,200	180	2.49
SHL66	Six	105x130	1.126	6.7540	2,200	125	—
85	Twelve	95x100	0.709	8.5068	2,600	185	4.21
87	Six	125x130	1.595	9.5720	2,400	180	—
90/100	Twelve	100x106	0.832	9.9903	4,000	400	—
92	Six	120x135	1.527	9.1610	2,400	180	—
101	Twelve	105x115	0.996	11.9494	3,800	510	—
116	Six	125x150	1.841	11.0447	3,000	265	2.52
120	Twelve	105x115	0.996	11.9494	3,000	300	2.98
140	Six	140x150	2.309	13.8540	2,400	250	—
148	Six	140x160	2.463	14.7780	2,400	260	—
150G	Six	150x160	2.827	16.9646	3,400	320	—
157	Twelve	115x125	1.298	15.5803	3,500	550	—
174	Twelve	125x130	1.595	19.1441	3,000	450	—
210	Twelve	125x145	1.779	21.3530	3,000	650	—
224	Twelve	125x145	1.779	21.3530	3,000	600	1.78
230	Twelve	130x145	1.924	23.0954	3,000	700	—
232*	Twelve	130x145	1.924	23.0954	3,000	1,100	—
233	Twelve	130x145	1.924	23.0954	—	—	—
234**	Twelve	130x145	1.924	23.0954	3,000	800	—
R234***	Twelve	130x145	1.924	23.0954	2,800	600	2.00

* Experimental engine with petrol injection and supercharger
* Experimental engine with petrol injection
*** Experimental diesel engine
HL High output engine

APPENDIX G Comparison of Armour Thickness

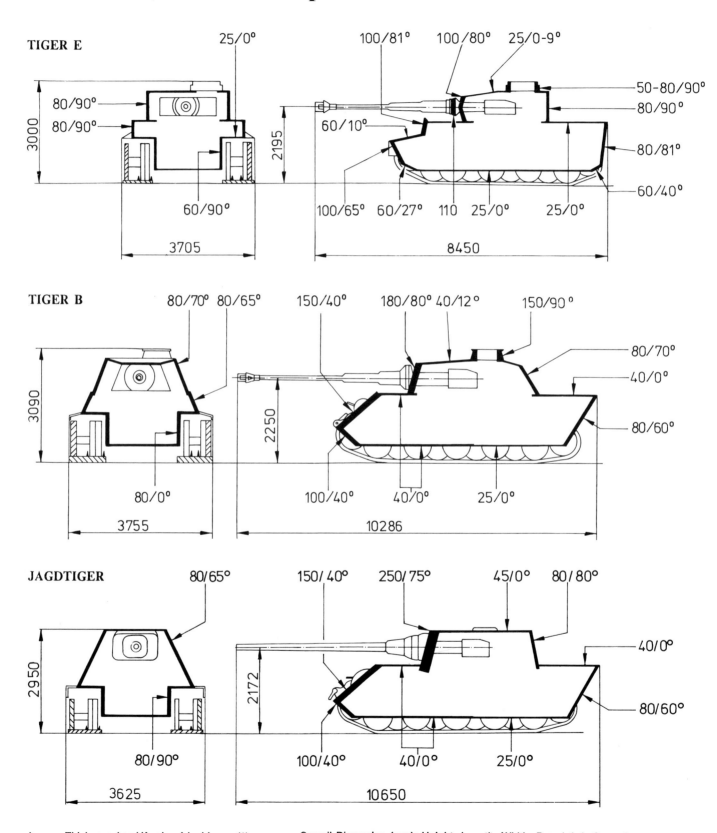

Armour Thickness (mm)/Angle of Incidence (°)   Overall Dimension (mm): Height, Length, Width, Barrel Axis-Ground

APPENDIX H
Organisation of Tank and Engine Directorate

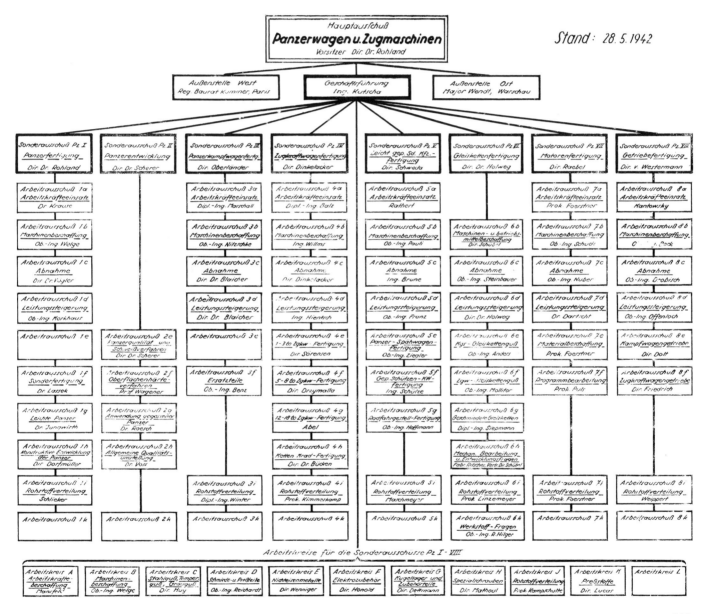

APPENDIX I Provisional Technical Terms of Delivery for the Chassis of the Mark VI Tank

(SdKfz . . .)
vom . . .

See page 1 for the Terms of Delivery and Standard Specification to be observed on this matter.

Observe

TL 21/2014 Technical Terms of delivery for armoured fully tracked chassis, without drawing

TL 21/6005 Technical Terms of Delivery for water tube type radiator, without drawing

TL 21/6009 Technical Terms of Delivery for brake linings made from special cast iron, according to design of Goetze, Burscheid, without drawing

TL 21/6014 Technical Terms of Delivery for shock absorbers for half and fully tracked vehicles, without drawing

TL 21/7007 Technical Terms of Delivery for searchlight mask, without drawing

TL 21/9002 Terms for the despatch of motor vehicles (accessories and instruments)

TL 21/9003 Technical Terms of Delivery for the installation and removal of interference suppressor and screening device to achieve ultra high frequency screening of chassis and superstructural parts of radio Command vehicle

TL 21/9007 Technical Terms of Delivery for special bolts for tanks, without drawing

TL 21/.... Technical Terms of Delivery for torsion bar suspension for tracked vehicles (still being worked on)

TL 1003 Technical Terms of Delivery for leather and fabric pockets, without drawing

TL 1006 Technical Terms of Delivery for wooden chests model II, without drawing

TL 4001 Technical Terms of Delivery for steel plate, without drawing

TL 4003 Technical Terms of Delivery for raw and preliminarily treated cast steel

TL 5000 Technical Terms of Delivery for fawn leather

TL 5005 Technical Terms of Delivery for chrome leather

TL 5006 Technical Terms of Delivery for sole leather (central part of hide)

TL 5008 Technical Terms of Delivery for smooth leather

TL 5110 Technical Terms of Delivery for undyed cotton tent material

TL 5118 Technical Terms of Delivery for unbleached field grey sailcloth, proofed and unproofed.

TL 5200 Terms for wood

TL 5901 Technical Terms of Delivery for blankets according to HgN 125 21

TL 6303 Terms for painting

TL 6311 Terms for phosphate rustproofing process

TL 9001 Terms for welding joints

TLM 0101 Terms for high stress steel joint welding

TL 9900 Testing materials: Chemical and mechanical tests

TL 9901 Testing materials: Steel and non-ferrous metals

HgN10710 General Manufacturing Regulations

HgN10740 Crowbars

HgN10741 Seams in leather, material, cellone i.a.

HgN11321 Permissible tolerance for measurements without tolerance specification.

TECHNICAL REQUIREMENTS

Stipulations as to the Delivery of Items

1. Chassis of Mark VI tanks after assembly list 021 Gr 39000 as well as subordinated designs and lists.
2. The chassis must fulfil the following requirements:
    (a) a completed chassis loaded with weight up to 32,000 kg in total on a straight road with a 3 degree gradient, a maximum speed at engine rpm of 3,000 of 24 km/h.
    (b) climbing ability forwards 30 degrees
            rearwards 45 degrees
    (c) a trench of traversable width
    (d) fording to a depth of 1.20m
    (e) terrain clearance of 0.450m
    (f) weight of completed chassis including fuel and oil but excluding instruments and accessories.
3. TLM0101 is the basis for the welding of all parts. Do not weld parts made of cast steel armour.

Acceptance

4. Undertake the following tests on all chassis:
- Test the central lubrication system to ensure all lubrication points connected to it are supplied with lubricant.
- Check the alignment of the bogie wheels
- Test setting of lighting system
- Reject unsatisfactory chassis either because of assembly or parts.

Testing of Materials

5. Undertake testing of materials in accordance with Annex 1.

Check on Measurements and Weight

6. Specially check the measurements in accordance with Annex 3.
7. Check weight by random sample (see number 2 following) and note it in the acceptance report.

Testing of Performance

8. The chassis are to be tested in accordance with the requirements laid down in numbers 2 (a) to (c).

APPENDIX J
Suppliers for the Tiger B Building Programme

Hull
Dortmund-Hoerder Hüttenverein, Dortmund
Friedr. Krupp, Essen
Skoda-Werke Pilsen, Werk Königgrätz
Gearbox
Zahnradfabrik Friedrichshafen Waldwerke Passau
Engine
Maybach, Friedrichshafen
Auto-Union, Chemnitz
Track
August Engels, Velbert
Turret
Wegmann & Co., Kassel
Fuel tanks
I. Arnold, Friendensdorf/Lahn
Hand lever and foot pedal actions
Bergische Achsenfabrik, Wiehl
Exhaust system
Karl Born, Aschersleben
Periscope
Dorst AG, Oberlind-Sonneberg
Sylbe und Ponndorf, Schmölln
Accelerator and choke linkage
Hermann Fesel, Zwiesel
Gearbox Ventilator
Hermann Fesel, Zwiesel
Track cover
Gotthardt und Kühne, Lommatzsch
Wilhelm Lenze, Neheim-Hüsten
Ventilation
Imperial GmbH, Meissen
Ammunition Storage
Richard Krahmer, Chemnitz
Schneider und Korb, Bernsbach
Driver's Seat
Wilhelm Lenze, Neheim-Hüsten
Ball-mounting — MG mounting
Arno Müller, Leipzig
Starter
Josef Münch, Brotterode
Hatch cover
O.D. Werk Willy Ostner, Branderbisdorf
Knee action shock absorbers
Scheidt & Bachmann, Rheydt
Bogie wheels
Diana Maschinenfabrik, Kassel
Driving sprocket
Bochumer Verein, Bochum

Bergische Stahlindustrie Remscheid
Ruhrstahl AG, Witten-Annen
Eisenwerke Oberdonau, Linz
Idler Wheel
Dingler, Karcher & Co., Worms
Ruhrstahl AG, Witten-Annen von Tongelsche Stahlwerke, Güstrow
Wittmann Ag, Hagen-Haspe
Knorrbremse AG, Volmarstein Deutsche Eisenwerke, Mülheim/Ruhr
Bogie wheel cranks
Rothe Erde GmbH, Dortmund
Stahlwerke Braunschweig GmbH, Watenstedt
Skoda-Werke, Pilsen. Eisenwerke Krieglach/Nierderdonau
Idler crank
Rothe Erde GmbH, Dortmund
Stahlwerke Braunschweig GmbH, Watenstedt
Track drive housing
Dingler, Karcher & Co., Worms von Tongelsche
    Stahlwerke, Güstrow
Deutsche Eisenwerke, Mülheim/Ruhr
Lindener Eisen-und Stahlwerke, Hannover
Pleissner GmbH, Herzberg/Harz
Gearbox cowling
Dingler, Karcher & Co., Worms
Meier & Weichelt, Leipzig
Deutsche Eisenwerke, Mülheim/Ruhr
Arched steel periscope shield
Ruhrstahl AG, Witten-Annen
Oberschlesische Hüttenwerke, Werk Malapane
Grating and protective capping
Dingler, Karcher & Co., Worms
Meir und Weichelt, Leipzig
Ruhrstahl AG, Witten-Annen
Torsion bars
Hösch AG, Hohenlimburg
Röchling GmbH, Wetzlar
Sprocket wheel toothed rim blanks
Charlottenhütte, Niederschelden/Sieg
Klöckner-Werke AG, Osnabruck
Steering Brakes
Suddeutsche Arguswerke, Karlsruhe
Ventilation fan drive
Ehrlich, Gotha
Turret drive
Ehrlich, Gotha
Electrical fittings
Bosch, Stuttgart

213

HENSCHEL & SOHN
G. M. B. H.
KASSEL

LOKOMOTIVE, KASSEL
KASSEL 241 51
FERNSCHREIBER 03 234
RB-NR. 0/0591/0013

BANKVERBINDUNGEN:
REICHSBANK, KASSEL, KONTO-NR. 42/63
DEUTSCHE BANK, FILIALE KASSEL
DRESDNER BANK, FILIALE KASSEL
COMMERZBANK, FILIALE KASSEL
BERLINER HANDELSGESELLSCHAFT, BERLIN
REICHS-KREDIT-GESELLSCHAFT, BERLIN
POSTSCHECKKONTO: FRANKFURT AM MAIN NR. 364 60

Maschinenbau
422 278 Auftrag-Nr.

Firma
Show Tsusho Kaisha, Ltd., T o k y o ,
über Fa. Showa Tsusho Kaisha, Ltd.,
B e r l i n .

Rechnung Nr. 10047

23. November 1943

KASSEL, den

XXXXXXX
Lieferung

XXXXXXXXXXXXXXXXXXXXXXXXXXXXXXXXX
Wir sandten für Ihre Rechnung und Gefahr am

als Wir führten die untenverzeichnete Lieferung aus.

Vorg.:

Lfd. Nr.	Stück	Gegenstand	Zeichnungs-Nr.	Stück-Preis *RM*	Gesamt-Preis *RM*
1		Panzerkampfwagen Tiger Ausführung E			
		gemäss Angebot der Firma Ilies & Co.			
		Berlin, vom ~~17.10.1943~~ 7. 10.1943 nebst			
		Ergänzung vom 11.10.1943		645.000,-	645.000,-

Die Zahlung hat zu 100% in freien
Reichsmark gemäss dem deutsch-japa-
nischen Zahlungsabkommen zu erfolgen,
und zwar bei Versandbereitschaft,
spätestens innerhalb von 2 Wochen nach
gemeldeter Versandbereitschaft.

MB Verk. Nr. 4 1000 S. 9. 43. K/0471

APPENDIX K Account for Tiger E sold to Japan

Construction Order Number
422   278

Account Number 10047   Kassel 23rd November 1943
We carried out the undernoted delivery.   Delivery

Item	Subject Blueprint Number	Price of Item RM	Total Price RM
1	TIGER TANK MODEL E in accordance with the quotation of the Firm of Lilies & Co Berlin dated 7.10.43 including the amendment of 11.10.43 The payment has to be made 100% in exempt Reichsmarks in accordance with German-Japanese payment agreement, namely when the item is ready for delivery and at the latest within 4 weeks after notification that the item is ready for delivery.	645,000	645,000

APPENDIX L Excerpts from *Tiger Primer*

The Tiger Primer was approved as service regulations (D656/27) by Colonel General Heinz Guderian, Inspector General of Panzer Troops on 1st August 1943. It represented the first and also undoubtedly best attempt to get away from the dry language of hitherto conventional Service regulations little understood by the soldier. It was a pocket-sized set of operating and combat instructions produced for the Tiger. It set out, in popular and humorous form and with the formality moderated by often spicy caricatures, jokes, moral sayings and much soldier's slang, the whole technical and tactical know-how of the Tiger and its practical aspects.

It turned something which was out of the ordinary and not easy to understand into exciting and diverting reading, awoke the joy of learning and was full of wisdom from the Front. At the same time, it assured the Tiger crews of the superiority of their weapon, assuming they used it properly, and made an important contribution to making the Tiger trusted and popular.

INDEX

The *filtercap* is leakproof but keep the air vent open.

> *Otherwise the engine will not run.*

Keep the *fuel tanks* and *fuel pipes* clean. Do not take the filter out.

> *Otherwise* the sight glasses and injectors will get covered in muck. They can both get in a bad state.

Keep *sight glasses* clear of dirt and water. Do not damage the gaskets rather replace them and put clean ones in. Tighten the sleeve nut well.

> *Otherwise* the Tiger will burst into flames or explode.

Therefore, fill up — but do not spill it.

> *Otherwise* The Tiger will burst into flames or explode.

Take care! When the fuel runs out — immediately turn over to the reserve tank; when the reserve tank is empty — immediately stop still and switch off the engine. 30 seconds of work!

> *Otherwise* fuel pipes and fuel pumps will be empty and after filling up no fuel will come through: unscrew the airfilter and its housing, dismantle the hollow carburettor screw, leave the electric pump running until fuel comes through. (Do not let it overflow). Put it all together again.
>
> An hour's work!

Illustration
530 litres = 27 Jerry cans = 3 barrels
Madgeburg–Berlin 140 kilometres by road (140 kilometres Strasse)
Madgeburg–stop 85 kilometres overland (85 kilometres Gelände

2*

9

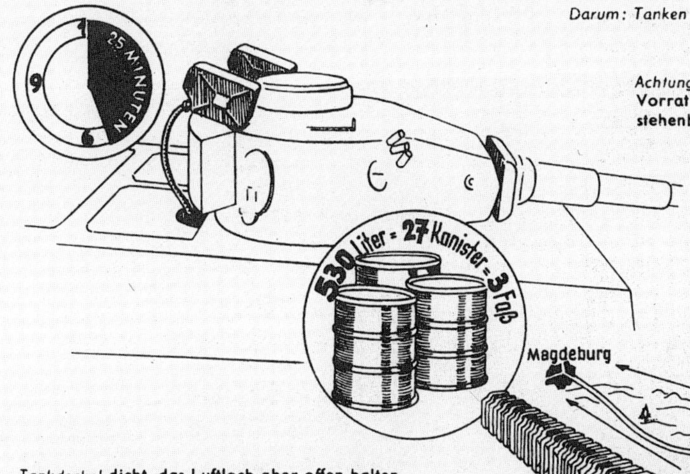

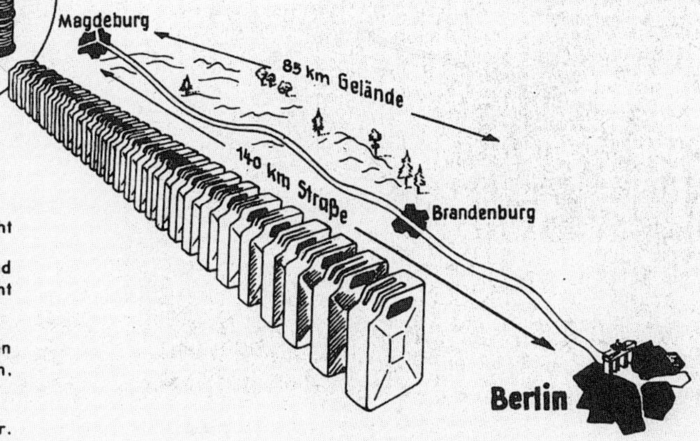

Tankdeckel dicht, das Luftloch aber offen halten,

   Sonst zieht der Motor nicht.

Einheitsbehälter und Schläuche sauber halten. Sieb nicht herausnehmen,

   Sonst verdrecken Schaugläser und Düsen. Du kannst beide schlecht erreichen.

Schaugläser von Schmutz und Wasser reinigen, Dichtungen nicht beschädigen, lieber auswechseln, sauber einsetzen. Hülsenmutter stramm anziehen,

   Sonst brennt oder platzt der Tiger.

Darum: Tanken — aber nichts danebengießen,

   Sonst brennt oder platzt der Tiger.

Achtung! Wenn der Kraftstoff zu Ende geht — sofort auf Vorrat umstellen; wenn Vorrat zu Ende geht — sofort stehenbleiben und Motor ausschalten, 30 Sekunden Arbeit!

Sonst werden Leitung und Kraftstoff-Pumpe leer, und nach dem Tanken kommt kein Kraftstoff: Luftfilter und Gehäuse abschrauben, Hohlschrauben am Vergaser abbauen, elektrische Pumpe laufen lassen, bis Kraftstoff kommt (nicht überlaufen lassen). Alles wieder einbauen.

   Eine Stunde Arbeit!

217

Motto: Benificent is the might of water
If you use Glysantine as you oughter

Water *is a coolant*

It washes round the crankcase like a fresh unending shower and carries off the heat produced by combustion and friction to the radiators. Besides, in Winter it stores up heat as an accumulator stores up current and in that way keeps the engine ready to start.

The Tiger needs 120 litres. At 85 degrees it feels in the pink.

Water is an Explosive

When you let it freeze into ice it expands by about 10 per cent. When the casing can take no more it will be burst open through natural causes. Ice bursts open rocks and iron.

The 120 litres becomes 132 litres and there is no room in a Tiger's stomach for that.

18

Therefore:

Motto: When you consider the Tiger tank
Its conduct is in the first rank

Drive but do it sensibly

26 *Revolutions in one minute in three-four time* is the way of a graceful man in a Viennese waltz. Then the music melts into your ear and blends with the rhythm of the movement. Slower is boring but if you turn too quickly then you become giddy and your lady partner will collapse from the heat.

2600 *Revolutions per minute in the four-stroke cycle* is what the Tiger loves. Then it gives the best return for its fuel. Your sensitivity, your ear and your rev. counter will tell you when you have brought your partner up to the correct rpm.

Never drive her at more than 3,000rpm otherwise you will overheat her. Water boils, oil ceases to lubricate, bearings, pistons and valves seize up — burnt out.

Therefore drive with your head not your backside.

Watch the regulation speed **1**	Water temperature **2** and oil pressure **3** (Sketch side 40)
Look for the best course,	but keep to your bearing,
Pussy foot away,	but get on with it,
Observe,	but keep an eye on your instrument panel,
Signal,	but listen for your engine and transmission!

On the move. Turn the gun to 6 o'clock and secure.

Buildings and walls. Do not drive through them. The debris from a wall looks better in a newsreel than on your rear end. Lots of rubble and dust gets sucked into the air filters, the radiator is clogged and stops cooling. The engine heats up and breaks-down.

38

Motto: Wohltätig ist des Wassers Macht,
falls Du an Glysantin gedacht.

Wasser

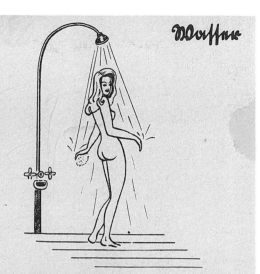

Wasser ist ein Kühlmittel

Es umspült wie eine frische Brause unablässig das Gehäuse und führt die Hitze, die durch Verbrennung und Reibung entsteht, zu den Kühlern. Es speichert im Winter außerdem die Wärme wie ein Sammler den Strom und hält dadurch den Motor startbereit.

120 Liter braucht Dein Tiger. Bei 85° fühlt er sich sauwohl

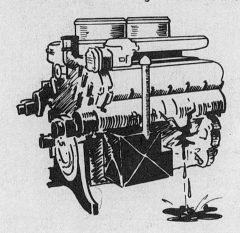

Wasser ist ein Sprengmittel

Wenn es zu Eis friert, dehnt es sich u.n 10% aus. Wenn die Wände nicht nachgeben können, werden sie mit Urgewalt gesprengt. Eis sprengt Felsen und Eisen.

Aus den 120 Litern werden dann 132 Liter, und die haben auch in einem Tigermagen keinen Platz.

Darum:

18

Motto: Der Tiger ist, wenn man's bedenkt,
ein Wagen, der sich prima lenkt.

Fahren, aber mit Verstand

26 *Umdrehungen in einer Minute im* **³/₄-Takt** macht der feine Mann beim Wiener Walzer. Dann schmilzt die Musik in Deinem Ohr und vermählt sich mit dem Gleichmaß der Bewegung. Langsamer ist langweilig, drehst Du aber zu rasch, dann wirst Du schwindlig und Deine Partnerin geht vor Hitze aus dem Leim

2600 *Umdrehungen in der Minute im* **4-Takt** liebt der Tiger. Dann leistet er für seinen Sprit am meisten. Dein Taktgefühl, Dein Ohr und Dein Drehzahlmesser sagen Dir, wann Du Deine Partnerin auf die richtigen Touren gebracht hast.

Jage sie niemals über 3000 U/min, sonst wird ihr zu heiß. Das Wasser kocht, das Öl hört auf zu schmieren, die Lager, Kolben und Ventile brennen fest — aus . . .

Darum fahre mit dem Kopf, nicht mit dem Hintern!

beobachte ständig Drehzahl **1**	Waserwärme **2** und Öldruck **3** (Bild Seite 40)
suche die beste Bahn,	aber halte die Richtung,
schleiche Dich an,	aber komme vom Fleck,
beobachte,	aber lies das Schaltbrett,
funke,	aber hör auf Motor und Getriebe!

Beim Marsch   Kanone auf 6 Uhr drehen und zurren.

Häuser und Mauern   fahre lieber nicht um. Die Mauertrümmer machen sich in der Wochenschau besser aus als auf Deinem Heck. Durch den Lüfter wird der ganze Schutt angesaugt, der Kühler wird eingedeckt und kühlt nicht mehr. Der Motor wird heiß und fällt aus.

219

38

Motto: A stoppage in the barrel of a gun
Seldom happens, isn't fun

To begin with

Trust your controls, keep your ammunition in good shape, clean the breech, ensure all moving parts work clean and remove oil from the barrel before firing and afterwards oil it liberally when it is warm to the touch.

Otherwise the gun will not fire.

Take care

That the muzzle cover is off, it is not blocked with ice

That camouflage and twigs are clear of the muzzle

That in a break in firing you have a look through the barrel

That at night you use a torch to clean it

That you remove splinters and refuse

When you load a hot gun during a break in firing.

Do not shoot

When the muzzle brake is loose or shot off
   It acts something like a sail and absorbs 70% of the recoil

When the recoil brake loses oil
   It acts like a shock absorber and absorbs air or does not work

Otherwise the barrel will burst

When the compressed air recuperator loses air or does not work
   It acts like a door closed and absorbs 5% of the recoil

When the recoil indicator sticks during a break in firing
   Shove it forwards after each shot

Otherwise the gun will backfire

When the split pin on the breach mechanism lever is missing or loose

However

With skilled gunners

Normally the gun will fire forwards

Moral: But the Panzer tankie can hardly credit
That not the target but *he* will get it.

55

The Tank's Claw

For each shell that you fire
   Your father has paid 100 RM in taxes
   Your mother has worked a week in the factory
   10,000 kilometres is a long way by rail.

Think of that before you shoot!

HE shells fired at an unidentified target 'on suspicion', a target which could be disposed of with an MG is a crime.

Tank shells fired at a useless range, at stricken tanks or badly aimed only produce a piece of chip carving in steel.

Tiger soldiers! Economise
   Make the most of the big Tiger! Let's Go!
   Rollers are cheaper than an MG!
   MG is cheaper than a gun!
   Return spent cartridge cases and bulk containers!

The Tiger guzzles fuel by the jerry can
Each litre must be carried 3,000 long kilometres.

Tiger Soldiers! Economise
   Be sparing with every litre
   Do not let the engine run unnecessarily
Do you know when your next fuel will come?

The Tiger with all its bits and pieces costs 800,000 RM and took 300,000 hours of work to build. 30,000 men had each to give a week's wages, 6,000 men had to work like slaves for a week just so that you can have a Tiger. They are working for you.

Tiger Soldiers!
   Think what you have in your hands!
   Stop her when you shoot!
   Outflank them with the Panzer claw!
   Strike down whoever strikes at her!

91

Motto: Hemmung im Kanonenrohr
kommt, Gott sei Dank, nur selten vor.

Die vielseitige Kanone

Vorweg

Prüfe Deine Leitung, pflege die Munition, reinige den Verschluß,
mach alles Bewegliche gängig, reinige und entöle das Rohr vor
dem Schießen und öle es hinterher dick, wenn es wieder hand-
warm ist.

Achtung

Mündungskappe ab, bei Eis auch die durchschießbare.
Tarnmittel und Zweige weg von der Mündung.
In Feuerpausen durchs Rohr gucken.
Nachts mit der Taschenlampe reinleuchten.
Sprengstücke und Rückstände raus.
Heißgeschossene Rohre in Feuerpausen entladen.

Nicht schießen

wenn die Mündungsbremse locker oder abgeschossen ist —
    sie wirkt wie ein Segel und bremst 70% des Rückstoßes ab,

wenn die Rohrbremse Öl verliert,
    sie wirkt wie ein Stoßdämpfer und bremst 25% des Rück-
    stoßes ab

wenn der Luftvorholer Luft verliert oder nicht arbeitet,
    er wirkt wie ein Türschließer und bremst 5% des Rück-
    stoßes ab,

wenn der Rücklaufmesser auf „Feuerpause" steht.
    Schiebe ihn nach jedem Schuß nach vorne

wenn der Splint am Öffnerhebel fehlt oder locker ist.

Indessen:

Bei geübten Schützen und auch.

Sonst schießt die
Kanone überhaupt
nicht

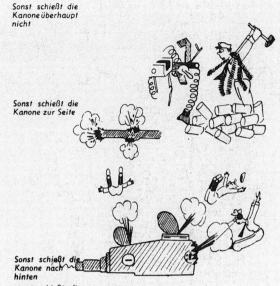

Sonst schießt die
Kanone zur Seite

Sonst schießt die
Kanone nach
hinten

sonst schießt die
Kanone nach vorn.

Moral: Nur ungern glaubt der Panzermann,
statt was zu treffen, selber dran!

55

Panzerklau

Für jede Granate, die Du verschießt,
    hat Dein Vater 100 RM Steuern bezahlt,
    hat Deine Mutter eine Woche in der Fabrik
    gearbeitet,
    ist die Eisenbahn 10 000 km weit gefahren!

Das bedenke vor jedem Schuß!

Sprenggranaten auf nicht erkannte Ziele „auf Ver-
dacht" verschossen, auf Ziele, die mit MG erledigt
werden können, sind ein Verbrechen.

Panzergranaten auf unbrauchbare Entfernung, auf
erledigte Panzer, oder schlecht gezielt verschossen,
geben nur Kerbschnitzarbeiten im Stahl!

Männer vom Tiger! Sparen!
    Nützt den dicken Panzer aus! Ran!
    Walzen ist billiger als MG!
    MG ist billiger als Kanone!
    Hülsen und Packgefäße abliefern!

Der Tiger säuft den Sprit kanisterweise.
Jeder Liter muß 3000 km weit gekarrt werden:

Männer vom Tiger! Sparen!
    Geizt mit jedem Liter!
    Laßt den Motor nicht unnütz laufen!
    Weißt Du, wann der nächste Sprit kommt?

*Der Tiger kostet mit allem Drum und Dran 800 000 RM
und 300 000 Arbeitsstunden. 30 000 Menschen müssen
einen ganzen Wochenlohn geben, 6000 Menschen
eine Woche schuften, damit Du einen Tiger be-
kommst. Sie arbeiten alle für Dich.*

Männer vom Tiger!
    Bedenkt, was Ihr in den Händen habt!
    Haltet ihn in Schuß!
    Panzerklau geht um!
    Schlagt ihn, wo Ihr ihn trefft!

221

GLOSSARY OF ABBREVIATIONS AND TERMS

ABBREVIATIONS

a/A	Old type, old model
A (2)	Infantry Branch of War Ministry
A (4)	Field Artillery Branch of War Ministry
A (5)	Foot Artillery Branch of War Ministry
A7V	Motor Transport Branch of War Ministry
AD (2)	General War Department Branch 2 (Infantry)
AD (4)	General War Department Branch 4 (Field Artillery)
AD (5)	General War Department Branch 5 (Foot Artillery)
AHA/AgK	General Army Office Motor Transport Office Group
AK	Artillery Design Office
AKK	Army Motor Transport Supply
ALkW	Army Lorries
ALZ	Army Freight Trains/Trucks
AOK	Army High Command
APK	Artillery Testing Commission
ARW	Eight-wheeled lorry
A-Typen	With all/four-wheel drive (Schell-type)
BAK	Balloon-Defence-Gun
BeKraft	Branch for Fuel and Oil for Motor Transport in the Field
BMW	Bavarian Engine Factory
Chefkraft	Head of Motor Transport in the Field
(DB)	Daimler-Benz
DMG	Daimler Engine Company
DTschr Krprz	German Crown Prince
E-Fahrgestell	Standard chassis
E-Personenkraft-wagon (E-Pkw)	Standard passenger vehicle
E-LKW	Standard Lorry
Fa	Field Artillery
FAMO	Vehicle and Engine Construction Company Ltd
Fgst	Chassis
FF-Kabel	Field trunk cable
FH	Field Howitzer
FK	Field Gun
Flak	Anti-aircraft gun
F.T.	Wireless/Radio/Telegraph
Fu	Wireless/Radio
Fu Ger	Wireless/Radio equipment
Fu Spr Ger	Intercommunication equipment
g	Secret
Gen St d H	Army General Staff
Gengas	Producer/Generator gas
G.I.d MV	General Inspectorate of Military Transport
G.Kdos	Military secret
gp	Armoured
gRs	State secret
gl	With cross-country capability
GPD	Rifle Testing Commission
Gw	Gun carriage
(H)	With engine at the rear
Hanomag Hanover	Engine Construction Joint Stock Company
HK	Half-track, half-tracked vehicle
H Techn VBl	Army Technical Regulations Sheet
HWA	Army Weapons Department
ID	Infantry Division
IG	Infantry Gun
In	Inspectorate
In6	Inspectorate of Motor Transport
1Kraft	Inspectorate of Motor Transport in the Field
1Luk	Inspectorate of Air and Motor Transport
K	Gun
K	Small (klein, -er, -es)
KD	Krupp Daimler
K.D.	Cavalry Division
KdF	Strength through Joy (Nationlist Socialist Organisation)
KdK	Commander of Transport troops
KFlak	Truck mounted anti-aircraft gun
Kfz	Motor vehicle
KM	War Ministry
KP	Motor Limber
(Kp)	Krupp
Kogenluft	Commanding General of the Air Forces
Krad	Motorcycle
KrZgm	Motortractor
KS	Fire Engine
Kw	Motor vehicle also fighting vehicle
KrKW	Ambulance
KOM	Motor omnibus
KwK	Tank Gun
l	Light
L/	Length of barrel expressed in calibres
le	Light
le FH	Light field Howitzer
le FK	Light field gun
lFH	Light field Howitzer
L I G	Light infantry gun
Le WS	Armed Services tractor
LHB	Left-Hoffman-Busch
lIG	Light infantry gun
LkW	Lorry
LWS	Land and water tractor
m	Medium
MAN	Augsburg-Nuremberg Engine Factory Joint Stock Company
MG	Machine-gun
MP	Machine pistol
MTW	Troop carrier
MunPz	Ammunition tank
n	Revolutions per minute
n/A	New type, new model
NAG	National Automobile Association
(o)	Commercial
ObdH	Commander-in-Chief of the Army
OHL	The Supreme Command
OKH	Supreme Command of the Army
OKW	Supreme Command of the Armed Services
PaK	Anti-tank gun
PD	Panzer Division
Pf	Sapper vehicle
Pakw	Motor car
PzF	Tank ferry
PzKpfwg	Tank
PzSpwg	Reconnaissance Tank
PzJg	Tank hunter
Pz Bef Wg	Command Tank
(R)	Caterpillar tracked/crawler tracked (vehicle)
R/R	Wheel-tracked (vehicle)
(RhB)	Rheinmetall Borsig
RS	Caterpillar/crawler tractor
RSG	Mountain caterpillar/crawler tractor

RSO	Caterpillar/crawler tractor, east (wheel tractor east)	sWS	Heavy military tractor	ve	Completely interference free
RV	Radio link	StuG	Assault gun	v/max	Maximum speed
Sankra	Ambulance	StuK	Assault gun	V	Muzzle velocity
s	Heavy	StuH	Assault Howitzer	VPK	Transport scientific Review board
sFH	Heavy field Howitzer	Tak	Antitank gun	VsKfz	Experimental Vehicle
schg	Transportable by rail	Takraft	Technical Branch of the Inspectorate of Motor Transport	VKz	Experimental Vehicle
Schlp	Tractor			ZF	Friederichshaven Gear Wheel Factory
Schf	With ability to float	TF	Carrier frequency (radio technology)	ZRW	Vehicle with tracked wheels
SdKfz	Special vehicle	Tp	Tropical model	Zgkw	(half-track) Prime-mover truck
Sfl	Self propelled (gun) carriage	Vakraft	Experimental Branch of the Field Motor transport (World War I) Experimental Branch of the Inspectorate of Motor Transport (Imperial Forces and Armed Forces)	WsPrüf/WaPrw	Ordnance Testing branch
Sf	Self propelled (gun) carriage			wg	With fording capability
S-Typen	With rear-wheel drive (Schell-type)				
SmK	Pointed bullet with steel core				
SPW	Armoured personnel carrier				
SSW-Zug	Siemens-Schukert-Factory-Association				

TERMS

Abdeckbleich	Access plate	Auschlag	Stop, detent	Dichtung	Packing
Abflussöffnung	Drain hole	Ausgleichscheibe	Shim, compensating disc or washer	Doppelklauenring	Double collar/guide ring
Ablass	Drain, outlet	Auspuffrohrmantel	Exhaust manifold casing	Doppelsperrventil	Check or stop valve
Ablasshahn	Drain cock	Auspufftopf	Exhaust silencer	drehen	To turn
Ablassöffnung	Outlet	Aussen	Outer	Drehbühne	Turntable, turret floor
Ablassschraube	Drain plug	Aussenlager	Outer or external bearing	Drehpunkt	Fulcrum
Absaugleitung	Drain/return pipes	Aussenlaufrad	Outer bogie wheel	Drehstabfeder	Torsion bar
Abnahme	Acceptance testing, inspection	Aussenstelle	Outpost	Dreh-zahlmesser	Tachometer, speedometer, rev. counter
Absperrklappe	Shut off valve	Ausserst	Extreme, farthest		
Abstandbuchse	Space bushing	Austritt	Outlet	Drosselklappe	Butterfly valve or gate, throttle valve, damper
Abstandhulse	Spacer tube	Auswechselbar	Renewable		
Abstandring	Spacer spacing collar			Druckfeder	Compression or pressure spring
Abtrieb	Output, power take off	Beigestellt	Provided, put in place, installed		
Abzug	Trigger (machine-gun)			Druckknopf	Control knob
Achtung!	Take care!	Beilagscheibe	Tab washer	Druckkugel	Ball thrust
Akku	(Abbr.) Accumulator, storage battery	Behälter	Tank, container	Drucklager	Thrust bearing/block/race
Allgemein	General	Belüflungsleitung	Pressure regulator pipe	Druckleitung	Delivery pipe
Andwendung	Application, employment, use	Beschaffung	Supply, procurement	Druckregulierventil	Pressure regulating valve
Angehoben	(pp. of Anheben) Lifted, raised	Beschleuniger	Accelerator, activator	Druckscheibe	Thrust washer
Anlasser	Starter, starting magneto	Betätigung	Control, operation, actuation	Druckschmierkopf	Grease nipple
		betragen	To amount to, measure	Druckstück	Thrust piece, pressure plate
Anlasskraftstoff	Primer (fuel)	Betrieb	Operation		
Anschlusschraubung	Screwed connection joint	Betriebsmittel	Machinery materials, rolling stock	Druckstange	Connecting rod, plunger, spindle
Ansicht	View, section, elevation	bis	Until	Durchlass	Outlet
Antrieb	Drive, driving gear, gearing	Blech	Plate, plank		
Antriebsflansch	Driving flange	Bodenstück	Breech plate	Einfachklauenring	Single collar, guide ring
Arbeitsausschuss	Works committee	Bodenventil	'sea cock', bottom valve	Entfernungsmesser	Range finder
Arbeitskräfte einsatz	Labour participation	Bremsbelag	Brake lining	erforderlich	Necessary, requisite, required
Arbeitskreis	Works group	Bremse	Brake		
Auflauf-flachen	Abutting surface	Bremsring	Brake ring	Einfülltrichter	Funnel, tube
		Bremsscheibe	Brake friction drive	Einfüllverschluss	Filler cap
Ausblickbohrung	Telescope/periscope aperture	Brems-trommel	Brake drum	eingebaut	Installed
Ausblich-stutzen	Telescope/periscope socket	Bremsträger	Brake bracket	einhängen	To hang, hook, suspend
		Brennstoff	Propellant charge	Einheit	Integral part
		Buchse	Bush(ing), bearing		
		Dämpfung	Cushioning, damping		
		Deckel	Cover, lid, cap		

einrückbar	Capable of being engaged	Geradeausfahrt	Driving straight ahead	Kegelradpaar	Pair of bevel gears
Einsatz	Application, use (military action, engagement)	Gerät	Apparatus, equipment, device, item of equipment	Kegelritzel	Bevel pinion
				Keil	Key, cotter, cotter pin, shim, dowel
Einspritzvorrichtung	Primer (fuel)	gemessen	(pp. of messen) to amount to, to measure	Ketten-abdeckung	Track cover
Einstiegluken	Entry hatch	geöffnet	Open		
Einstellmarke	Adjustment mark	Gesamtgewicht	Total weight	Ketten-antriebsflansch	Track driving flange
Eintritt	Inlet	geschlossen	Closed	Kettenspanner	Track tension adjuster
Entkuppler	Declutcher, uncoupler, disconnector, disengager	geschmiedet	Forged (metal)	Klauenkupplung	Dog clutch
		Geschwindigkeits-messer	Speedometer, tachometer, rev. counter	Klemmhülse	Collet
Enlüfterschraube	Vent screw			Kolben	Piston
Entwicklung	Development			Konuskupplung	Cone friction clutch
Ersatzteile	Spare parts	Geschwindigkeits-regelung	Speed control or adjustment	Kopfschutz	Protective head cushion, brow pad
fahren	To travel	Gestänge	Rod	Kraftfahr-wesen	Motor transport service
Fahrbremse	Wheel brake	Getriebe	Gearing, gear unit, transmission — power or gear	Kraftstoff	Fuel
Fahrersehklappe	Driver's vision port			Kraftstoffbeh(alter)	Fuel tank
Fahrgestell	Chassis			Kraftstoffemfüllöff-nung	Fuel filler neck
Fahrschalter	Commutator or reversing switch	Getriebeblock	Gearbox unit	Kraftstoffhahn	Fuel cock
Fahrt	Travel			Kugel	Ball bearing
Fahrtrichtung	Direction of travel	Getriebebelüftung	Gearbox ventilation	Kugelblende-MG	Machine-gun ball-mounting
Fahrzeuge	Vehicle	Getriebe-kühlLuft	Gearbox cooling air		
Feder	Spring			Kugelschale	Sliding joint
Federsbuchse	Spring bush, spring eye bushing	Getriebe-nummer	Gear unit number	Kühler	Radiator
		Gleiskette	Caterpillar track	Kühlerblock	Radiator core
Federteller	Spring washer	Grauguss	Grey or cast iron	Kühlluftaustritt	Cooling air outlet
Feldregler	Field rheostat or regulator	Gummi-dichting	Rubber seals	Kühllufteintritt	Cooling air inlet
Felgenkranz	Rim (of wheel)	Guss	Casting	Kühlluftgebläse	Cooling air blower
Fernther-mometer	Water temperature gauge			Külluftleitung	Cooling air duct
				Kühlmantel	Cooling jacket
Fertigung	Production	Hahnstellung	Fuel cock position	Kühlwasser-einfüllöffnung	Radiator water filling opening
feststehend	Stationary	halbkreisf(örmig)	Semi-circular		
Festellmarke	Locating key	Haltebremse	Blocking brake	Kühlwasserregler	Thermostat
Feststellschraube	Locating screw, locking device	Haltefeder	Retaining spring	Kühlwasser-überdruckventil	Cooling water relief pressure valve
		Halterung	Support, mounting		
Feuchtigkeitsemp-findlich	Sensitive to damp	Halte-schraube	Clamping bolt	Kühlwasserüber-tragung	Cooling water exchange/transfusion
Feurhöhe	Height of gun barrel axis from ground	Haltestift	Locking pin, plunger		
		Handrad	Hand wheel		
Feuerlöscher	Fire-extinguisher	hängtdurch (durch-hangen)	Sagging, hanging down	Kupplungsgabel	Clutch fork
Flanschwelle	Flanged shaft	Hauptausschuss	Main directorate, central committee	Kupplungsgestänge	Clutch linkage
Flur	Floor			Kupplungs-hebel	Clutch pedal
Flussigkeitsgetriebe	Hydraulic transmission	Hauptdüse	Main jet		
Frage	Question	Haupterregung	Main energisation	Kupplungsmuffe	Clutch coupling sleeeve, coupling box
Fremderregung	Separate energisation	Hauptkupplung	Main clutch		
		Hauptschalter	Main or master clutch	Kupplungsschiebe	Clutch slide
Gabelhebel	Forked lever, cut-out (slotted) lever	Hauptstromwicklung	Main current winding	Kupplungsstücke	Coupling
		Hebel	Lever	Kupplungs-welle	Clutch shaft
Gabelwelle	Forked (steering arm) shaft	Hilfstrieb	Auxiliary drive wheel, traversing handwheel	Kurbel	Crank
		hinter	rear	Kurzschluss	Short circuit
Ganghwähler	Gear preselector (lever)	Hochdruckraum	High pressure chamber		
Gasgeber	Accelerator	Hohlwelle	Hollow shaft		
Geblasehauptleitung	Ventilator or trunking			Labyrinthdichtung	Labyrinth seal
gefederte	Spring loaded	Innenlaufrad	Inner bogie wheel	Lagerbüchse	Bearing (bush[ing]), axle box, journal box
gegossen	Welded				
Gehäuse (deckel)	Housing, casing (cover), cowling	Kampfraum	Fighting compartment	Lagerung	Bearing
		Kegel	Core, bevel, tapered sleeve or socket	Lammellenträger	Disc carrier
Gep(anzert)	Armoured			Laufradreifen	Bogie wheel tyre
Gelenkwelle	Drive-shaft			Laufwerk	Running gear

Leerlaufraste	Idling notch	
Leerweg	Free play	
Leicht	Light (weight)	
Leitrad	Idler wheel	
Leistungssteigerung	Increase in performance or efficiency	
Lenkantrieb	Steering input	
Lenkbremse	Steering brake	
Lenkgetriebe	Steering mechanism	
Lenzpumpe	Bilge pump	
Lichtmaschine	Lighting dynamo	
link	Left (direction)	
Linkslauf	Anti-clockwise rotation	
Lüfter	Ventilation fan or blower	
Lüfterantrieb	Fan drive	
Lüftergetriebe	Fan gear unit/gearing/power transmission	
Lüfterkupplung	Fan coupling	
Lüfterschalthebel	Ventilation fan control lever	
Luftfilter	Air filter	
Luftschieber	Air valve or damper	
Magnetzünder	Magneto	
Mantelrohr	Jacketed barrel	
Maschinenbeschaffung	Machine procurement/supply	
Mass	Measurement	
messen	To measure	
messbar	Measureable	
MP Klappe	machine pistol port	
Mitnehmer	Carrier, cam	
Mittenhohlrad	Annular gear	
Mittenvollrad	Sun gear	
Motor	Motor, engine	
Motorraumbelüftung	Engine room vent(ilation)	
Motorraumentlüftung	Engine room venting	
Mundungsbremse	Muzzle brake	
Munition	Ammunition	
Nabenverschlussklappe	Hinged hub cover	
nachstellen	To adjust	
Nachstellmutter	Adjusting net	
Nichteisenmetall	Non-ferrous metal	
Niederdruckraum	Low pressure chamber	
Notaustieg	Emergency chamber	
Nullwelle	Intermediate shaft	
oben	Upper	
Oberflächenhärteverfahren	Surface hardening process	
od(er)	or	
Öffnung	Opening, inlet, aperture, port	
ohne	without	
Ölablassschrauber	Oil outlet screw	
Ölablaufrohr	Oil drainage pipe	

Ölbehälter	Oil tank, reservoir	
Öldruck	Oil pressure	
Öldruckbremse	Hydraulic brake	
Öldruckmesser	Oil pressure gauge	
Öleinfullrohr	Oil filler pipe	
Ölfilter	Oil filter	
Ölkuhler	Oil cooler	
Ölrucklauf	Oil return line	
Ottomotor	Carburettor or spark ignition engine	
Panzer	Armour plate	
Panzerdeckel	Armoured cover	
Panzerglasblock	Bullet proof glass vision block	
Panzerwagen	Armoured car, tank	
Pendelrollenlager	Self-aligning roller bearing	
Pressstoffe	Plastic/moulded material/compound, compressed material	
Programmbearbeitung	Work scheduling	
Pz-Führerkuppel	Tank commander's cupola	
Qualität	Quality	
Rad	Wheel	
Rädertrieb	Gear drive	
Reihe	Series	
recht	Right (direction)	
Rechtslauf	Clockwise rotation	
Regen	Rain	
Reibglocke	Friction jacket	
Richtschütze	Gunner	
Richtungshebel	Reversing handle	
Ringlagerung	Ring supports	
Ringmutter	Eye, annular or ring nut	
Ritzellagerung	Pinion bearing	
Rohstoff	Raw material	
Rolle	Roller (bearing)	
Rollenkäfig	Roller cage	
Rollenlager	Roller bearing	
Rücklaufleitung	Return pipe	
Rückschlagklappe	Check, relief or non-return valve or non-return flap	
Rückschlagventil	Check, relief, non-return or back pressure valve	
Rückwarts	Back(wards), reverse	
Rückzug(s)feder	Release spring	
Rutschkupplung	Release clutch, slipper clutch	
Sammler	Accumulator, battery	
Schaft	Shaft, shank, stem	
Schaltausloser	Trip switch	
Schaltbrett	Switchboard	
Schaltbrett leuchten	Switchboard light	
Schalter	Switch	
Schaltgebel	Shift fork	
Schaltgestänge	(Gear) shifting linkage	

Schaltgetriebe	Gear shift mechanism	
Schalthebel	Control (lever)	
Schaltkasten (schlüssel)	Ignition key	
Schaltsäule	Switch column	
Schaltrohr	Switch conduit	
Schaltstellung	Switch position/indicator	
Schaltzylinder	Control, cylinder	
Scharnier	Hinge, joint	
Schauglas	Sight glass	
Schauloch	Inspection hole	
Scheibenkupplung	Disc clutch	
Schema	Diagram, scheme, plan, model	
Scherenfernrohr	Scissors telescope	
Schlecht	Bad, poor	
Schleife	Slide	
Schmieden	To forge (metal)	
Schmiere	Lubricant, lubricating oil or grease	
Schmierbatterie	Lubricant distribution system	
Schmierschlauch	Flexible lubrication pipe	
Schmutzwasserklappe	Dirty water valve	
Schnitt	Section, cut, profile	
Schraubenfeder	Spiral, helical or coil spring	
schützen	To protect	
Schutzglas	Protective, armoured glass	
Schweissverfahren	Welding process	
Schwenken	Rotate, revolve, tilt	
Schwingarm	Swing arm, cranked axle	
Schwungkraftanlasser	Inertia starter	
Schwungrad	Flywheel	
Seegering	Circlip lockring	
Seelenrohr	Inner tube of gun liner	
Sehschlitz	Vision port	
Seite	Side	
Seit(lich)	Side, lateral	
Seitenvorgelege	Final drive	
Seitenwelle	Side shaft	
Selbstätig	Automatic	
Serie(n)	Series, serial	
Servoschieber	Servo slide valve	
Sicherheitsventil	Pressure relief valve, safety valve	
Sicherungsblech	Locking or anti-twisting plate	
Sicherungskarten	Fuse box	
Simmering	Oil seal, retaining ring	
Sonderausschuss	Special committee	
Spähwagen	Scout car	
Spannschraube	Breech ring securing collar	
Sperring	Locking ring	
Sperrschieber	Check valve	
Sperrventil	Check valve, stop valve	
Spindelmutter	Spindle nut	
Sprengring	Circlip, spring ring	
Stahlguss	Cast steel, steel castings	
Stärke	Power	

Starkstrom-Technik	High voltage current technology
Staubring	Dust shield
Stellung	Position
Steuerkasten	Steering frame
Steuerschieber	Servo valve spool, distributing slide valve-servo-piston
Stirnradvorgelege	Spur wheel reduction gearing
Stosse	Shock, jolt
Stossdämpfer	Shock absorber
Sturmgeschütz	Assault gun
Stutzwelle	Intermediate shaft
Temperguss	Malleable (cast) iron
Trennwand	Bulkhead
Trichter	Funnel
Triebad	Driving sprocket
Trommel	Drum
Turmantrieb	Turret (turning) gear
Turmblende	Mantlet
Turmkugellager	Turret ballrace
Turmrichtung	Turret direction
Turmschwenkwerk	Turret traversing mechanism/gearbox
Turmzielfernrohr	Turret binocular sight
Überbrückungsplatte	Bridging plate
Uberlagerungtrieb	Superimposed drive
unten	Below, beneath, down
unter	Lower
umgekehrt	Reciprocal
Umkehrfeldregler	Reversing field rheostat/regulator
umlaufend	Rotary
Umlaufgetriebe	Planetary gear, epicyclic gear, sun and planetary gear
Umlaufrad	Planetary gear wheel
Umlaufrad-Träger	Planetary carrier
Umlaufrich-tung	Circumferential direction
Umschalthahn	Change over cock
Umschalthebel	Change lever
Umstellung	Change, conversion
Ventil	Valve
Ventilbatterie	Battery of fuel cocks
Verbindungsleite	Connecting pipe
Verdichtung	Compression
Verdrängerkolben	Recuperator piston
Vergaser	Carburettor
Verlängerungsnabe	Hub extension
Verschluss	Breech block (gun)
Verschlusseschraube	Screw plug, drain plug
Verteilung	Distribution, allotment
Verzahng-Verzahnung	Toothing
Verzögerer	Retarder, restrainer, delayer
volle	Fully, maximum
Vorgang	Process
Vorgelegewelle	Counter shaft
Vorrichtung	Mechanism
Vorsitzer	Chairman
vorwärtz	Forward
Wahlhebel	Selector lever
Wasser	Water
Wechselgetriebe	Transmission gear
weit	Far
Welle	Shaft, axle
wenden	To turn
Windhutze	Air scoop
Winkelblech	Angle sheet iron
Winkelhebel	Crank, angle lever
Winkelgetriebe	Mitre gear
Zahnkranz	Turret rack
Zahnring	Toothed ring
Zubehör	Accessories
Zugang	Access
Zugkraft-wagen	Half-track
Zugmaschine	Tractor
Zuleitung	Feed pipe
Zusatzlaufrad	Additional bogie wheel
zwischen	Between
Zwischenkammer-ventil	Inter-chamber valve
Zwischenplatte	Intermediate plate
Zwischenrad	Idler gear
Zwölfuhrzeiger	Clockdial target direction indicator, azimuth indicator
Zylinderstift	Straight or cylindrical pin

BIBLIOGRAPHY

Aders, Erwin	*Memoirs* (unpublished)	Oswald, Werner	*Motor Vehicles and Tanks of the Imperial Armed Forces, the Armed Forces of Nazi Germany and the Federal Armed Forces*
Boelcke, Willi A.	*German Armour in the Second World War*		
Caruso, Otto	*Tiger in the Mire*	Schausberger, Norbert	*Armour in Austria 1939-1945*
Chamberlain, Peter & Ellis, Chris	Profile: *Mark VI Tank Tiger I (H)*	Schubert, H. & Wagner, C.	*German Tank Troops 1939-1945*
Crow, Duncan & Icks, Robert J.	*Encyclopaedia of Tanks*	Senger, F. M. von & Etterlin	*German Tanks 1926-1945*
Feist, Uwe	*Tigers in Action*	Spielberger, Walter J. & Feist, Uwe	*Mark VI Tank Tiger I and Tiger II (King Tiger)*
Fey, Will	*Tanks in Front-Line Action*	Spielberger, Walter J.	*The Mark VI Tank and its Variants*
Guderian, Heinz	*Memories of a Soldier*	—	Profile: *Panzerjäger Tiger (P) Elephant*
Halder, Franz	*War Diary*	—	*The Motor Vehicles and Tanks of the Austrian Army*
Icks, Robert J.	*Tanks and Armoured Vehicles*	Stoves, Rolf	*The 1st Panzer Division*
Magnuski, Janus	*Wozy Bojowe (Armoured Vehicles)*	OFFICIAL	*Tiger Primer*, Inspector General of Tank Troops 01.08.1943 (Service Regulations D656/27)
Munzel, Oskar	*German Tank Troops up to 1945*		
Mellenthin, F. W. von	*Panzer Battles*		
Nehring, Walther K.	*The Story of the German Tank Corps 1916-1945*		

A faithful facsimile of the Tiger Primer is published by Motorbuch Verlag, Stuttgart, Germany. The wording reads:

> 'For Platoon Leaders
> and Tiger Folk
>
> 'D656/27
>
> 'Tiger Primer
> . . . loud quick-fire hot stuff!'

INDEX OF VEHICLES